The Logic of Legal Argumentation

Multi-modal argumentation with its logical, emotional, visceral and kisceral arguments is an important addition to logical argumentation, especially when real-life situations are considered. It does not discard logic but adds other modes of argumentation to complement it, to emphasize the realistic environments of communication. In this sense, the multi-modal theory is important for the area of legal argumentation, where even in the reasoning of judicial decisions traces of a flesh-and-blood personality, who decided the case and wrote the reasons, can be found.

This book presents a comprehensive analysis of this informal logic in legal argumentation and its practicality within the law. It argues that by building on the dialectical and rhetorical models of legal argument, the former being important for clear cases while the latter for unclear ones, the multi-modal theory of legal argumentation brings together logic and psychology in a holistic or integral perspective. The approach is not only descriptive, identifying the traces of alternate arguments in judicial decisions, but is also normative, presenting the criteria for evaluation that multi-modal arguments need to face to attain validity in the legal context.

The work will be of interest to academics and researchers in the areas of Legal Theory, Legal Linguistics, Philosophy of Law, and Communication Studies.

Marko Novak is Professor of Law in the European Faculty of Law at New University, and Management and Law College (MLC) Ljubljana, Slovenia.

Law, Language and Communication
Series Editors

Anne Wagner is Professor of Legal Semiotics and Research Professor at Centre de Recherche Droits & Perspectives du Droit, équipe René Demogue, Lille University, France. She is the Editor-in-Chief of the International Journal for the Semiotics of Law (Springer) and President of the International Roundtables for the Semiotics of Law. She has been awarded the National Research Grant for her research career. Her main research interests include semiotics, verbal and non-verbal sign system analyses, language and law, legal culture and heritage, legal translation, legal terminology, and legal discourse studies.

Vijay K. Bhatia, formerly Professor of English, City University of Hong Kong, is now Adjunct Professor at Chinese University of Hong Kong, and Visiting Professor at the Hellenic American University, Athens (Greece). He is also the founding President of the Languages for Specific Purposes and Professional Communication Association for Asia-Pacific. His research interests include Critical Genre Analysis, academic and professional discourses in legal, business, newspaper, and promotional contexts; ESP and Professional Communication; simplification of legal and other public documents; intercultural and cross-disciplinary variations in professional genres.

This series encourages innovative and integrated perspectives within and across the boundaries of law, language and communication, with particular emphasis on issues of communication in specialized socio-legal and professional contexts. It seeks to bring together a range of diverse yet cumulative research traditions in order to identify and encourage interdisciplinary research.

The series welcomes proposals – both edited collections as well as single-authored monographs – emphasizing critical approaches to law, language and communication, identifying and discussing issues, proposing solutions to problems, offering analyses in areas such as legal construction, interpretation, translation and de-codification.

Titles in the series

Language and Legal Judgments
Evaluation and Argument in Judicial Discourse
Stanisław Goźdź-Roszkowski

The Logic of Legal Argumentation
Multi-Modal Perspectives
Marko Novak

For more information about this series, please visit: www.routledge.com/Law-Language-and-Communication/book-series/LAWLANGCOMM

The Logic of Legal Argumentation

Multi-Modal Perspectives

Marko Novak

Routledge
Taylor & Francis Group
LONDON AND NEW YORK

First published 2024
by Routledge
4 Park Square, Milton Park, Abingdon, Oxon OX14 4RN

and by Routledge
605 Third Avenue, New York, NY 10158

Routledge is an imprint of the Taylor & Francis Group, an informa business

British Library Cataloguing-in-Publication Data
A catalogue record for this book is available from the British Library

ISBN: 978-1-032-55784-7 (hbk)
ISBN: 978-1-032-56077-9 (pbk)
ISBN: 978-1-003-43376-7 (ebk)

DOI: 10.4324/9781003433767

Typeset in Galliard
by Apex CoVantage, LLC

Contents

Preface and Acknowledgments

As a lawyer I have been trained, and spent a number of years in a professional environment believing, that legal argumentation is exclusively about logic and the verbal "game" of "logical compulsion." Then as a legal scholar, I witnessed from time to time legal argumentation models built on symbolic logic. Even though I respected their theoretical value, I was skeptical of their practical application to the everyday justification of legal and mostly judicial decisions. What I missed and wanted to find at that time was a model of legal argumentation through which it would be possible to, on one hand, theoretically reflect judges' daily work justifying their decisions and, on the other hand, remain close enough to real-life situations in the need to adjudicate.

In 2015, I attended an international conference on legal argumentation and rhetoric, the so-named Trento Days on Rhetoric, at the University of Trento, Italy, where I listened, among others, also to Leo Groarke's paper on visual argumentation entitled "Modes of Arguing, logophilia, and the limits of language." What fascinated me in that talk was not only Leo's ability to present complex issues clearly and simply, but the mere fact that there can exist non-verbal (multimodal) arguments incorporating non-verbal premises, which can be even presented in a logical form (*modus ponens*). When returning home, I dug deeper in the cyberspace about multimodal argumentation and ran into Michael Gilbert's multi-modal argumentation (with his four modes of logical, emotional, visceral, and kisceral arguments). That resonated as quite familiar to me due to my past work dealing with Carl Jung's psychological typology,[1] his four cognitive functions (i.e., thinking, feeling, sensation, and intuition) to explain the embeddedness of the phenomenon of law in psycho-social environments. Gilbert's approach to argumentation looked like a perfect example of how different cognitive functions often "speak" through the logical language when we justify even our most rational statements. Accordingly,

1 Novak, Marko. 2016. *The Type Theory of Law*. Cham: Springer. By the way, in a personal conversation with Claudio Duran several years later, Claudio told me that already in the early 1990s when Gilbert had appeared with his multi-modal theory of argumentation, he pointed to its resemblance with Jung's types.

I went on a mission to prove the existence of, and also find justification for, such multi-modes used in the legal context.

In the past years I presented the materials appearing in this book, in whatever form they were at a certain point, at several international conferences. In 2016, I attended a rhetoric conference, the Days of Ivo Škarić, on Brač island, in Croatia, where I discussed the beginnings of what was to become my multi-modal legal argumentation with different argumentation scholars, of whom I should mention first of all Leo Groarke. Leo has become a constant discussant on the issues of multi(-)modal argumentation, always interested in my work and ready to encourage further pursuits. There I also met Paul van den Hoven, Gabrijela Kišiček, and, once again, the Trento "triplets" (Maurizio Manzin, Federico Puppo, and Serena Tomasi). Over the past years, I discussed my multi-modal work with Maurizio, Federico, and Serena at different conferences (ISSA,[2] ECA,[3] GTR[4]) across Europe, as well as at my several Erasmus teaching exchange visits to Trento. Running into them seems to have been a necessary step in my career, bringing me to the rhetorical approach to legal argumentation.

Furthermore, I also presented my multi-modal findings at several legal argumentation conferences ("LegArg") in Ljubljana, at the New University, and discussed them in particular with several Slovene colleagues. Then, I also presented that work at the University of Zagreb, on the occasion of my Erasmus exchange visit, in Luka Burazin's jurisprudence class. Also, I presented on visual legal argumentation at a general legal theory conference (organized by the Central and Eastern European Network of Jurisprudence – CEENJ) at the Comenius University in Bratislava, Slovakia,[5] and at a legal argumentation conference at Masaryk University in Brno, Czechia.[6] My visit to Bocconi University in Milan, and the presentation of a paper in Giovanni Tuzet's and Damiano Canale's classes also needs to be mentioned in this context.

However, a breakthrough event in this project was definitely a several-week research visit to the University of Windsor (and CRRAR) in May 2019. Thanks primarily to Chris Tindale, my host, I had an excellent opportunity for research and presentation of my work, to other CRRAR scholars such as Douglas Walton, Hans Hansen, Anthony Blair, and others. The paper I presented there, and which was later commented on by Tindale, was published in *Argumentation and Advocacy* and is now, in a substantially revised form

2 One of my first papers on the topic was presented at the 2018 ISSA.

3 A paper that is now Chapter 6 of this book was presented at the 2019 ECA conference in Groningen, the Netherlands.

4 An initial version of my article on the multimodality of trademarks, which is now Chapter 7 of this book, was presented at the 2022 GTR.

5 The paper presented there was then published as "Visual as Multi-Modal Argumentation in Law" in 2021 *Bratislava Law Review*, 5 (1): 91–109. I thank the editors for their permission to republish it in this book.

6 There I presented a paper on emotional argumentation, which is now Chapter 7 of this book.

especially concerning the first part, Chapter 3.[7] That was then followed in the same year by the publication of an article in *Informal Logic*.[8]

What also needs to be mentioned in the context of this book, is the 2022 OSSA Summer Institute dedicated to the 20th anniversary of Gilbert's multi-modal argumentation. During a week of lectures and discussions we had a chance to exchange our views on Michael's work with Michael himself, Chris Tindale, Claudio Duran, David Godden, and Linda Carozza. Thus, my article, which now appears in Chapter 4,[9] which was then published in *Informal Logic*, in a special issue devoted to Michael's work, was greatly inspired by that Summer Institute.

Further, I need to thank Assimakis Tseronis for reading and extensively commenting on my paper that now appears as Chapter 7 of this book. That is to some extent a different kind of (multimodal) argumentation than Gilbert's. However, since there are overlaps and common points with multi-modal argumentation, I decided to include it in this book.

Lastly, I need to thank all the anonymous reviewers of my work, who helped a lot with their directions in building my ideas. I also need to thank my students at home and abroad for the incessant motivation I get for my work while communicating with them. Finally, and of course, the greatest acknowledgment goes to my family for their love and support over the years.

7 Novak, Marko. 2020. "Multi-Modal Argumentation and Rhetoric in Judicial Proceedings." *Argumentation and Advocacy*, 56 (1): 41–60.

8 Novak, Marko. 2020. "Rooting Gilbert's Multi-Modal Argumentation in Jung, and Its Extension to Law." *Informal Logic*, 40 (3): 383–421.

9 Novak, Marko. 2022. "Kisceral Argumentation in Law: Between Past and Present." *Informal Logic*, 42 (3): 623–652.

Introduction

Approaching (Legal) Argumentation: A Historical Background

After the "invention" of formal logic, in particular deductive syllogism, of demonstrative value, for the purpose of theoretical (scientific) reasoning in the *Prior Analytics*, Aristotle devoted his study to practical reasoning or argumentation (in the *Topics* and *On Sophistical Refutations*), where he discussed dialectic.[1] Finally, in *Rhetoric*, he introduced the idea, arguing that: "Rhetoric is a counterpart of dialectic." While (formal) logic was important for discussing arguments in their static capacity of the premises and their inferential relationship establishing truth, dialectic introduced their (i) dynamic or procedural aspect through the exchange of views by two opposing sides in a dialogue; as well as (ii) logic that is not formal but presumptive and defeasible, establishing a probability of the premises. Finally, what rhetoric in the Classical tradition brought to the argumentative situation was the role of the audience to be persuaded by orators, not only by the means of *logos* but also *ethos* (the arguer's credibility) and *pathos* (the audience's sentiments), thereby joining logic and psychology (Frost 2005) into one package.

After the Middle Ages period, rhetoric as a method of argumentation went into decline to be increasingly regarded as dealing primarily with matters of style (*elocutio*) (Kennedy 1994). At the same time, with modern-age philosophers logic ascended. It was not until recently that the logical model was seriously challenged by the rhetorical model in Perelman's work. But logic and rhetoric could also be complementary, and this kind of discussion was continued by Wenzel (1979), based on analyzing Habermas's discursive theory. According to Wenzel, what is typical for the logical approach is to view the argument as a product; rhetoric focuses on argument creation as a process in the broadest term possible, while dialectic emphasizes a procedure in which the argument is developed with all the procedural rules to follow. He also stressed that

1 The logical works of Aristotle (i.e., *Categories*, *On Interpretation*, *Prior Analytics*, *Posterior Analytics*, *Topics*, and *Sophistical Refutations*) were compiled into a set of six books called the Organon around 40 BC (Lloyd 1968).

DOI: 10.4324/9781003433767-1

the three models are not necessarily sharply divided between themselves but: "[T]hose three interests, and the disciplinary perspectives which serve them, are not separable along sharp lines; they interpenetrate one another in complex ways" (Wenzel 1979, 85). Thus, is their integration possible at least to some extent? Perhaps in a theory that could be called integral (theory of argumentation).

The mentioned triplet of logic, dialectic, and rhetoric of ancient origin have also been reflected in numerous modern approaches to legal argumentation, which can be classified as logical, dialectical,[2] and rhetorical (Feteris 1999, 15–21). Legal logicians have traditionally focused on legal arguments with respect to their formal logical validity as a "criterion of rationality for legal argumentation" and logical systems (such as syllogistic, propositional, predicate, or deontic logic) used to reconstruct legal arguments composed of legal rules, facts, and legal decisions (conclusion) (Feteris 1999, 15–16). In the 1990s, certain formal logicians became interested in the cross-section of AI and law (Feteris 2017, 33).

Furthermore, legal dialecticians have emphasized the procedural aspects of a discussion or dialogue developing certain rules for rational discussion, such as legal theorists interested in the pragma-dialectic theory of argumentation (Feteris 1999, 20; Feteris 2017, 201 et seq.).[3] Different legal scholars also interested in the dialectical approach have focused on the so-called external justification of legal decisions dealing with material aspects in order to justify the premises selected in the internal (formal logical) justification of such decisions as acceptable (Wróblewski 1974). Alexy added to that the so-called procedural criteria of rationality, such as the principles of consistency, efficiency, testability, coherence, generalizability, and sincerity (Alexy 1989).

Legal rhetoricians, the most prominent of them still being Perelman, have brought the importance of audience to the focus of legal argumentation, and the audience's reception of legal arguments as the criteria to accept legal argumentation. Within that tradition, certain authors have applied the classical rhetoric of Ancient Greece and Rome to the modern judicial environment (Frost 2005), while others have only used elements of rhetoric to complete their dialectical theories, following the example of strategic maneuvering (by van Eemeren (2010) and his Dutch colleagues).

In the mid-1990s, Michael Gilbert introduced the concept of multi-modal argumentation, by which he wanted to broaden the scope of argumentation theory by adding three alternate modes: the emotional mode dealing with emotions, the ***kisceral*** mode dealing with intuitions, and the ***visceral*** mode focusing on physicalities. His alternate modes are ways or channels of our

2 Feteris used the adjective "dialogical" (1999, 19), which has a similar meaning with "dialectical," at least in the context as it is used here.

3 A similar approach to what can be considered as dialectic but from a perspective of informal logic was taken by informal logicians of the Windsor school of argumentation (Puppo 2019).

communication and argumentation, in addition to the logical mode prevailing in traditional argumentation theory (Gilbert 1994). His multi-modal theory of argumentation was meant to be descriptive, explaining the way in which people argue in real-life situations, but he also upgraded it to become normative, under the concept of coalescent argumentation (Gilbert 1997). The normativity of that approach was in that the arguers are obliged to coalesce with their claims, negotiate and finally reach an agreement rather than win over the other. This is made possible by the fact that our positions, in which our claims are only their "icons," are multi-modal such that we may agree according to one mode but disagree with respect to another mode. Unlike dialectical argumentation, which is antagonistic, making certain arguers to win over their counterparts, coalescent argumentation is synthetic and conciliatory, leading to a compromise.

What benefits could Gilbert's theory of multi-modal argumentation bring to legal argumentation? It seems to be precisely the same thing that it brought to traditional argumentation theory, which is its expansion beyond the traditional logical frontiers. Furthermore, with its rhetorical aspects, it especially rejuvenates rhetorical discussions in legal argumentation, beyond classical rhetoric and Perelman's approach. As a response to the development of new technologies, the visceral mode extends the framework of traditional argumentation and rhetoric. Moreover, a holistic or integral consideration of dialectical and rhetorical models of argument is reinterpreted in a new perspective. By grounding Gilbert's multi-modes in Jung's psychological type theory, logic and psychology are brought closer in a new light shed on their interrelation, since the cross-sections between rational and non-rational dimensions of people's behavior and attitudes have been put in another framework by contemporary cognitive science and neuroscience.

Legal argumentation is quite a complex phenomenon. It basically refers to every legal claim (conclusion) that is supported by legal reasons (premises being either legal rules/norms/principles or facts and evidence). It embraces different (i) arguers, either parties to legal proceedings (lay or professional, such as public prosecutors), lawyers (also state attorneys representing the state), other persons representing the parties, or judges to convince and persuade superior judges. Also, it includes different (ii) audiences, public servants in administrative procedures, or judges of various levels deciding in court proceedings. We could add to that also lay persons constituting, for example, a board of some association in which there is a dispute. Furthermore, there are (iii) different legal arguments, some consisting of legal rules and facts (in administrative and ordinary judicial proceedings) and some of only legal rules (constitutional and statutory in constitutional review). Moreover, there is a difference between (iv) oral and written advocacy, oral before a judge or jury and written in the reasoning of briefs, judgments, and administrative decisions. Thus, those who write about legal argumentation need to be specific about which aspect they deal with since different modes from within the ambit of multi-modal argumentation are relevant for legal argumentation in a different manner. For example, it is very difficult to find traces of emotional argumentation in legal texts written by professional lawyers unless we read concurring opinions by highest-court judges where traces of rhetorical figures having an emotional impact can sometimes be found. However, it is another issue when oral advocacy is considered, especially when cases are decided by juries. Moreover, when we take into account alternative dispute resolution, emotional argumentation is something that is expected by, for example, mediators who need to deal with a dispute in its entirety, not only from the logical mode's aspect.

Although multi-modal argumentation could be relevant in several different contexts of the phenomenon of law, in this book I mostly focus on what can be considered the toughest part of it to show the presence of multi-modal argumentation – the reasoning of court judgments. This is to be one of the most formal and official features of legal business. If multi-modal arguments can to some extent even be found in such a formal setting, this would indicate their even more exuberant presence in other less official legal frameworks.

The Book's Content

The present book is a result of not only my own theoretical research but also of the analysis of many judicial decisions together with the students in my legal theory class. It consists of seven chapters with the following content. Chapter 1 is titled "Gilbert's Multi-Modal Argumentation, Jung's Psychological Typology, and the Law." It introduces the reader to Gilbert's multi-modal argumentation, in which I found an argumentative channel for my lifetime interest in Jung's psychological types, which I had relied on to also develop a general theory of law (see Novak 2016). Furthermore, Chapter 1 introduces the four multi-modes into the framework of legal argumentation. What is of special importance in this work for legal argumentation theory is the introduction of the multi-modal alternate modes (in addition to the logical mode, also the visceral, kisceral, and emotional modes) into the traditionally conceived "fortress" of law as formal and rational, in other words, logical. This, however, makes the logical element in law in no manner superfluous but merely supplements it by rejuvenating, more or less, the rhetorical means of persuasion, moreover, by adding "physis."

Chapter 2, "Multi-Modal Argumentation in Judicial Decisions," builds on the previous chapter by going deeper and more specifically into the matter of multi-modal theory of legal argumentation. In terms of the scope and areas of the presence of multi-modal arguments in the judicial domain, it could be considered as a core of the book. Moreover, this chapter does not only emphasize the rhetorical dimension of multi-modal arguments in the judicial context, being the most formal and official of all the legal frameworks, but also their dialectical aspect. The dialectical concept of legal argument is close to what O'Keefe (1977) designated as argument 1 (argument "made"). In such a manner, we discuss arguments trying to show how they work as "products," independent of the speaker as much as possible. We present them as being made by sentences, claims, evidence, etc., and are able to deal with them symbolically and schematically. However, O'Keefe also spoke of argument 2 (argument "had"). As such, it is characterized by natural language, imprecise formulations, power differentials, and weird moves like non-sequiturs that are completely normal in a human interaction. In such a manner this kind of argument is closer to the rhetorical concept of argument. Although having dialectical dimensions, multi-modal argumentation is, with its emphasis on the alternate modes, close to a rhetorical tradition. In the context of law, it helps us disclose hidden spots between logic and psychology, thereby presenting somewhat of a bridge to cross that gap. It, however, helps us realize that such kinds of "spots" may be valid complements to traditional argumentation. While dialectical argumentation is useful and necessary to decide as well as reconstruct clear legal cases, its rhetorical counterpart is closer to what is really there in unclear legal cases. Finally, this chapter also brings many examples of the alternate modes used in specific legal cases.

Chapter 3, "Visual as Multi-Modal Argumentation," elaborates on problems associated with visual argumentation, which is mostly discussed by argumentation scholars subscribing to multimodal argumentation, being another approach studying multiple modes of argumentation. Apart from the findings of multi-modal argumentation theory, it is an essentially different but to an important extent similar and converging field of argumentation theory, its most known proponent being Leo Groarke. Although the multimodal argumentation follows important findings from social semiotics that are taken into consideration, which in addition to the verbal mode identifies a number of non-verbal modes, this chapter is nevertheless mostly grounded on the multi-modal approach of analysis.

Chapter 4, titled "Kisceral Argumentation in Law: Between Past and Present," demonstrates how kisceral argumentation has much more been used in pre-modern societies as a valid means for backing judicial decisions. It particularly depends on the internal dimension of (moral) conscience and inner highest norms one relies on. Apart from some legal systems that still rely much on religious rules, such as Islamic law, its use in modern times, due to the predominance of very much codified legal systems that, through the prism of moral pluralism, may view such inner conscience as potentially arbitrary, has more or less been confined to the frameworks of rhetorical argumentation, where in addition to explicit legal provisions all sorts of values are argued about in various decisions of highest courts in particular.

Chapter 5 deals with "Emotional Argumentation Law, and ADR." Although emotional argumentation has already proved itself as a valid and, especially in the real world, a frequent manner of arguing among people, it seems to be the most problematic mode of (multi-modal) argumentation in the legal and, even more, judicial domain where judges have a special institutional commitment of impartiality. Therefore, in the reasoning of judicial decisions, unlike trials, emotional arguments are much subordinated to the logical mode of argumentation. However, it is possible to find traces of such in the reasoning of at least certain judicial decisions to the extent of constituting their argumentative value, however, from a rhetorical perspective (the so-called arguments backed by emotions). Moreover, we also can find real emotional arguments but in the context of ADR, which is alternative to much more formal court proceedings.

Further, Chapter 6 is titled "The Legal Appraisal of Multi-Modal Arguments." This chapter brings a normative dimension to the book, without which it would only remain at the level of descriptive. We need to be aware that every specific field or system of argumentation has its own rules of argument evaluation. The legal field of argumentation has its own specific rules, which need to be followed if legal justifications want to pass their review in the legal context. Because many multi-modal arguments are able to stand that test, this assures us that it is worthwhile to consider them, or simply become more familiar with their appearances in the law.

Finally, Chapter 7 is titled "Multimodal Argumentation in EU Trademark Disputes." It builds on certain findings by the aforementioned multimodalists, whose work overlaps to some extent with Gilbert's visceral argumentation. But the approach to the analysis here is mainly multimodal. EU trademark law has traditionally mostly included word and figurative trademarks, but also shape and other trademarks. Recently sound, motion, hologram, and multimedia trademarks have been included, which brought additional argumentative problems. This chapter also deals with the classical Sabel test that the EU Court of Justice applied to resolve (multimodal) argumentative problems in trademark disputes.

References

Alexy, Robert. 1989. *A Theory of Legal Argumentation*. Oxford: Oxford University Press.

Feteris, Eveline T. 1999. *Fundamentals of Legal Argumentation: A Survey of Theories on the Justification of Judicial Decisions*. Dordrecht: Kluwer Academic Publishers.

Feteris, Eveline T. 2017. *Fundamentals of Legal Argumentation: A Survey of Theories on the Justification of Judicial Decisions*. Dordrecht: Springer.

Frost, Michael H. 2005. *Introduction to Classical Legal Rhetoric: A Lost Heritage*. Aldershot: Ashgate.

Gilbert, Michael A. 1994. "Multi-Modal Argumentation." *Philosophy of the Social Sciences*, 24 (2): 159–177.

Gilbert, Michael A. 1997. *Coalescent Argumentation*. Mahwah: Lawrence Erlbaum Associates, Publishers.

Kennedy, George A. 1994. *A New History of Classical Rhetoric*. Princeton: Princeton University Press.

Lloyd, Geoffrey E. R. 1968. *The Critic of Plato. Aristotle: The Growth and Structure of His Thought*. Cambridge: Cambridge University Press.

Novak, Marko. 2016. *The Type Theory of Law*. Cham: Springer.

O'Keefe, Daniel J. 1977. "Two Concepts of Argument." *Journal of the American Forensic Association*, 13: 121–128.

Puppo, Federico (Ed.). 2019. *Informal Logic: A "Canadian" Approach to Argument.* Windsor: The University of Windsor.

van Eemeren, Frans H. 2010. *Strategic Maneuvering in Argumentative Discourse. Extending the Pragma-Dialectical Theory of Argumentation.* Amsterdam: John Benjamins Publishing Company.

Wenzel, Joseph W. 1979. "Jürgen Habermas and the Dialectical Perspective on Argumentation." *Argumentation and Advocacy*, 16 (2): 83–94.

Wróblewski, Jerzy. 1974. "Legal Syllogism and Rationality of Judicial Decision." *Rechtstheorie*, 5: 33–46.

1 Gilbert's Multi-Modal Argumentation, Jung's Psychological Typology, and the Extension of Multi-Modality to Law

1.1 Introduction

Argumentation theory has become de-logicalized in recent decades: it is now commonplace to consider not only logical modes, arguments, and reasons but also emotional, intuitive, visceral, contextual and other factors. Rather than relying on static arguments, it is increasingly concerned with dialogic interactions (Gilbert 2004, 245).[1] A more realistic approach to arguments, one which emphasizes their interrelated and intermingled character, requires an understanding of specific modes and the nature of their interactions. In terms of its breadth or the scope of different modes of argumentation, Gilbert's concept of multi-modality seems to have gone the farthest.[2] To understand multi modes, it is especially useful to be familiar with psychological typology and one of the most influential and still widely used in practice is that of Jung.[3] With the advent of neuroscience and cognitive psychology, Jung has enjoyed something of a revival.

Yet is multi-modal argumentation theory also relevant for legal argumentation? The context of legal argumentation is about a particular professional arena, one in which both arguers and audiences are more restricted by certain normative constraints than in other fields of argumentation. Thus, it is necessary from the outset to admit that the logical mode of argumentation dominates the field and that logic (in its informal variant) is an idealized form of argumentation. Logical argument is the blueprint of a reasoned and patterned way of thinking in the area of law. However, both arguers and audiences in the legal context are individuals who enjoy multi-modality in communication and

1 Consider here O'Keefe's famous distinction between argument 1 (*making* it) and argument 2 (*having* it) (O'Keefe 1982).

2 There is another kind of multi-modality, written as "multimodality" (without a hyphen), which deals with visual, aural, and other similar modes. Their most famous proponent is Leo Groarke.

3 It is impossible to refer the reader to all the references emphasizing the importance of Jung's psychology in contemporary psychoanalytic theory and practice. It suffices to refer the reader to the website of the International Association for Analytic Psychology (IAAP 2022) in order for them to obtain a glimpse of its magnitude.

DOI: 10.4324/9781003433767-2

argumentation to its full extent. Therefore, in legal practice, in real live communication and argumentation, it can be observed that other modes are also used to justify legal positions, at least to some extent.

Multi-modal argumentation is a relatively new approach in argumentation theory. It focuses not only on logical means of argumentation but also on emotions, intuitions, and physicalities, based on the senses, as specific sources of reasons. Apart from the traditional, i.e., "logical" mode of argumentation, there are other modes. A classical approach to argumentation and reasoning suggests that arguments are essentially rational (or at least "reasoned") and that social context (including various psychological factors) as well as other matters that influence the argumentation process are mostly irrelevant to the notion of an argument (Gilbert 1997, 76).

The founder of the four modes of multi-modal argumentation, the Canadian philosopher Michael Gilbert, introduced (i) the logical mode based on linear, analytical, in short, informal logical (or critical) thinking; (ii) the emotional mode, grounded on emotions; (iii) the visceral mode, in which we argue by means of the physicalities that we experience through our senses; and (iv) the kisceral mode, which is based on our intuitions, hunches, etc.[4] Gilbert called these the "alternate modes" (Gilbert 1994).

In my discussion of multi-modality, I understand his four modes according to Jung's psychological typology and his four cognitive functions: thinking, feeling, sensation, and intuition (Jung 1971). In my view, Jung's psychological types are crucial to any understanding of Gilbert's modes. Jung would also add that the number four (as in his four modes) is not just any number, but a general and universal dimension of human cognition, something that cannot only be discussed philosophically but also used clinically in psychotherapeutic practice.

Gilbert's modes are important because they seem to have been the broadest description of multi-modality to date, and it is crucial to connect them with Jung's psychological types in order to fully and universally understand people's cognitive functions. From a comprehensive point of view, argumentation is not only about arguments as "products" but also their creators – the arguers and the audiences to whom they are addressed (Tindale 2004). Jung was not particularly interested in argumentation, but his types help us realize how the alternate modes differ psychologically from the logical mode, which is important in order to understand arguers and audiences when they deal with arguments, whether dialectically or rhetorically. However, since Gilbert's

4 What defines the mode are different sources of reasons or premises, such as logical thoughts, emotions, physicalities, and intuitions. Gilbert claims mode is a "way of communicating, a form or expression, a style of imparting information" (Gilbert 2020). Still, arguments made within such modes are built in a logical manner. This comes as no surprise as, according to Jung, our thinking function by which we analyze things around us is importantly about logic. Even though all the three alternate modes are genuinely and mostly non-verbal, Gilbert further argues that is not their essential feature (Gilbert 1994).

terminology has become established in the field of argumentation, I have decided to retain it.

If multi-modality has already been proven as a legitimate account of various argumentative situations, it is questionable whether it can be relevant for the context of law, understood as a social arena with strong formal and institutional constraints. Unsurprisingly, the dominant mode of legal proceedings and argumentation is the logical, traditionally considered the ideal mode in law. To this effect, a central topic in legal argumentation theory in recent decades has been the dialectical approach. However, since legal stakeholders are people and not logical or subsumption "machines," they also embrace other cognitive functions (or "alternate modes"), traces of which we may find in their argumentation. Although they tend to express themselves by means of the logical mode, in order to be as close as possible to the legal norms on the basis of which they argue, we can also find traces of the use of other modes in their reasoning.

Thus, the fact that alternate modes are present in the legal context follows from certain legal briefs, as well as in the reasoning of judgments. In lawyers' briefs and certain court judgments, we can find multi-modal arguments from the visceral mode. Moreover, we can find traces of "strategic manoeuvring" (van Eemeren 2010) or rhetorical *logos*, as well as those based on emotions (*pathos*), and values (*ethos*), as rhetorical means of persuasion. Accordingly, it seems that, based on the notion of multi-modal argumentation, there can be found certain rhetorical aspects of legal argument in addition to their dialectical dimension.[5]

It has already been well-established that "logic is something but not all" in the context of law (Haack 2007), and the idea can be traced back to the American Legal Realists. Thanks to the findings of multi-modal argumentation theory, it seems to be possible to emphasize this older point in a new perspective, one which is more structured and nuanced than previous attempts. In such a way, not only are the alternate modes established to a certain extent in the field of law, but legal logic also profits given that its realistic role in the justification of legal decisions is emphasized. To date, only a few attempts have been made to utilize Groarke's version of multimodality in the analysis of legal material but, to the knowledge of this author, none from Gilbert's theory of multi-modal argumentation.

5 I understand the "logical" mode *sensu lato*, encompassing aspects of both formal ("linear") and informal ("non-linear") logic. That could be accompanied by rhetorical logos. Moreover, the word "dialectic" can be used in two different meanings, which depend on the context of particular usage. In *sensu lato*, by using the term dialectic, it could mean "minor logic," to distinguish it from formal (demonstrative) logic. In *sensu stricto*, when using the term in the legal context, by dialectic it could also mean "procedure" (or dialogue) in which arguers try to establish the premises of a legal deductive syllogistic argument (logic *sensu stricto*). The dialectical dimension is then juxtaposed with the "rhetorical," whose goal is to use the famous triplet of *logos*, *ethos*, and *pathos* (and I am adding to those "*physis*") as the means of persuasion.

The existence of multi-modal argumentation is a far from novel idea. The purpose of its creation was to extend the traditional logical mode of argumentation to other non-logical and generally non-verbal modes of argumentation (Gilbert 1994).[6] Gilbert designated the emotional, visceral, and kisceral modes in order to distinguish them from the logical mode (Gilbert 1994). They very much resemble the findings of Carl Jung concerning psychological typology and his cognitive functions of thinking, feeling, sensation, and intuition (Jung 1971). If for "claims" within the logical mode their "reasons" are logical thoughts and inferences, concerning the emotional mode we have emotions, the kisceral mode, intuitions, and the visceral mode, physicalities. Jung's four cognitive functions are universal. As such they are potentially relevant for every situation, not only cognitive but also communicative and argumentative. There is no communication and argumentation without prior cognition, which to an important extent determines the direction in which we decide to argue about certain issues. In the context of such, people might back their standpoints with logical, emotional, kisceral, or visceral reasons. Accordingly, to have proper "alternate" arguments, as Gilbert calls them (Gilbert 1994), at least one premise must be in such a mode (either emotional, kisceral, or visceral).

In real life situations, there is a number of such examples, which were already emphasized more than 25 years ago (Gilbert 1994).[7] Yet the relevance of all three types of alternate arguments for legal and judicial procedures and legal argumentation has not been discussed (in one place) until recently (Novak 2020).

In modern law, formal rationality (Weber 1978) has prevailed, and there are legitimate reasons for that to ensure important social values, such as order and stability, trust in the law and its predictability, along with equality. Hence, there is no doubt about the greatest importance of the logical mode in the area of law (and legal argumentation). Thus, special rules of substantive and procedural law are enacted in order for courts with mostly professional judges to decide upon the most important social disputes, so their decisions have very important consequences for the whole of society. Hence there is a need for these decisions to be properly made and reasoned and, therefore, the basic rule of the legal context emphasizes its strong institutional and normative constraints. If a legal dialogue is about communicating on the basis of legal norms, legal argumentation cannot be free from using them.

But although the logical mode is certainly the most important, it is not omnipotent. There appear problems that need to be addressed additionally to examine the possibility of traditional (i.e., logical) legal arguments being

6 Kress even asserted that multimodality is "the normal state of human communication" (Kress 2010, 1; Tseronis 2018, 41).

7 However, his first lecture on multi-modal argumentation is said to be in the Department of Philosophy at York University in 1988 (Gilbert 2020).

influenced by multi-modality. From multi-modality, the so-called alternate modes are especially interesting, particularly in terms of seeing how they interact with the predominant logical mode in law and what kind of dynamics they bring to the static character of traditional legal arguments.

In Section 1.2, I briefly outline the basics of Gilbert's multi-modality – especially for the reader interested in argumentation who is perhaps unfamiliar with the historical roots of multi-modal argumentation. Section 1.3 connects Gilbert's multi-modality with Jung's psychological typology, which seems fundamental to any understanding of the dimension and operation of different modes. In the same section, based on the overlaps between Gilbert and Jung, I explain how I understand multi modes, the arguments based within them, and their semiotic resources. Subsequently, a longer Section 1.4 introduces how alternate modes (i.e., emotional, kisceral, and visceral) add argumentative and rhetorical flesh to the logical skeleton in the legal context. Finally, the conclusion presents situations in which alternate modes are not always simply subordinated to the logical mode but also help determine its content.

1.2 Gilbert's Multi-Modal Argumentation

The multi-modal[8] theory of argumentation appeared as a critique of formal (logical) reasoning. It stressed the point that human beings, when making decisions and arguing about them, are necessarily multi-dimensional,[9] not one-sided "machines." According to multi-modal theory, the requirements for argumentation as stressed by formal logicians are quite far from what goes on in reality when people make and justify their decisions. Thus, the multi-modal approach maintains that there are also modes other than logic that people use to argue.

One of the ideas of multi-modality (or multimodality) that is also used in the context of argumentation is decentering language as a favored manner of meaning making (Groarke 2015a, 142) and adding, not replacing, the importance of (other) "signs" for (social) communication. Multi-modality describes communication practices in terms of the textual, aural, linguistic, spatial, and visual resources – or different modes – used to compose messages (Murray 2013). It is about the use of several modes, the collection of which contributes to how multi-modality affects different rhetorical situations, or opportunities to increase an audience's reception of an idea or concept (Lutkewitte 2013). In Gilbert's multi-modality, unlike Groarke's, the semiotic

8 There is a question of whether the word multi-modality should be written using a hyphen or without, as multimodality. Gilbert suggested that it is better to use a hyphen than not, in order to stress the fact that there are other modes of communication and argumentation rather than just the logical. The word multimodal was borrowed from social semiotics (see Kress 2010).

9 Groarke maintains that divergent modes of arguing, including non-verbal arguing, correspond to a theory of different modes of intelligence, such as the one outlined by Gardner (Gardner 2011; Groarke 2015b).

resources of the modes are not limited to non-verbal expressions but may also be verbal.

One of the forerunners of multi-modality in argumentation was certainly Michael Gilbert,[10] and it is his version of multi-modality that interests me here the most. Gilbert associated arguments with a "wider notion of communication between people," including "non-verbal communications or contextual ramifications" (Gilbert 1994, 159). In this regard, Gilbert also referred to Willard's definition of an argument as "a form of interaction in which two or more people maintain what they construe to be incompatible positions," and to his position that arguers "use any or all of the communication vehicles available to them" (Willard 1989, 92). Gilbert concluded, following such a broad view, that an argument can be anything that is communicated and used to convince or persuade (Gilbert 1994, 162). He understood argumentation as a process of producing arguments and, in a very broad manner, communication as being any activity of making meaning. This was very important in order to connect the notion of argumentation to communication, especially concerning non-verbal communication. According to multi-modal argumentation theorists, this necessarily implies that the "reasons" used to support a claim can also be of a non-rational character.[11]

To be able to include non-verbal communication within the notion of argumentation, he needed to subscribe to a wider concept of argumentation and rationality since, in his opinion, people argue with whatever sorts of material, evidence, modes of communication, maneuvers, and fallacies are available to them. To supplement rationality, he preferred to refer to reasonableness, instead of irrationality, since the latter had overly negative connotations (Gilbert 1994, 160). In his opinion, this more realistic approach to argumentation goes beyond the rational (which he associates with the logical), beyond deduction and induction, and beyond the rationalistic and scientific tradition and therefore he called this traditional mode of argumentation the logical mode. But he wanted to expand our modes of argumentation beyond the logical, since he opined that the logical mode of argument is what argumentation theorists believe ought to be used (normative), while he was more interested in what forms of arguments are actually used (descriptive).

In his view, citing O'Keefe (1982), it is, firstly, true that all arguments are ultimately linguistic or even linguistically expressible since there are no non-linguistic arguments. But, secondly, if there is non-verbal communication, then where there is communication there can be argumentation and so any mode of communication can serve as a mode of argumentation (Gilbert 1994, 73). As a matter of fact, Gilbert subsequently departed from the necessity of linguistic explicitness, admitting that this is not a necessary condition of an argument. According to him, any argument can be enthymematic and thus a

10 His seminal paper, published in 1994, was titled "Multi-Modal Argumentation."

11 "Rational" in the narrow sense of informal logic's linearity.

"translation" from the verbal to the nonverbal is only an analogue or shadow of it (Gilbert 1997, 85).

In general, multi-modal theorists claim that specific modes cannot be translated into other modes. Here we can find a great similarity with Jung's cognitive functions, which I use in the continuation as a psychological correlation or explanation of Gilbert's multi-modality. For those functions (i.e., thinking, feeling, intuition, and sensation) Jung claimed the following: "The intellect proves incapable of formulating the real nature of feeling in conceptual terms, since thinking belongs to a category incommensurable with feeling; in fact, no basic psychological function can ever be completely expressed by another" (De Laszlo 1990, 257–258).

In Gilbert's view, besides the logical mode of argumentation, which he identified as the traditional one, there are three other non-logical modes of argumentation: the emotional, the visceral, and the kisceral (Gilbert 1994, 161). All three are non-verbal modes but can be linguistically explicable to a greater or lesser extent. Although the logical mode has traditionally been the grand mode, it is frequently reductionist, providing only mechanistic interpretation of various phenomena that can be more precisely communicated in other modes, where physicalities, emotions, and intuition could be more precise than words (Gilbert 2020).

Furthermore, Gilbert claims that his theory of multi-modal argumentation is a model since in reality nothing is only in one mode. And in real life we communicate with messages, not propositions, words, actions, etc., that are packed with all sorts of information. Thus, message is the essential unit of communication, and modes are tools for understanding the meanings of a communication (Gilbert 2020).

The emotional mode normally deals with emotions as a means of communication, and thereby argumentation (Willard 1989), that is used to convince or persuade, and hence we can speak of emotional arguments. What is essential in understanding the emotional mode according to Gilbert, is that the "emotions which are expressed in or by an argument are more important that the words being used for that" (Gilbert 2022, 490), since "the message is in the emotion, not in the discursive element" (Gilbert 2022, 495). Furthermore, Gilbert highlighted the visceral mode of argumentation, which stems from the area of the physical (and our senses), such as visual arguments and arguments based on touch (Gilbert 1994, 169–172).[12] Although not rational in the narrow sense, both the emotional and visceral modes can be "linguistically

12 In the framework of the visceral mode as discussed by Gilbert, other arguments based on our sensations could be added, such as auditive arguments and arguments based on smelling and tasting, as discussed by Groarke (Groarke 2015b, 2018). More precisely, if Gilbert's visceral mode encompassed at the beginning only the physical, such as gestures, what was thereafter added was also environmental, political, and social aspects, including physical configurations, power relations, cultural considerations such as class and gender, and even weather (Gilbert 2020).

explicable" (O'Keefe 1982), are able to be communicated, and may be used to "effect some difference in another person." Thirdly, the last mode that Gilbert mentioned is called the kisceral (from the Japanese term "ki," also said to originate from Chinese, which means spirit or energy) and covers intuitive and non-sensory arenas, thus intuitive arguments (Gilbert 1994, 173). In such a manner, these intuitive arguments are vehicles of communication, conviction, or persuasion. According to Gilbert, the kisceral is a mode that relies on the intuitive, the imaginative, the spiritual, the religious, the mystical, and the revelatory and extra-sensory. It covers a wide range of communicative phenomena, such as hunches, feelings, and coincidences (Gilbert 1994, 173).

1.3 Multi-Modality and Jungian Psychological Typology

In Gilbert's view, a claim includes "icons for positions that are actually much richer and deeper" (Gilbert 1995, 839) and include reasons – in the case of the logical mode of arguing (the classical CR ["claim" and "reason"] analysis) – or some other similarly supporting material (such as attitudes, beliefs, feelings, and values) (Gilbert 1995, 837), which are not necessarily rational in the narrow sense of the word. Gilbert maintained that "understanding position requires exploration of all the available modes of argumentation, from the logical, emotional, visceral, and kisceral aspects of a view" (Gilbert 1995, 843), which is what he called multi-modal argumentation.

Gilbert's four modes very much resemble Jung's four cognitive functions. I claim that Jung's psychological typology is very important to understand Gilbert's modes. Cognition as a psychological term explains how people take in information through their perception, and how they evaluate such data. One of Gilbert's main intentions was to show that the traditional rational approach to argumentation, which is mainly based on a logical manner of arguing, is only one of the approaches he typically called logical (Gilbert 1994, 161). Comparing Gilbert's logical mode of argumentation with Jung's cognitive function of thinking, we may find many similarities.

To be honest, Gilbert is not particularly convincing in terms of explaining why there should be precisely four types of modes within multi-modal argumentation. He merely argued the following:

> by explicitly opening up means of argument that are not logical we come closer to capturing the richness of everyday disputing. One might, of course cavil at my categories. Perhaps there should be five modes, or seven of them. Future discussions will, I hope, examine these possibilities.
> (Gilbert 1994, 176–177)

Therefore, is this number four simply a "magical number" that Gilbert simply plucked from the ether?

I believe that this is not the case. For example, the number four was also used by Jung to describe the four cognitive functions (i.e., thinking, feeling, sensation, and intuition) in the framework of his psychological type theory. The purpose of using Jung and his type theory here is to support the idea that Gilbert's number four has a firm grounding in Jung's theory of cognition, which is today widely used by clinical psychology and psychoanalytical practice and has to a certain extent been confirmed by the findings of neuroscience.[13]

Accordingly, using Jung's four cognitive functions seems more than useful to ground and further develop the idea of fourness in Gilbert's multi-modal argumentation. And we need psychology to discuss argumentation in order to better understand arguers and audiences as real people that are engaged in the process of argumentation, rather than only focusing on the argument as a product of such (Tindale 2004).

Furthermore, there are other similarities between Jung's types and Gilbert's modes, not just the one related to thinking and the logical mode. In Jung's view, a sensation is determined by the perception of our senses and is in such a manner empirical; thinking, once again, is a rational model of analysis and logic; intuition is our "sixth sense"; and feeling is a rational evaluative cognitive function, but quite connected with our emotions.[14] Apart from the logical mode, according to Gilbert, there are also visceral, kisceral, and emotional modes as "alternate modes." Following Jung, the four cognitive functions consist of two rational (thinking and feeling as the functions of evaluation) and two "irrational"[15] ones (sensation and intuition being the functions of perception) (Jung 1971, 330–407). For Jung, all four functions are equally important for individuals and society but certainly differ in this regard in the various

13 For example, Kahneman introduced the idea of the fast-thinking System 1, one which "operates automatically and quickly, with little or no effort and no sense of voluntary control." There is also a System 2, which "allocates attention to the effortful mental activities that demand it, including complex computations. The operations of System 2 are often associated with the subjective experience of agency, choice, and concentration" (Kahneman 2011, 20–21). That is very similar to what Jung discussed concerning active and passive thinking (Jung 1971, 342–346). On the basis of Kahneman, Greene discussed the idea of fast and slow morality. The first is based on our automatic settings, where we base our decisions on moral intuitions and emotions, while in the second settings we rely on our practical rationality. The automatic setting refers to our gut reactions as biological imperatives that can be good for ourselves and our tribes over others, and as such is biased (Greene 2013, 15, 328). Further, Haidt emphasized the strong role of intuition in peoples' decision-making (Haidt 2013). Moreover, close to Jung, Mercier and Sperber claim that in people's cognition what comes first is intuition or perception, and with the second evaluation being reasoning. Or, more precisely, they claim that "reasoning is not an alternative to intuitive inferences; reasoning is a use of intuitive inferences about reasons" (Mercier, Sperber 2018, 133).

14 In *The Type Theory of Law* (2016), Novak analyzes legal phenomena through the four Jungian cognitive functions.

15 In Jung's psychological theory, irrationality does not have a negative connotation; it only points to the opposite side of rationality. However, since argumentation theory is much more sensitive to the term "irrational," I rather keep using "non-rational," instead of irrational, to be more coherent with the field's terminological canon. Another alternative could be "reasonable" or even "rational in the broad sense."

matters that they deal with. Jung's idea was that we always perceive "matters" corporal or incorporeal either more by sensation or predominantly by intuition, and that we always make evaluations based on thinking or feeling, taking into consideration the fact that feeling seems to be more connected with emotions, while thinking is closer to logic. Moreover, among people there are the so-called rational types, such as "thinkers" and "feelers," in whom their rational cognitive functions of thinking or feeling predominate over their non-rational functions of intuition and sensation. But we also have "intuitors" and "sensors," in which the relation between the dominant non-irrational functions and their rational functions is quite the contrary (Jung 1971).

Thus, Jung's approach to cognition was holistic in a manner similar to Gilbert's multi-modal approach to argument. Moreover, although their terminology with respect to "mode" and "function" is different, they meant very similar things by these terms.

What Jung included in his type theory is that from among the four functions in every individual, (only) one is dominant, one inferior, another secondary, and a fourth of tertiary importance. Thus, the thinking type would predominantly subordinate his cognition to the rational evaluation of what he or she perceived. The feeling type would focus his or her perception on personal consideration very much taking into account his or her emotions, which would aid his or her consideration. The sensing type would primarily emphasize his or her sensory perception of the situation, and then he or she would try to evaluate such, considering that his or her evaluation would be very much (or even predominantly) influenced by sensation. Finally, the intuitive type would proceed in a similar manner to the sensing type; however, not from outside inwardly but, vice versa, from within herself or himself, his or her insights, outwardly.

It follows that different cognitive functions necessarily influence other cognitive functions in people (for example, the non-rational impact on the rational ones and vice versa) to some extent since we are personalities in which the relevance of different cognitive functions, although they might have a certain hierarchy in terms of their impact on us, cannot be strictly separated. In such a manner, this seems to suggest that Jung's psychological types basically confirm Gilbert's position that reality-oriented argumentation is necessarily multi-modal.

My claim is that by knowing Jung's psychological types we can better understand what Gilbert wanted to say to us with his four modes of arguing. Concerning a potential overlap between Jung's functions and Gilbert's modes, a short explanation seems to be in order. If we have four different functions of cognition, why should we not have four different types of arguing or four modes of communication to address the cognition of others? What can be perceived and evaluated can also be communicated and argued.

Jung's "functions" of cognition could also be understood as "modes" of cognition. His four cognitive functions (or modes) are universal. As such, they are potentially relevant for every situation, not only cognitive but also communicative and argumentative. There is no communication and argumentation without prior cognition, which to an important extent determines at least the potential direction in which we decide to argue about certain issues. In the context of such, people might back their standpoints with logical, emotional, intuitive, or sensory reasons. Consequently, different means of persuasion, such as existing in the realm of rhetoric, have developed on the basis of the different means of cognition that people share.

One word of caution is needed here. Jung's understanding of feeling is not simply emotions but something he considers as a rational function of evaluation. Jung did not study emotions very much, but he paid attention to them in his theory of complexes. Nonetheless, I have found certain elements of emotions in his cognitive function of feeling. The fact that Jung's concept of feeling included, to some extent, a special relation, or at least a consideration of emotions, follows from his description of feeling in connection with a particular way of valuation in terms of "acceptance or rejection" ("like" or "dislike"), which seems to be a kind of evaluation in which different emotions are taken into account. In this respect Jung used the notion of "valuation by feeling." Furthermore, in connection with feeling, he used the word "mood" that can also be described as a particular state of mind based on emotions. He also asserted that when the intensity of feeling increases it turns into an "affect," which is also a state of strong emotions. However, he differentiated between "active feeling (e.g. loving)" and "passive feeling (e.g. being in love)." Moreover, he spoke of feeling in conjunction with expressions "speaking to the heart" and "human warmth," words that are easily associated with emotions (Jung 1971, 256–258, 601).

There have been a number of post-Jungians who have confirmed the important connection between feeling and emotions in their research, since this very link separates feeling from thinking as an "impersonal" cognitive function. Thus, Isabel Briggs Myers emphasized the said connection by claiming that what is typical for feeling types is, for example, that they "value sentiment above logic; are usually personal, being more interested in people than things; if forced to choose between tactfulness and truthfulness, will usually be tactful; suppress, undervalue, and ignore thinking that is offensive to the feeling judgments" (Briggs Myers, Myers 1995, 68). Similarly, among the five facets

Table 1.1 A comparison of Gilbert's argumentative modes with Jung's cognitive functions

Gilbert's Modes of Argumentation	*Jung's Modes of Cognition Functions*	*Jung Cont'd*
Logical	Thinking	Rational/evaluation
Emotional	Feeling	Rational/evaluation
Visceral	Sensation	Irrational/perception
Kisceral	Intuition	Irrational/perception

of feeling, Quenk mentioned "empathetic (focusing on relationships), compassionate (considering unique and personal needs of individuals rather than objective criteria to be most important in actual decision making); accepting (using kindness and tolerance of others); and tender (the use of gentle persuasion and a personal approach to gain others' agreement)" (Quenk 2009, 11). All the aforementioned examples indicate a serious consideration of emotions by feeling, albeit in a rational manner.

In his theory of the soul, Jung located emotions in a more primitive location. They are involuntary and reactions to certain (external) events and are connected either with the conscious mind (ego), such as experiencing fear because of a physical danger, or with individual unconsciousness[16] (in relation to complexes) (Cope 2006), or with collective unconsciousness (concerning archetypes). According to Jung, the emotions cannot be separated from cognitive functions, and they definitely influence them since they are connected to a certain extent. This precise notion has been confirmed in recent years by neuroscience, where scientists established the location of emotions in the more primitive parts of the brain (the limbic system), whereas cognitive functions are part of the more developed parts (the cortex) (Eagleman 2015).

Thus, at least according to Jung, feeling is different from emotion because it is rational and voluntary while emotion is non-rational and involuntary but, as generally claimed (Novak 2016, 27–28), it is still much closer to emotions than thinking, which is also a (rational) function of evaluation that is more based on objective evaluation and detached from (personal) emotions. Thus, in my opinion, the emotions have an important role to play in how feeling is used as a cognitive function, so I am quite certain that there is a strong parallel between Gilbert's emotional argument and Jung's feeling.

Similarities between Gilbert and Jung are not only about the (i) list of four modes (or functions), but also (ii) how specific modes interrelate. For Jung, people rationally evaluate non-rational intuitions and sensations as perceptions by thinking or feeling in order to establish, communicate, or argue what they mean for them. This seems to conform with Gilbert's idea that non-logical modes can also be rationally presented in the logical C-R form of an argument. In line with an emotional argument, if A loves B (reason), he would like to kiss her (claim). For a visceral argument, if I see a bear fast approaching me (reason), I become very afraid (claim). Finally, for a kisceral argument, I have a strong intuition that there is a God (reason), so I have a need to pray (claim).[17] Although it seems that all of the previously mentioned situations

16 In a different piece of research, neuroscientists established that people are subject to "implicit biases" that are developed in early childhood and influence any adult activity that is thus not backed merely by conscious consideration, so emotional arguments, in particular, have deep connections with arguers' biases (Carozza 2016, 2). This is quite similar to what Knox claims about "image schemas" as the basis for the integration of archetypes in childhood (Knox 2003).

17 Considering that there are disagreements involved in the previous situation, such that arguments are exchanged and argumentation thereby provided.

could be fully rational, only their argument structures are such; their premises or reasons are the results of non-rational cognitive processes. However, the premises are the ones that determine the mode. According to Jung, sensations, intuitions, and emotions are non-rational and thus, translated in the language of Gilbertian modes, only the logical mode will be entirely rational. However, if the non-logical arguments can be rational per se when it comes to the non-logical modes taken independently, they cannot be so in the context of law. To be rational in the context of law, both modes and arguments must be indispensably connected with legal provisions as the premises or reasons of the logical mode.

In multi-modal argumentation scholarship, different theorists understand the concept of mode differently. In order to avoid confusion, let me now explain what I mean by the following concepts: argumentation, mode, argument, and semiotic resources. I view argumentation as a social, externalized, communicative act, one that can be externalized in the form of arguments (C-R), by using different semiotic resources, and the reasons, as essential parts of arguments, that one may want to externalize and that can refer to four different modes. Thus, a mode is a way of arguing (Groarke 2015b, 140) in which, according to multi-modal argumentation theory, reasons need not be strictly rational – in the traditional sense of the word being close to logic. Thus, the reasons for our claims can also be emotions, intuitions, and physicalities, since modes of arguing may be seen as people's externalized modes of cognition, as their psychological properties. Finally, the semiotic resources by which we express our arguments can be numerous: verbal (words) and non-verbal (pictures, sounds, smells, bodily expressions, tastes, touches, etc.).

In this regard, see Table 1.2:

Table 1.2 Multi modes, arguments, and semiotic resources

Mode	*Reasons/Premises for a Claim*	*Semiotic Resources*
Logical	Rational thoughts	Mostly verbal
Emotional	Emotions	(Non)verbal
Visceral	Physicalities	(Non)verbal
Kisceral	Intuitions	(Non)verbal

Accordingly, non-logical modes are not substantially rational, thus we perceive their premises on the basis of non-rational functions, such as sensation and intuition, rather than thinking. However, according to Jung, we generally evaluate them rationally because we are also rational beings. According to Jung, both rational and non-rational functions are present in every human being. What makes us different is the predominance of either perception or evaluation. But it seems to be perfectly reasonable, if not rational, to argue emotionally in emotional situations, viscerally in visceral situations, and kisccerally in kisceral situations. The alternative modes have their own criteria of validity. This kind of evaluation will even "survive" the RSA test (relevance, sufficiency, acceptability), borrowed from informal logic, concerning specific audiences (Gilbert 2020). However, what passes in the event of law could be another issue.

With respect to law, there is a prevalent institutional requirement that legal norms are to be applied to cases in a logical (strictly rational) manner. Concerning such, there are two possibilities with respect to deciding legal cases and justifying the decisions thereof: (i) we are entirely successful in rationally considering all those non-rational reasons (taken into consideration by legal provisions) that have been foreseen by the law as part of the legal provisions and eradicate those that have not been foreseen by the same, which would be the position of an idealized form of legal argumentation; or (ii) we are not fully successful in the former for various reasons, which would follow from a more realist form of legal argumentation, one that is supported in this book.

1.4 The Four Modes and Law

1.4.1 Introduction

Taking into consideration the fact that Gilbert's and Jung's approaches overlap to an important extent, and that Jung's psychological typology is an excellent way to understand Gilbert's modes of argumentation, I have decided to keep Gilbert's terminology with respect to the four modes because that theory of argumentation is well established and around 30 years old.

Are the previously presented modes appropriate for what goes on in law, legal procedures, and legal argumentation? At first glance, it seems that the context of legal argumentation is about a particular professional field, in which both arguers and audiences are restricted by legal provisions as some kind of contours only in the framework of which they are allowed to argue. But then both arguers and audiences in the legal context are people with a full range of abilities for multi-modality in communication and argumentation. Then, legal arguments could be discussed rhetorically as "dense human occurrences involving both arguers and audiences, not at all independent of their users" (Gilbert 2020). To what extent is multi-modal argumentation relevant for the area of law and legal argumentation?

As outlined and explained earlier, apart from what Gilbert calls the logical mode, there are also other modes that are important for people's communication and therefore also argumentation. When it comes to law, however, it is important to see whether the so-called alternate modes (i.e., the kisceral, emotional, and visceral modes) are present in legal procedures, and if, to what extent, and what role (at all) (should) they have in law as a relatively formal discipline of resolving peoples' conflicts.

In the following section, I first briefly present the logical mode, being the most important mode in law and legal procedures, and, second, discuss the presence of the three other modes, their potential overlap with the logical mode, and the possibility of their separation.

1.4.2 The Logical Mode

It is no surprise that law, legal decision-making, legal justification, and argumentation are importantly connected with logic in all respects. Legal decision-making and justification had had a logical form even before logic as a special word was invented. A kind of deductive reasoning seems to have even predated modern civilization. Imagine an existing local (legal) custom in a tribal society stipulating that person A, who insults person B, needs to give them a hen as compensation being a universalist premise. If that had actually occurred, causing a dispute to arise between A and B (the particularist premise),[18] in reaching his decision the chief of a tribe as the arbitrator of that dispute, if he found out that what was argued had indeed been committed, would most probably subsume the act of insulting under the local custom and order B to deliver the hen to A as compensation. That was deductive syllogism even before Aristotle, who first described it in his *Analytics*.

The logical mode as it is understood here is in no manner exhausted by deductive syllogism, as that would also apply to other modes as a manner of making inferences. From the other modes the logical mode differs not as much with respect to inference but concerning the premises – how they are made, in a linear and analytical manner. From the primitive deductive syllogism as depicted earlier, the civilization had made a huge progress. They became more or less institutionalized (MacCormick 2005). Be it statutes in civil law or precedents in common law, both the universalist premises are created in a very organized process of parliamentary debates and judicial proceedings, for which linear, that is "straight-line" or sequential, reasoning and analysis is typical. Moreover, in judicial proceedings, brute facts of a case are carefully analyzed before they constitute the lower premise. Not only judges but also lawyers participate in this rather complex way of creating the premises. Even lay persons need to imitate the legal professions if they want to be successful when arguing their cases before courts.

Accordingly, it comes as no surprise to claim that the logical mode is from all the modes the mode to begin with when we want to learn any lesson about legal argumentation. It has traditionally been considered as the only (by formalists) or at least dominant (for non-formalists) mode of legal procedures and legal argumentation. By this mode, Gilbert and Jung, who actually used a similar concept of "active thinking," both meant linear[19] and analytical

18 See discussion about universalist and particularist premises in defense of some modest scope of deductivism in MacCormick (2005).

19 Sometimes Gilbert even prefers "linear" to "logical" (arguments), and also uses "clinical" (i.e., analytically or coolly dispassionate) (Gilbert 1995), whereas Jung also calls it *ratio* to differentiate it from intellect (Jung 1971, 481).

reasoning that is as systematic as possible and verbal in particular. What should be pointed out from the previous characterization of this mode is certainly logic, at least in the sense as understood by *quasi*, informal logic or critical thinking.[20] Part and parcel of this mode is the deductive syllogistic argument as the "backbone" of legal proceedings, making it possible for facts and legal norms to meet at some point so that we are able to designate a situation evaluated thereby as legal (or not legal). It is the prototypical argument of this mode and represents one of the major processes in law, i.e. the application of law. The deductive syllogistic argument is composed of a major premise, where lawyers place legal norms, and a minor premise, including facts, and the evaluation of whether facts and norms meet being the conclusion. At least at the level of a framework, this argument is indispensable for any procedure that wants to be in conformity with the rule of law. Legal argumentation theory understands it to be crucial for justifying the so-called clear (or easy) cases in the internal context of justification (Alexy 1989).

However, in unclear cases we can have ambiguous, vague, or gapful legal norms in the major premise, or an uncertainty in the minor premise as to whether facts correspond to selected legal norms in order to qualify as facts to match legal facts. Thus legal argumentation theory claims that in such a situation, we need to go through a process of external justification (Alexy 1989), and (i) interpret legal provisions, or (ii) additionally establish facts to meet legal facts on the basis of evidence meeting specific standards of proof. Even in its informal variant, logic is definitely one of the most important aspirations to be pursued when normativity in law and legal argumentation is desired. However, realistically speaking, there are also other modes applicable in law and legal proceedings apart from the predominant and most typical logical mode, which may be called alternate modes, the role of which in the context of law will be presented next.

Once one departs from the "safe" area of internal justification, which is the gist of the logical mode, one steps onto a slippery path of external justification with a thin dividing line between the legal and the extra-legal. This is not to say that alternate arguments are not used in clear cases. But in clear legal texts, their place is within legal provisions. For example, a picture is used as evidence in a trial to prove the existence of a fact that has already been envisaged in the relevant statute as a legal fact. Therefore, by virtue of its being clear, a legal text restricts the possibilities of the application of non-legal arguments, which has not been foreseen to be used. However, as soon as there occurs a major problem of "translating" alternate modes into the logical one, the case might become an unclear one.

20 One interesting definition of that kind of thinking reads as follows: "Critical thinking is a metacognitive process that, through purposeful, self-regulatory reflective judgment and application of a number of sub-skills (i.e. analysis, evaluation and inference), when used appropriately, increases the chance of producing a logical solution to a problem or a valid conclusion to an argument" (Dwyer 2017, 73).

Various canons and arguments of interpretation have traditionally been used by jurists to justify claims that their decisions were as close as possible to the legal text (as the most important institutional constraint in the legal field) in situations in which the text was not clear. Contemporary legal theory is aware that we cannot expect some kind of mechanical jurisprudence from our judges, they need to be creative when deciding unclear legal cases, which would fall within a framework of some kind of material justification rather than the formal. This stems from the assumption that it is impossible for a judge to simply deduce a legal solution from premises in situations in which they are not clear.

The previously presented picture of law has traditionally drawn on the basis of the predominance of (rational if not logical) reasons that need to predominate over (non-rational) emotions, intuitions, senses, etc. It has an important rationale and is normatively very important for dealing with clear cases. It is an indispensable tool to safeguard against arbitrariness, unpredictability, vagueness, ambiguity, gaps, etc. Essentially it is everything that can be understood as safeguarding against legal instability (unpredictability and uncertainty). It is an important link with legal norms and the overarching legal value of the "rule of law" (the "parent" of all legal norms). However, there is a problem with this picture of law in unclear cases in which the traditional legal mode is unable to legally justify judicial behavior by the so-called internal means (including the facts given to meet legal facts, the legal norm selected, and the final legal inference or conclusion made).

In an unclear case in which the internal means of justification are exhausted, the premises and conclusion need to be justified by the so-called external means, at least external concerning their clear meaning, which is lacking and needs to be determined *a posteriori*. We therefore need to reach out to the legal context in which the premises are situated. This context is basically a legal system in which we have legal principles and legal values in addition to legal rules from legal texts, in which different individual and social values are embedded. The just mentioned non-formal dimension of the logical mode can be called material or substantive because it goes beyond the formal context of selecting the premises and making a final inference thereupon. Thus, realistically speaking, such a material dimension necessarily accommodates part of the alternate modes.

This version of less clear legal language is all the more appropriate for the application of multi-modal alternate modes and their arguments in the context of law, since the logical "restriction" applying in clear cases is much less firm. The alternate modes enable people to go beyond legal language, or just fill in its blank content.

As a matter of fact, to be clearer about what I mean by the logical mode in the context of law, an additional adjective, "legal," could be added to the syntax "logical mode" so the whole concept could be termed "legal logical mode." That would emphasize the particular character of legal logic, which is indispensably connected with legal norms, their provisions, legal facts, and texts as more or less verbal. However, for the matter of simplicity of my multi-modal terminology, I most often retain the expression "logical mode."

1.4.3 Facing Legal Institutional Constraints

In (modern) law, seen as a separate social system of legal norms, people have traditionally argued on the basis of legal norms from statutory, constitutional, and executive regulations provisions as well as the case law of courts. As a result, specific legal arguments developed on the basis of legal texts, or at least in (close or more relaxed) connection with them. In this respect, Perelman and Olbrechts-Tyteca discussed the relevance of starting points (Perelman, Olbrechts-Tyteca 1969), and the pragma-dialectical theory of argumentation of institutional constraints (Feteris 2017), in the case of law – legal provisions, the consideration of which is necessary in order to argue legally.[21] This issue is of paramount importance for legal argumentation, and disrespecting it leads to erroneous legal argumentation. The so-called errors in law include not only the absence of any legal provision referred to but, much more frequently, erroneous or improper legal norms being referred to in legal proceedings. Thus, in the context of law, the indispensable institutional starting points include both substantive as well as procedural legal provisions, since only both of them constitute complete legal texts as the necessary grounds in legal proceedings.

Moreover, logic and logical frameworks for making legal inferences and justifying them, whether they be simple or complex, have always been crucial for the legal world. This seems to be an axiom, at least regarding modern law. In order for the rule of law to apply, at least from the formal and internal point of view, in the context of the internal justification of legal decisions (Alexy 1989), the logical syllogistic argument seems to be an overarching form of legal argument. As a result, future legal practitioners are taught as early as in the first year of their schooling that the lower premise of the ("concrete") facts of a specific case must match the upper premise of a legal norm in order to come to a legal conclusion. However, in many legal cases, simple deduction as a method of formal logic does not suffice since we have to additionally work on the premises (i.e., externally justify them (Alexy 1989)), often in the manner of informal logic. Accordingly, in the legal context, along with the deductive argument, which may even be called the "skeleton" legal argument, we could also add to such arguments of systemic, linguistic, historical, or a similar character, to additionally explain the legal premise, and evidence to help establish the factual premise.

Considering the fact that not only typical logical and verbal arguments as traditional legal arguments can constitute arguments, but also other multi-modal arguments such as visual arguments, it is necessary to establish whether

21 MacCormick would add that this makes "a restricted version of the arguable character of law" (MacCormick 2005, 17).

these alternate arguments can be valid ones in the legal context. In any consideration of this question, I should stress from the outset that, unlike general social communicative situations in which multi-modal argumentation can apply to its fullest extent, this is not entirely the case in the legal domain. As already mentioned, law as a social subsystem has additional formal requirements, "starting points" or "institutional constraints." Therefore, this "golden" rule applies when we enter a legal discussion, which also applies to legal argumentation: in order for discussion and argumentation to be valid in legal terms, one should argue by means of legal norms (legal rules and legal principles) only (or in connection with such). This follows from the overarching principle of the (modern) rule of law as the law based on legal norms.

To argue legally, one needs to assert a claim that is recognized by a legal norm: otherwise his or her claim is rejected, and no legal argumentation ensues. The same rule applies to all participants in legal argumentation, whether they be parties, judges, prosecutors, or attorneys. All arguers and audiences participating in the legal discussion must follow this rule in order to make valid legal arguments.

Does this mean, therefore, that we need to discard the role of multi-modal argumentation in the legal domain altogether? I do not think so, and we will see next that by including multi-modal rhetorical argumentation it becomes relevant in combination with legal norms as institutional constraints.

This could be one of the answers to Groarke's question of how to differentiate between appropriate and inappropriate multi-modal arguments in the legal context (Groarke 2017). Therefore, to argue legally is to argue on the basis of legal norms, to subsume factual situations under them, and make legal conclusions. This is the basic requirement of the rule of law, as an ideal legal approach that is normative in character. Thus, the alternate arguments can also be appropriate in legal argumentation when, in a stronger or weaker manner, they are reasonably connected to legal norms. If they are not, they become erroneous.

Let us see which other modes may be present in the legal context, how these modes interact with the logical mode, how they influence it (whether consciously or unconsciously) (Posner 2008), and determine when the alternate modes fall within the legal framework and when they are to be found outside of it.

1.4.4 The Kisceral Mode

I have already mentioned Gilbert's approach of including the kisceral as a specific mode in his multi-modal argumentation. Further, I have also explained that what he considers kisceral is very similar to Jung's intuitive (Jung 1971, 398–403).

Even if we are dealing with a separate kisceral mode and intuitive arguments, we need to present them in a logical form (the claim-reason structure) in order to analyze them. From all of the mentioned multi modes and their arguments, the kisceral mode as here understood in its intuitive dimension is the most elusive and therefore the most problematic. The problem lies in its externalization: it simply cannot be communicated to one's audience by means of intuitive semiotic resources, which would be the most "natural" resources for that mode. We quite easily communicate (and argue about) stuff from the logical mode (for example, by (verbal) logical statements), the visceral mode (for example, by visuals, voices, movements), as well as the emotional mode (for example, by expressing our emotions). But with the kisceral mode, it is different. How can we express a thing such as intuition, which as a rule is an internal and introverted matter? The fact that we do have intuitions, that intuition is an important psychological function of perception, that there are not only some fleeting hunches but important moral intuitions that go all the way at least to basic archetypes and that they are reasons for our claims is one thing. But quite another thing is whether we are able to communicate them to our audiences. To do so we need to make use of the other modes (i.e., the logical, emotional, and visceral modes) through which we express our intuitive reasons. The non-intuitive modes' semiotic resources are usually close to the "stuff" of their reasons, that is, logical reasons are communicated as a rule by means of logical sentences composed of (rational) thoughts, emotional through (non)verbally expressed emotions, and visceral through pictures, sounds, etc. The problem with the kisceral mode is that it does not have "its own" semiotic resources. Still, we can communicate it by means of semiotic resources that are more natural to other modes.

It is the rhetoric[22] of values that provides the requisite grounds to enable the use of kisceral arguments. The text of a legal provision, being the primary source of the logical mode and especially in hard legal cases, becomes exhausted and there is no other way for judges than to rely on their (moral) intuitions. Dworkin claimed that in hard cases judges rely on their moral integrity (Dworkin 1978) as responsible persons who have been entrusted with an important job by their societies. In the framework of moral integrity, there is a prominent place in particular for moral intuitions as a priori elements of such integrity and only the a posteriori rational evaluation of such intuitions. The externalization of judges' (moral) intuition is presented in values that they read in unclear legal provisions as the necessary premises for legal

22 I understand rhetoric in a classical Aristotelian sense, embracing logos, ethos, and pathos as the means of persuasion, with logos being the most important, although far from the only, means of persuasion (Aristotle 2004). When logos somewhat "runs out," in the legal domain, that would be a case when the legal provisions to be applied are not really clear and there are no prior precedents, it is the arguers' credibility (ethos) that might persuade the audience. Moreover, the arguers also try to be effective in their arguing, thereby also employing non-rational means of persuasion. For how classical legal rhetoric can be still applied in modern situations, see Frost (2005).

decision-making. Through their rhetoric of values (or "ethos") they try to steer[23] the discussion into a certain direction such that the unclear legal provisions would be understood in a certain manner, of which several of them are considered reasonable.

At least in civil-law legal systems, judges pledge to uphold the constitution and statutes and to adjudicate impartially using their "conscience" when sworn in to their judicial office. So what does their conscience mean in this respect? I believe it is their moral intuition on the basis of which in unclear cases in which the legal text runs out, they find a necessary premise in it. But the problem is that their moral intuition might depend on the different moral values they uphold: and we can have both liberal as well as conservative values – all of which are moral. When the aforementioned canons of interpretation and arguments are concerned, there is more room for judges to rely on their different values and intuitions when using arguments in the framework of the evaluative-teleological group.[24]

According to Perelman and Olbrechts-Tyteca:

> In a legal proceeding, the tendency to judge according to the law is combined with that of judging on the basis of equity . . . he is not entirely immune to arguments addressed to him as a member of a particular, but not specialized, social group or a member of the universal audience: this appeal to his moral sense may had him to discover new arguments.
> (Perelman, Olbrechts-Tyteca 1969, 104)

In his later work, Gilbert developed the idea of kisceral further. His approach to this issue, as well as to multi-modality itself, is descriptive, as is appropriate for real arguers. Gilbert was aware that the kisceral is an elusive area of cognition as it can be based on intuitive, imaginative, religious, spiritual, as well as mystical aspects. Thus, he understands its controversial character but, having cited some historical quotes from famous philosophers and scientists, concluded, firstly, that "an appeal to intuition is philosophically, mathematically, and scientifically acceptable, and, secondly, these intuitions are amenable to argument" (Gilbert 2011, 164). However, my understanding of the kisceral is more restricted, as I focus merely on intuition as a cognitive function in terms of its description by Jung.

Although Gilbert initially maintained that his approach to multi-modality, including the kisceral, was descriptive, he also could not resist the temptation

23 Van Eemeren would say "strategically maneuver," although he only recognizes the role of rhetoric in the field of logos (van Eemeren 2010).

24 The famous comparative study of various national approaches to statutory interpretation made by the "*Bielefelder Kreis*" indicated four groups of arguments, including linguistic, systemic, teleological/evaluative, and transcategorical (argument from intention) (MacCormick, Summers 1991, 512–516).

to discuss it normatively. Thus, he developed "a number of criteria that can be used to judge intuitions." Thus, upon the importance of application of the principle of defeasibility, he further referred to persuasibility, consequentiality, and evidential responsibility as those "procedural" criteria that may be used when separating reliable intuitions from false ones (Gilbert 2011, 166–169). More on the assessment of the modes, also in the legal context, follows in a subsequent chapter of this book.

In *The Type Theory of Law* (Novak 2016), in which the author discussed the relevance of Jung's psychological types for law, he pointed to two versions of intuition. Jung defines intuition (Lat. *intueri*, to look at or into) as the function that mediates perceptions in an unconscious way. He sees it as a kind of "instinctive apprehension," knowledge that "possesses an intrinsic certainty and conviction." Furthermore, he considers intuition to be either subjective or objective depending on whether it stems from the subject or is somewhat related to the object, as well as abstract or concrete, whether it is directed to inner ideational connections or outside facts (Jung 1971, 269–270).

Novak's understanding of intuition in relation to law is twofold. First, he refers to the so-called extraverted intuition as the one that helps people quickly find possible connections between external objects as the so-called insights into the possibilities of these connections or relations (Jung 1971, 368), which he calls "instrumental intuition" (Novak 2016, 96). Kahneman calls this type of intuition "expert intuition" (Kahneman 2011, 11–12). In the legal arena, the sense ("feeling") of law or Rechtsgefühl designates a situation in which an experienced lawyer, one with a certain degree of knowledge and experience already obtained, quickly "guesses" what a legal solution would be when initially faced with a factual situation brought to him or her by a client. This quick "consultation" between the facts of a legal case and the legal norm, the two premises of deductive argument, is intuitive in this phase. However, for a serious opinion to be made, such guesses must be followed up by a rational analysis of the resolution of the legal problem, which is reasoned in an analytical and linear manner in the reasoning of a legal decision/opinion.

The other kind of intuition, which Novak calls "creative intuition" (Novak 2016, 96) from Jung's introverted intuition (Jung 1971, 400), is related to perceptions from within ourselves. It is connected to what Plato called ideas, Jung termed archetypes, what other philosophers named abstract ideals, and Kant coined as noumena. According to Jung, introverted intuition is related to the images arising from what he calls archetypes: "the accumulated experiences of organic life in general, a million times repeated, and condensed into types" (Jung 1971, 236).

In the area of argumentation theory, like Gilbert, Robinson rejects the experimentalists' claim that intuitions are not valuable as reasons. Instead he argues that intuitions are the best kind of evidence for judgments about moral responsibility, and distributive justice. According to him, any argument about moral responsibility would either appeal directly to intuition, or else rely on a premise that itself appeals directly to intuition (Robinson 2014, 158).

As this work is about multi-modal argumentation in the legal domain, a more common version of such intuitively perceived meta-norms in the field of law would be (legal) values, as a kind of established category for such in the framework of legal philosophy. They are certain concepts, beliefs, and goals that we value as our personal orientations and are (non)rational and semi-conscious.

According to psychological theory, an individual's values and thus social values, assuming that those perceived and evaluated first at the individual level are then communicated and debated at the social level, are (non)rational: emotional, cognitive, and (un)conscious. What influences their formation are (i) biological, genetic, and evolutionary factors (Musek 2000, 276–277). Various genetic studies have demonstrated that it is not only our temperaments and personality features that are under the influence of hereditary factors but also our viewpoints, convictions, and values (Eysenck 1990a, 1990b). There are also mechanisms in people representing connections between genetic activity and environmental influences. Thus we also have (ii) cultural, social, and educational formation of values (Musek 2000, 277–278). Then there are (iii) motives and our needs that shape our values, as well as our emotions. Finally, (iv) cognitive factors also influence value formation (Musek 2000, 278–292).

Through values as a kind of higher premises or norms we evaluate various material things, concepts, and other phenomena such as food, beverages, clothes, transportation, life, freedom, peace, responsibility, order, religion, family, marriage, etc. People make value judgments when they evaluate (or judge) certain phenomena by resorting to the mentioned values they incorporate half-consciously. Through intuition, which according to Jung is a non-rational cognitive function, we have (non)rational access to our (personal and social) values as those values that we integrate as the major premises for our life and activities.

We have internalized social values at some point in our lives, and they have become our personal values, those which we share with other people and recognize (un)consciously. For example, some prefer more responsible attitudes toward society (respecting social security and equality) over individual freedom, and vice versa. Law as a social discipline is concerned mostly with values of this kind, which do not appear necessarily as meta-norms and, most certainly not, as explicitly legal norms. Such values appear in the "background" (being inexplicit) of many legal norms, usually legal principles that are fundamental and indeterminate (Guastini 2014, 77–81).

Whenever the application of legal provisions is considered, these hidden (intuitively perceived) premises, acting as enthymemes that are not explicitly written in the legal text, may become important when we evaluate legal norms. This is more probable the more abstract, general, vague, and gappy the legal provisions are. In such a manner, these values determine judges' evaluation of explicit legal provisions in certain manners. There is an extensive literature on how the ideology of judges enters their decision-making through their value judgments based on either principles or policies.[25] In unclear cases, deduction "runs out" and the premises need to be recreated, first by rational means, although it is impossible to exclude value judgments. This is because value judgments can be hidden behind a rational judgment as a kind of logical "decoration" for a true value judgment as the main impetus or stimulant for such a final judgment.

Let me provide an example at this point. In *Plessy v. Ferguson*, 163 U.S. 537 (1896), Plessy, who claimed to be seven-eighths white and one-eighth black, refused to comply with a demand that he sit in the black railway carriage rather than the one for whites. A Louisiana statute namely required railroad companies to provide "equal but separate accommodations for the white and colored races." A passenger using facilities intended for the other race was made criminally liable. Plessy was persecuted under the statute when he failed to leave the coach reserved for whites. The state supreme court upheld the constitutionality of the statute (Stone et al. 1991, 488–490). He then appealed to the US Supreme Court.

In 1865 the Thirteenth Amendment to the US Constitution was adopted prohibiting slavery throughout the United States. It also gave Congress the power to enforce its provisions through appropriate legislation; however, it did not prohibit states from discriminating against blacks, which many states did through enactment of so-called Black Codes, which restricted their rights. One such code was the aforementioned Louisiana statute. Finally, the Fourteenth Amendment to the US Constitution was adopted to provide a constitutional basis for imposing (federal) civil rights, such as equal protection before the law, on the states (Stone et al. 1991).

Affirming the state legislation to allow separate railway carriages for whites and blacks, the Court majority held that the state legislature may have properly concluded that the law would preserve the public peace and good order. That was within the competency of the state legislature in the exercise of their police powers, following established usages, customs, and traditions in that state. Justice John Marshall Harlan dissented from the majority. By taking the equal protection clause literally, he argued that

> in respect of civil rights, common to all citizens, the Constitution of the United States does not, I think, permit any public authority to know the race of those entitled to be protected in the enjoyment of such right. . . . Our Constitution is color-blind, and neither knows nor tolerates classes among citizens. In respect of civil rights, all citizens are equal before the law.
> (Stone et al. 1991)

Surprisingly, Harlan had been a slave owner and defender of slavery as a Whig, but he then changed his position dramatically to become the "lonely

25 For one such notable example, see Kennedy (1996).

dissenter" in *Plessy*. Beth suggests that for years Harlan's private racial attitudes had been more liberal than his public statements, which were fueled by "a partisan enthusiasm and the desire to win elections . . . with a resulting split between the private and the public man" (Beth 1992, 105). According to Thompson, there are numerous factors in Harlan's background that might have softened his racial attitudes. Although he owned household slaves, Harlan's father abhorred the brutality of the system. John's wife wrote in a memoir that John had imbibed "a deep dislike of involuntary servitude in any form" from his father and teachers. Her own distaste for slavery also may have influenced his views, too. Then there was John's slave half-brother Robert, who was treated to some degree as a member of the family. According to some accounts, his father once tried, unsuccessfully, to send Robert to school along with his other children. That knowledge may have made him more sensitive to racial injustice. Moreover, there was the terrorism that the Ku Klux Klan and similar groups inflicted upon blacks in Kentucky immediately following the war, which also pushed Harlan toward the Republicans. He was appalled by the arson, beatings, and murders, and the revulsion he felt was reinforced by his friendship with a leading Republican, who as US Attorney for Kentucky prosecuted the white terrorists (Thompson 1996).

Accordingly, from the previous accounts, we can see how Justice Harlan's private system of values and moral intuitions, also accompanied with his family members' views and changed social circumstances, progressed to break his onetime public positions. Consequently, he began seeing the equal protection clause differently than the other seven judges (one was missing from the verdict). His intuitive (moral and (non)rational) reasons must have played an important part in that, which could also be grasped from his dissent in *Plessy*.

In Groarke's view, expressions of value are usually multimodal because their language is uncertain, unclear, vague, and elusive, which causes problems for expressing them in exact words. This is also a problem in the area of legal reasoning, especially because concerning the judgments of value, "the complications that arise for language in the realm of value further limits the adequacy of language" (Groarke 2017, 24–25).

Harlan's rhetoric of values suggests his dissent to the audience and a different reading of the US Constitution than the majority one, something which eventually led to its overall change of opinion about the "equal but separate" notion thereafter. In connection with such, it might seem to be a pretty ordinary claim that moral factors influence judicial decision-making. However, by pointing to a specific kisceral mode within a multi-modality theory of legal argumentation, I would like to show its distinct character in comparison with the logical mode. This contributes to greater transparency in decision-making and its justification since, on one hand, it stresses the importance of judges' creativity, and, on the other hand, it reveals that judges may potentially hide behind the letter of the law in unclear cases.

1.4.5 The Visceral Mode

Under the so-called visceral mode, I understand everything that is perceived by our five senses: in essence, seeing, hearing, tasting, touching, and smelling. Thus, communication and argumentation are based on sensory messages, as reasons on the basis of which we make claims. For example, in a communication with B, A claims that B is loud because A hears strong voices made by B ("reasons" for his "claim"). But B would deny that.

The adjective "sensory," in terms of which I understand the visceral according to Jung's description of sensation, basically reduces Gilbert's visceral since the latter is broader. It refers not only to all the physicalities that we sense and may argue upon, including all the five senses, but also the environmental issues, such as political and social aspects, power relations, physical configurations, etc. (Gilbert 2022, 490).

Jung understood sensation as

> the psychological function that mediates the perception of a physical stimulus. . . . It is related not only to external stimuli but to inner ones, that is, to changes in the internal organic processes. It is perception that is mediated by the sense organs and body-senses. . . . Since it is an elementary phenomenon, it is given *a priori* and, unlike thinking and feeling, is not subject to rational laws.
>
> (Jung 1971, 276–277)

He differentiated further between concrete and abstract sensation. Concrete sensation is related to the external objects as seen by a subject, whereas abstract sensation can be termed aesthetic and is found chiefly among artists. Concrete sensation never appears in a pure form but is always mixed up with ideas, feelings, and thoughts (Jung 1971, 276–277). Furthermore, according to Jung: "Objects are valued in so far as they excite sensations, and, so far as they lie within the power of sensation, they are fully accepted into consciousness whether they are compatible with rational judgments or not. The sole criterion of their value is the intensity of the sensation produced by their objective qualities" (Jung 1971, 213).

Following multi-modal argumentation theory, in the framework of this mode there are visceral arguments that have mostly non-verbal reasons of their own, those which can be linguistically explicable, but their verbal equivalent cannot fully express their entire dimension. If there exists some kind of "translation" of such between the modes, it is often very general, shallow, and superficial. People do indeed "translate" (or at least transfer) non-rational information that they receive (perception) into rational information (evaluation). However, the problem is that this kind of translation can never be literal and is only an approximation.

Duran claims that in the event of visceral arguments "the main thrust of the arguments is constituted by physical expressions," which means that its essence is physical. However, he continues, "what is meant by argument is not this physical base but the intellectual activity involved" (2020, 9). Thus, "the thrust of the argument goes beyond the purely physical expressions of the utterance." For that reason, he cites to psychologies who specialize in empirical research on hand gestures. They developed the so-called Information Packaging Hypothesis holding that "gesture helps speakers package information into units appropriate for verbalization." They discuss special "spatio-motoric thinking" that "provides an alternative informational organization that is not readily accessible to analytical thinking." In producing speech, "the two modes of thinking are coordinated and tend to converge" (Duran 2020, 10; McNeill 2015, 163). Jung would probably not be surprised by this kind of "sensational intelligence," based on empirical research as he would say in his theory of psychological types that sensors like athletes are more sensorily intelligent than intuitives or thinkers.

Groarke argues that "words are clumsy instruments" unable to entirely encapsulate what was communicated not only by visual multi-modal arguments but also by other multimodal arguments in general (such as sounds, tastes, smells, values, and other non-verbal properties) (Groarke 2017, 16). Kjeldsen would add that a picture as such would be a "thick" representation of its content in comparison with the words describing it being a "thin" representation of the same (Kjeldsen 2015, 200).

But how and where is this mode important for law, legal procedures, and, ultimately, legal argumentation?

For example, it is particularly important for the area of evidence assessment in a particular area of establishing (visceral) facts (see also van den Hoven, Kišiček 2017). It generally concerns the minor premise of a deductive syllogism, in the framework of which it is the role of evidence to prove that the facts of a case indeed meet legal facts – the "facts" of a relevant legal norm. When it comes to seeing or visual argumentation, suppose A is charged with the criminal offense of fraud for having sold a fake painting of a famous painter as the original one. To prove this in court, an expert would appear to testify about the fake nature of the painting. He would describe certain details to demonstrate that there are visual differences between the original and the fake in order to prove the fraudulent act. These differences as visual arguments are described in words, but it is questionable whether they can be full (or literal) translations of the visual into words. In borderline (unclear) cases, linguistic categorization or conceptualization can go either way by missing certain important points.[26]

26 Groarke reports a case, known as the Keane controversy, in which the court was to decide who the real painter was in a dispute between two painters about the authorship of a work. To determine this, the court made the two artists paint the same painting again in front of the court. However, only one artist complied with the court's request, while the other excused himself on account of some pain in his arm. Finally, the first artist painted the painting in a

Neuroscientists would say that the senses are "translated" in the brain into words, yet gestures and words may tell different stories. In this context, Sigman points to a football player being tested by means of a verbal description of how to take a free kick (Sigman 2017, 224–225). In everyday life we take such "translations," e.g., from images into words, for granted, but in unclear situations judges sometimes need a few experts to interpret the images to them, as in the case, for example, of determining whether a footprint found at the crime scene belongs to the defendant.

Furthermore, concerning the sense of hearing and auditive arguments, van den Hoven and Kišiček presented an interesting case of Stanley "Tookie" Williams, a former gang leader, sentenced to death in 1979 and then executed in 2005. They analyzed a video clip as a part of a 2005 campaign to urge the then governor of California, Arnold Schwarzenegger, to grant clemency to Williams. Convinced that he should have been pardoned by the governor, they claimed that the prosodic information, such as "pitch, pitch range, voice quality, intonation, tempo, loudness, emphasis, accentuation, and (non-)fluencies of the speaker (i.e. Williams)," which cannot be translated into words, showed that Williams had become "re-socialized" and thus a better person while in prison for such a long time. They mainly associated such prosodic features with emotions (*pathos*) and ethics (*ethos*) (van den Hoven, Kišiček 2017).

The basic problem concerning these alternate arguments is how we "translate" them into verbal and most often logical arguments for the reason of their application in law. The problem is that such "translations" or transpositions are only approximate, and the less approximate the transposition of some alternate argument into the legal one is, the less room there is for legal certainty and a greater possibility of a legal decision being reached in one way or another, especially in unclear cases. Instead of translation, we could perhaps speak about the "transformation" from one mode to the other.

1.4.6 The Emotional Mode

People who participate in legal proceedings, whether as professionals or interested parties, are far from being only rational, they are also emotional beings. This makes life more colorful and thus richer; however, emotions are generally not the most appropriate ways of communication and argumentation in law and legal procedures, which tend to be rational, objective, and impartial – at least when seen from a judicial perspective, which is one of the most important points of view in law.[27] Frankly, legal procedures not being such is not only a

manner that completely resembled the original, thus she passed the court's test and the case was decided in her favor (Groarke 2017, 17).

27 In the last decade especially, scholarship dealing with law and emotion has been growing fast (the most prominent author in the area being Maroney (2011a, 2011b, 2012)). Based on neuroscientific and psychological findings that emotions are deeply intertwined with the process of reasoning, scholars want to demystify the traditional picture of law as necessarily

problem for the emotional mode but also for other non-logical modes, such as kisceral and visceral modes.

The emotional mode deals with emotions, such as love, affection, anger, hatred, etc. In such a mode people make claims supported by emotional premises. In an ideal linear, logical, systematic, and rational mode of legal procedures, there is usually no significant room for emotions as sole or independent criteria for legal decisions and legal arguments. But realistically, it is people that argue in legal procedures and listen to arguments from other people, decide upon them, and then justify their decisions on the basis of legal norms. Thus, we cannot expect from judges to entirely eliminate the presence of their emotions in decision-making because that is impossible, which is also scientifically proved. However, we still expect from them to be impartial, not siding with either party solely due to their sympathy or anger for that party. Otherwise they might be biased, legally erroneous, or violative of rules of judicial ethics. Accordingly, instead of the traditional ideal of the dispassionate judge, a new ideal has been proposed in the law and emotional scholarship – that of the emotionally well-regulated judge (Maroney, Gross 2014).

Gilbert calls emotional argument "one in which the feelings being communicated by the participants are more important than the words being used to communicate those feelings." He further points to "the relative importance of the words versus the feelings they express that is crucial" (Gilbert 1995).

As already indicated, from a normative point of view, in the framework of legal procedures, they are required not to rely solely on emotions as independent criteria for legal decisions, as judges could appear to be biased (not impartial). It is certainly not possible to get rid of emotions and "dehumanize" a person in such a manner, but judges are asked to subordinate their emotions to rational arguments (i.e., verbal and most often logical) because this is what legal premises require in order for a rule of law to be followed.

Emotions *per se* are not "hostile" to law when they are part of legal norms. It is especially constitutional values and human rights that were built on the basis of strong public emotions (such as liberty, equality, etc., with which strong emotions might be associated). In his Constitutional Sentiments, Sajo argues the following:

> Widely shared moral judgements are summarized and fixed as vague values and principles of the constitution and set constitutional principles.

dispassionate. Maroney also cites Justice Brennan (Maroney, Gross 2014). Even more than 30 years ago, a justice of the US Supreme Court, William J. Brennan, held that judges should recognize passion in themselves, which he described as the "range of emotional and intuitive responses to a given set of facts or arguments, responses which often speed into our consciousness far ahead of the lumbering syllogisms of reason." In his opinion, this would keep judges closer to human reality and prevent law from becoming sterile (Brennan 1988, 9). It seems eerily reminiscent of Kahneman's fast and slow thinking, some 20 years before it was formulated!

> These priorities are needed to solve otherwise hard-to-treat complex problems. . . . Values animated by moral sentiment have specific regulatory power here: moral values preclude the consideration of some of the consequences of value-driven decisions. Protected values operate as emotion-backed constraints on choice.
>
> (Sajo 2011, 42–43)

Accordingly, there is no problem with using emotions to back legal norms. A problem appears when they are used to circumvent or undermine legal norms.

In performing their judicial function impartially, judges should not be biased, a very typical version of which is emotional bias. To avoid situations in which this might occur, legal systems provide for the possibility of their recusal. There are (i) absolute reasons for recusal in which, if they are in very close relations with certain people (such as spouses, children, parents, brothers and sisters, etc.), they must request their recusal from deciding the case. With regard to (ii) relative reasons for recusal, they need to request their recusal from a case if they decide that their emotions could make them biased. Thus, the law has envisaged the problem and provided solutions but only for the gravest or most common situations of emotional bias. What about all other cases in which parties do not know about judges' relations that specific people or judges are not aware of being emotionally biased? We could say, following Kjeldsen (Kjeldsen 2015, 200), that legal provisions are much "thinner" than the emotional situations they are supposed to deal with rationally. This gives parties, attorneys, and even judges tremendous potential for their rhetorical strategies.

For example, according to Bandes (2016), there are at least two areas where it is interesting to study implicit emotional norms: one is remorse, the other rape. First, several studies found that when a defendant does not look suitably remorseful, his or her sentence is likely to be harsher. A particularly harsh price is paid in such situations by those facing capital punishment (Haney, Sontag, Costanzo 2010). Second, it is generally believed that rape victims should act hysterically, rather than seeming calm shortly after the crime, so one victim was even charged with perjury for reporting a rape, largely based on her flat emotional response (Miller, Armstrong 2015). Moreover, a study demonstrated that judges in Minnesota adjudged rape victims most credible when they expressed compassion or forgiveness for their assailant, rather than anger (Schuster, Propen 2011).

Therefore, to act legally in such emotionally explicit situations, and to rely solely on legal arguments, judges would need to overcome their emotional arguments or, if they feel that they are unable to do so, request their recusal from the case. But that is often not easy, and we are frequently not even aware of the impact some emotional arguments have on us, especially when it happens semi-consciously or even unconsciously. We may think that we can handle an emotionally sensitive situation but that might only be our rationalization as a psychological defense mechanism. In a real situation, just like other people, judges are not immune to all of these influences. As professionals they are trained and experienced to avoid such situations and know how to overcome them, but it is impossible to say that they would do the right thing in a hundred percent of cases. It is more realistic to say that, just like all other people, they are fallible too, and it is more likely that they will slip up the more complicated the case is and when the premises for making use of inference are unclear.

The previous findings present a challenge for argumentation theory, at least one that is more rhetorically oriented. Thus, we will no longer deal with emotions in law in a black-and-white manner but will study "gray areas" of how the emotional mode and emotional arguments interrelate with the logical mode and arguments and will determine what are acceptable, non-erroneous, emotions in the law. This is because, to date, the sharp emotion versus reason dichotomy has clouded the issue of how arguments actually persuade (Bandes, Salerno 2014).

That judges are also emotional in their decision-making is one issue, but quite another is to analyze this from the justification of their judgments, which is primarily the interest of legal argumentation theory. Indeed, especially in their dissenting opinions,[28] one can find examples where they are more personal and use emotions as rhetorical devices or figures (pathos) to try to steer the understanding of legal provisions in a certain direction. For example, from the history of US constitutional law, Holmes's dissenting opinion in *Lochner v. New York*[29] was to some extent emotional when he stressed the following:

> The Fourteenth Amendment does not enact Mr. Herbert Spencer's Social Statics. . . But a constitution is not intended to embody a particular economic theory, whether of paternalism and the organic relation of the citizen to the State or of laissez faire. It is made for people of fundamentally differing views.
>
> (*Lochner v. New York*, 198 U.S. 45, 1905 in Stone et al., 795–796)

1.5 Conclusion

We generally have one crucial mode in the context of law, namely, the logical mode, and three other seemingly less relevant modes that we call alternate

28 Frost also finds judges' dissents as having rich potential in terms of studying their rhetorical strategies (Frost 2005, 111–138).

29 Mr. Lochner was convicted of permitting an employee to work for him more than the statutory maximum of 60 hours per week. Lochner appealed, claiming the law violated his freedom of contract under the Fourteenth Amendment, as part of the due process clause. Deciding on the issue of whether a state may have generally prohibited private agreements to work more than a specified number of hours, the US Supreme Court found no violation of the Constitution, deeming that the general right to contract in business was clearly part of the individual liberty protected by the Fourteenth Amendment (Stone et al. 1991, 790–796).

modes. Although they should have no decisive importance in the context of law, albeit from an idealized point of view, realistically speaking they keep appearing all the time in a broader context of decision-making and argumentation as they remain present in both arguers and audiences that consist of people as multi-dimensional individuals.

As a rule, the four modes influence one another and overlap in the process of argumentation all the time. However, to have a non-erroneous relation between non-logical modes and the logical mode from the point of view of the rule of law and legal validity, in their decisive capacity they need to be subordinated to the logical mode, that is, to legal premises, the major one consisting of a legal norm and the minor one including (concrete) facts, and there needs to be a meeting thereof to form a legal conclusion. This is certainly true if we know what legal premises actually require in a specific case. The non-logical modes may be relevant for a legal case if the logical mode allows room for their relevance and to the extent it does so: (i) the visceral mode is important in certain cases, in the epistemic as well as rhetorical sense, for establishing the lower premise in particular with regard to evidence; and (ii) the kisceral and emotional modes add an important rhetorical dimension to the legal premises.

All of the previous examples of the alternate modes would be completely useless if we are certain that all of them can fully be translated into the logical mode. We would simply say that all these alternate modes simply need to be subordinated to the logical mode if they want to have any relevance in legal argumentation, that is, to the one that is verbal, logical, and rational in the traditional sense of the word (i.e., *logos* – being both logical and verbal). But if we are not fully sure about that, by understanding that there is a certain gap between an idealized legal situation and what actually occurs in legal reality, we have to take into account the possibility that the alternate modes that appear in legal procedures are not always fully subordinated to the logical mode. As a result, they can thus influence how it is used, which is more common in hard or unclear legal cases in which legal premises are unclear, ambiguous, and gappy. This opens up a certain space for the relevance of rhetoric and rhetorical dimensions (including *pathos and ethos*) when arguing in legal procedures. In such decisions there are several possible solutions, which all need to be in accordance with the law, and alternate non-legal modes can also influence the understanding of legal premises.

Lawyers who represent their clients in numerous court proceedings every day are very aware of the rhetorical value of the mentioned alternate modes and their arguments. They know logic is only one part of the "story" and thus they prepare strategies for how to influence judges. In doing so, they are not concerned with idealized legal argumentation's requirements, which uphold logical results, but rather in its realistic outcomes. This applies particularly, but not exclusively, to their strategies in unclear or hard cases.

Gilbert's multi-modal theory of argumentation played a very important role in demonstrating that there is no single mode of argumentation, but rather it is in fact multi-modal. This created a more holistic approach to arguments in which we should consider logic as only a skeleton of the whole body of an argument (Carozza 2016, 8). Further, Jung's psychological types are needed to better understand the psychological grounding of the mentioned modes and to justify the number enumerated.

All of this is intended to convey the idea that logical, linear, or clinical arguments only exist in theoretical models, whereas in reality, in real-life situations, we have multi-modal ones, where different modes and their arguments influence each other incessantly.

Last but not least, I would like to conclude this chapter with a note on the comparison between multimodal and multi-modal argumentation made for the first time in the argumentation community by Groarke. He finds the two approaches complementary. Referring to Tseronis and Forceville (2017), he emphasized that the authors there establish nine different modes (written language, spoken language, visuals, music, non-verbal sounds, gestures, olfaction, taste, and touch) by also linking them with social semiotics (Groarke 2022, 507–510). Moreover, he finds the greatest overlap between the multimodal and the multi-modal argumentation in the visceral mode of the latter. He finds it as a *material mode*, in which arguers use various materials to construct arguments when they perform an act of arguing, while he understands the logical and emotional modes as the *modes of rationality*, in which arguers assess arguments on the basis of logical or emotional criteria. Finally, he sees the kisceral mode also as a mode of rationality, rather than as a material mode, on the basis of which arguers have intuitions within their private state of mind, which are disclosed only as their reports about such states. In that, he found a similarity with the logical and emotional modes as modes of rationality (Groarke 2022, 513–517).

I basically agree with his classification of the logical and emotional modes as the modes of rationality, and the visceral mode as a material mode, as that would correspond to what I discussed earlier when linking Gilbert's modes with Jung's cognitive functions. However, when it comes to the kisceral mode, I do not agree with Groarke and his classification of this mode as a mode of rationality. According to the previous description of Jung's cognitive function of intuition, I would see it as a material mode, like the visceral mode, whose "material" as information directs our rationality to think in a certain direction. This would also follow Gilbert's finding that with respect to many kisceral arguments, their experience of discovery is the same as the justification (Gilbert 2022, 500). This perfectly matches Jung's idea that there are two cognitive functions of thinking (the logical mode) and feeling (the emotional mode) as evaluation, and two of sensation (the visceral mode) and intuition (the kisceral mode) as perception.

References

Alexy, Robert. 1989. *A Theory of Legal Argumentation*. Oxford: Clarendon Press.
Aristotle. 2004. *Rhetoric*. Mineola, New York: Dover Publications, Inc.
Bandes, Susan. 2016. "What Roles do Emotions Play in the Law?" http://emotionresearcher.com/what-roles-do-emotions-play-in-the-law/ (30.1.2019).

Bandes, Susan, Salerno, Jessica. 2014. "Emotion, Proof, and Prejudice: The Cognitive Science of Gruesome Photos and Victim Impact Statements." *Arizona State Law Journal*, 46: 1003–1056.

Beth, Loren P. 1992. *John Marshall Harlan: The Last Whig Judge*. Lexington: University Press of Kentucky.

Brennan, William J. 1988. "Reason, Passion, and the 'Progress of the Law'." *Cardozo Law Review*, 10: 3–23.

Briggs Myers, Isabel, Myers, Peter B. 1995. *Gifts Differing: Understanding Personality Type*. Mountain View, California: Davies-Black Publishing.

Carozza, Linda. 2016. "Emotional Arguments: What would Neuroscientists and Psychologists Say?" *OSSA Conference Archive*, 74. https://scholar.uwindsor.ca/ossaarchive/OSSA11/papersandcommentaries/74 (20.10.2018).

Cope, Theo A. 2006. *Fear of Jung: The Complex Doctrine and Emotion*. London: Routledge.

De Laszlo, Violet S. 1990. *The Basic Writings of C. G. Jung*. Princeton: Princeton University Press.

Duran, Claudio. 2020. "Diversity in Argumentation Theory." *Paper Presented at the 12th OSSA Conference, CRRAR*, Windsor: Windsor University, 1–14.

Dworkin, Ronald. 1978. *Taking Rights Seriously*. Cambridge: Harvard University Press.

Dwyer, Christopher P. 2017. *Critical Thinking, Conceptual Perspectives and Practical Guidelines*. Cambridge: Cambridge University Press.

Eagleman, David. 2015. *The Brain: The Story of You*. Edinburg, London: Canongate.

Eysenck, Hans J. 1990a. "Biological Dimensions of Personality." In Pervin, Lawrence A. (Ed.). *Handbook of Personality: Theory and Research* (244–276). New York: Guilford.

Eysenck, Hans J. 1990b. "Genetic and Environmental Contributions to Individual Differences: The Three Major Dimensions of Personality." *Journal of Personality*, 58: 245–261.

Feteris, Eveline T. 2017. *Fundamentals of Legal Argumentation*. Dordrecht: Springer.

Frost, Michael H. 2005. *Introduction of Classical Legal Rhetoric: A Lost Heritage*. Aldershot, Burlington: Ashgate.

Gardner, Howard. 2011. *Frames of Mind: The Theory of Multiple Intelligences*. New York: Basic Books.

Gilbert, Michael A. 1994. "Multi-Modal Argumentation." *Philosophy of the Social Sciences*, 24 (2): 159–177.

Gilbert, Michael A. 1995. "What is an Emotional Argument? Or Why Do Argument Theorists Quarrel with Their Mates?" In van Eemeren, Frans H., Grootendorst, Rob, Blair, Anthony J., Willard, Charles A. (Eds.). *Analysis and Evaluation: Proceedings of the Third ISSA Conference on Argumentation* (Vol. II, 3–12). Amsterdam: Sic Sat.

Gilbert, Michael A. 1997. *Coalescent Argumentation*. Mahwah, New Jersey: Lawrence Erlbaum Associates, Publishers.

Gilbert, Michael A. 2004. "Emotion, Argumentation, and Informal Logic." *Informal Logic*, 24 (3): 245–264.

Gilbert, Michael A. 2011. "The Kisceral: 'Reason and Intuition in Argumentation'." *Argumentation*, 25: 163–170.

Gilbert, Michael A. 2020. "Understanding the Embrace of Fallacy: A Multi-Modal Analysis." *12th OSSA Proceedings: Evidence, Persuasion & Diversity*. https:scholar.uwindsor.ca/OSSAarchive/OSSA12/ (25.5.2021).

Gilbert, Michael A. 2022. "Multi-Modal 2020: Multi-Modal Argumentation 30 Year Later." *Informal Logic*, 42 (3): 487–506.

Greene, Joshua. 2013. *Moral Tribes. Emotion, Reason, and the Gap Between Us and Them*. London: Atlantic Books.

Groarke, Leo. 2015a. "Going Multimodal: What is a Mode of Arguing and Why Does it Matter?" *Argumentation*, 29: 133–135.

Groarke, Leo. 2015b. "Modes of Arguing, Logophilia, and the Limits of Language." *CERMEG*. www.cermeg.it/2014/12/01/giornate-tridentine-di-retorica-15-%E2%80%93-gtr15-save-the-date-call-for-papers/ (27.7.2017).

Groarke, Leo. 2017. "Multimodality and the Law." In Manzin, Maurizio, Puppo, Federico, Tomasi, Serena (Eds.). *Multimodality and Reasonableness in Judicial Rhetoric*. Studies on Argumentation & Legal Philosophy/2. Trento: Università degli studi di Trento, Quaderni della Facoltà di giurisprudenza.

Groarke, Leo. 2018. "Auditory Arguments: The Logic of 'Sound' Argument." *Informal Logic*, 38 (3): 312–340.

Groarke, Leo. 2022. "Gilbert as Disrupter: Modes (of Many Sorts) in the Theory of Argument." *Informal Logic*, 42 (3): 507–520.

Guastini, Riccardo. 2014. *La sintassi dei diritto*. Torino: Giappichelli editore.

Haack, Susan. 2007. "On Logic in the Law: 'Something, but not All'." *Ratio Juris*, 20 (1): 1–31.

Haidt, Jonathan. 2013. *The Righteous Mind: Why Good People Are Divided by Politics and Religion*. New York: Vintage Books.

Haney, Craig, Sontag, Lorelei, Costanzo, Sally. 2010. "Deciding to Take a Life: Capital Juries, Sentencing Instructions, and the Jurisprudence of Death." *Journal of Social Issues*, 50: 149–176.

International Association for Analytical Psychology (IAAP). 2022. www.iaap.org (2.12.2019).

Jung, Carl G. 1971. *The Psychological Types*. London: Routledge.

Kahneman, Daniel. 2011. *Thinking, Fast and Slow*. London: Penguin Books.

Kennedy, Duncan. 1996. *A Critique of Adjudication*. Cambridge: Harvard University Press.

Kjeldsen, Jens. 2015. "The Rhetoric of Thick Representation: How Pictures Render the Importance and Strength of an Argument Salient." *Argumentation*, 29: 197–215.

Knox, Jean. 2003. *Archetype, Attachment, Analysis: Jungian Psychology and the Emergent Mind*. London: Routledge.

Kress, Günther. 2010. *Multimodality: A Social Semiotic Approach to Contemporary Communication*. London: Routledge.

Lutkewitte, Claire (Ed.). 2013. *Multimodal Composition: A Critical Sourcebook*. Boston: Bedford/St. Martin's.

MacCormick, Neil. 2005. *Rhetoric and the Rule of Law*. Oxford: Oxford University Press.

MacCormick, Neil, Summers, Robert. 1991. *Interpreting Statutes*. Aldershot: Ashgate.

Maroney, Terry. 2011a. "The Persistent Cultural Script of Judicial Dispassion." *California Law Review*, 99: 629–681.

Maroney, Terry. 2011b. "Emotional Regulation and Judicial Behavior." *California Law Review*, 99: 1485–1555.

Maroney, Terry. 2012. "Angry Judges." *Vanderbilt Law Review*, 65: 1207–1286.

Maroney, Terry, Gross, James. 2014. "The Ideal of the Dispassionate Judge: An Emotion Regulation Perspective." *Emotion Review*, 6: 142–151.

McNeill, David. 2015. *Why We Gesture?* Cambridge: Cambridge University Press.

Mercier, Hugo, Sperber, Dan. 2018. *The Enigma of Reason: A New Theory of Human Understanding*. London: Penguin Books.

Miller, Christian T., Armstrong, Ken. 2015. "An Unbelievable Story of Rape." *Pro Publica and the Marshall Project*, December 16. https://propublica.org/article/false-rape-accusations-an-unbelivable-story (31.1.2019).

Murray, Joddy. 2013. "Composing Multimodality." In Lutkewitte, Claire (Ed.). *Multimodal Composition: A Critical Sourcebook*. Boston: Bedford/St. Martin's.

Musek, Janek. 2000. *Nova psihološka teorija vrednot*. Ljubljana: Educy.

Novak, Marko. 2016. *The Type Theory of Law: An Essay in Psychological Jurisprudence*. Cham: Springer.

Novak, Marko. 2020. "Multi-Modal Argumentation and Rhetoric in Judicial Proceedings." *Argumentation and Advocacy*, 56 (1): 41–60.

O'Keefe, Daniel J. 1982. "The Concepts of Argument and Arguing." In Cox, Robert J., Willard, Charles, A. (Eds.). *Advances in Argumentation Theory and Research* (3–23). Illinois: AFA/SIU Press.

Perelman, Chaïm, Olbrechts-Tyteca, Lucie. 1969. *The New Rhetoric: A Treatise on Argumentation*. Notre Dame: University of Notre Dame Press.

Plessy v. Ferguson. 1896. 163 U.S. 537.

Posner, Richard. 2008. *How Judges Think*. Cambridge: Harvard University Press.

Quenk, Naomi L. 2009. *Essentials of Myers-Briggs Type Indicator Assessment*. Hoboken, New Jersey: John Wiley & Sons.

Robinson, Robert C. 2014. "The Role of Intuitions in Moral and Political Arguments about Justice." *ISSA: 8th International Conference on Argumentation*, Amsterdam: University of Amsterdam.

Sajo, Andras. 2011. *Constitutional Sentiments*. New Haven, London: Yale University Press.

Schuster, Mary L., Propen, Amy. 2011. *Victim Advocacy in the Courtroom: Persuasive Practices in Domestic Violence and Child Protection Cases*. Boston: Northeastern University Press.

Sigman, Mariano. 2017. *The Secret Life of the Mind*. New York: Little, Brown and Company.

Stone, Geoffrey R. et al. 1991. *Constitutional Law*. Boston, Toronto, London: Little, Brown and Company.

Thompson, Charles. 1996. "Plessy v. Ferguson: Harlan's Great Dissent." *Kentucky Humanities*, 1.

Tindale, Christopher W. 2004. *Rhetorical Argumentation, Principles of Theory and Practice*. Thousand Oaks, London, New Delhi: SAGE Publications.

Tseronis, Assimakis. 2018. "Multimodal Argumentation: Beyond the Verbal/Visual Divide." *Semiotica*, 220: 41–67.

Tseronis, Assimakis, Forceville, Charles (Eds.). 2017. *Multimodal Argumentation and Rhetoric in Media Genres*. Amsterdam: John Benjamins.

van den Hoven, Paul, Kišiček, Gabrijela. 2017. "Processing Multimodal Legal Discourse; The Case of Stanley 'Tookie' Williams." In Manzin, Maurizio, Puppo, Federico, Tomasi, Serena (Eds.). *Multimodality and Reasonableness in Judicial Rhetoric*. Studies on Argumentation & Legal Philosophy/2. Trento: Università degli studi di Trento, Quaderni della Facoltà di giurisprudenza.

van Eemeren, Frans H. 2010. *Strategic Maneuvering in Argumentative Discourse*. Amsterdam: John Benjamins Publishing Company.
Weber, Max. 1978. *Economy and Society*. Berkeley: University of California Press.
Willard, Charles A. 1989. *A Theory of Argumentation*. Tuscaloosa, Alabama: University of Alabama Press.

2 Multi-Modal Arguments in Judicial Decisions

2.1 Introduction

Having established the link between Gilbert's multi modes and Jung's psychological type, to understand a psychological basis of the "human" element in the framework of argumentation, the discussion continued with the presence of alternate modes in the legal domain, especially concerning judicial reasoning. Now it seems important to take a closer look at how these alternate modes work along the logical mode and typical legal arguments. What is their place in dialectic and rhetorical legal arguments? How do legal texts being part of the upper premise of legal logical syllogism allow for the presence of the alternate modes? How does the presence of multi-modal arguments determine the lower (epistemic) premise?

In Section 2.2, I discuss the general problem of multi-modal arguments appearing in the legal context and stress that there are three different levels of justification (legalistic, legal-systemic, and meta-legal) depending on which type of legal cases we deal with, from clear to unclear to very unclear ("ideologic") ones. The differentiation between the dialectic and rhetorical modes of arguments that begins in this section continues into Section 2.3. Then, in Section 2.4, I emphasize their difference with respect to different models and types of legal argumentation. Section 2.5 presents all four multi-modes in the context of various legal situations and legal acts, emphasizing either the dialectical or rhetorical character of arguments utilized. Finally, in Section 2.6, I include a discussion about "genuine" multi-modal arguments and arguments "about" multi-modality, which is important to add a rhetorical dimension to the discussion of multi-modal argumentation in the legal context, to supplement the dialectical dimension.

2.2 Three Models of Legal Argument

From Aristotle onwards, the notion of an argument has traditionally been discussed in three different models: the logical, dialectical, and rhetorical.[1] In

1 His different models of arguments in *Posterior Analytics*, *Topics*, and *Rhetoric* are part of the cultural heritage of Western civilization. The three models were first re-emphasized in modern times by Wenzel (1990).

DOI: 10.4324/9781003433767-3

the framework of interaction among the constitutive elements of argumentation, namely arguers, argument, and audience, each of them is centered on one of these features: the logical model focuses on arguments, the dialectical model addresses arguers, and the rhetorical is concerned with the audience. Moreover, the logical model stresses the importance of an argument as a product, the dialectical model discerns the procedural significance of an argument in a dialogue, and the rhetorical model emphasizes argument in a process "used in argumentative communications between arguer and audience" (Tindale 2004, 4–8). Within the ambit of modern legal argumentation, all three models have been emphasized.

A typical meaning of logic is twofold: formal (*logica maior*) and informal (*logica minor*). As formal logic is more used for artificial language rather than law, for which natural language is typical, I understand logic, whenever I do not use the adjective "formal" in front of it, in a more informal manner, namely as dialectic. Formal logic is "limited to the examination of demonstrative methods of proof" (Perelman, Olbrechts-Tyteca 1969, 13), which requires that its premises must be true and is not suitable for an area of human activity, where only arguable (probable) premises can be established. Such an area is, for example, also the area of law, in which practical, rather than theoretical, rationality is used for the resolution of people's disputes.

Therefore, dialectic would be more appropriate for legal usage than formal logic because we deal with a natural language in which it is almost impossible to achieve formal precision. Thus, (i) dialectic can be, in the Aristotelian sense, understood as *logica minor*. But there can be (ii) another understanding of dialectic, namely procedure or dialogue. Here, I am mainly concerned with dialectic in the sense of "informal logic" (or *logica minor*), which I use to designate my first model of legal argument, namely the dialectical model. With respect to the multi-modal theory of legal argumentation, we will normally find it in the logical mode of such. As it follows in the subsequent section, we would typically find it in relatively clear cases, where the premises of a deductive syllogism are more or less clear and are simply applied as such. The fact that clear cases can get messy does not deny the existence of routine cases, which legal practice would certainly confirm. By the premises, I mean the upper premise, where arguers place legal provisions, and the lower premise, including facts (backed by evidence) necessary for the legal provisions to be applied.

What about the rhetorical model of argument in the context of legal argumentation? Well, when the premises are no longer clear, and cease to "speak for themselves," we need further justification from the arguers about which legal provisions need to be selected, how they are to be interpreted, and also additional evidence if those already produced do not secure a clear epistemic picture. There seem to be two different levels: one more direct where arguers try to find (legal) "systemic" arguments to persuade their audience, and the one that is in the background at a meta-legal level.

Accordingly, there are in general three typical models of legal argument, applicable to clear and unclear cases. In the continuation, I describe each of them, establish criteria for their differentiation, and provide some examples of their application.

2.2.1 *The Dialectical Model*

As to the dialectical or, in a sense, logical model, there have been different approaches by theorists analyzing legal arguments from the perspective of syllogistic, propositional, predicate, deontic, etc. logic, who built logical models of ideal legal arguments (Feteris 2017, 25–28). In a similar manner, MacCormick asserted the importance of (logical) deductivism and syllogistic argument (with the upper premise being the legal norm, the lower premise representing facts, and the conclusion being a legal decision) for the rule of law (MacCormick 1994, 2005). He termed the use of the syllogistic argument to be the first order of the justification of a legal decision, which is the manner in which clear cases are resolved. Alexy made a similar claim, preferring to describe it as the internal criteria of justification (Alexy 1989, 218–226). Both their approaches with respect to the first level of legal justification have been considered and followed by the mentioned dialectical model of legal argument.

The word dialectic, and adjective dialectical, has been frequently used in modern argumentation theory, mostly in a dialogical or procedural sense. For example, the pragma-dialectical theory of argumentation has built a number of procedural rules to follow in order to resolve disagreements in a reasonable way. Here I do not use the word dialectic in the same sense. There is no need to develop specific procedural criteria when it comes to legal argumentation because, in the context of law, we already have very detailed procedural codes, including dozens of rules that need to be followed in order to avoid legal errors. Instead, it is more important to develop additional procedural criteria to resolve disagreements in areas that have not been that institutionally regulated. Clear procedural rules are also dealt with under the first level of the logical (more precisely dialectical) justification of judicial decisions. Therefore, in that context, we have a kind of double deductive syllogism, including both the substantive and procedural upper premises (including substantive and procedural legal provisions), which determine the legal correctness of both substantive and procedural lower premises, the first being facts and the second a specific step made in the proceedings.

Deductive syllogism in which the upper premise is presented by a legal provision, and the lower premise is a factual situation, as understood through the prism of the selected legal provision (i.e., the legal norm), is a cornerstone of the most essential legal thinking. By such, any particular act in the legal domain, either brute facts, which through the prism of a selected legal provision and thereby the legal norm become concrete facts, or judicial decisions challenged at an appeal, are subsumed under the universalist premise, and a legal conclusion (most typically judgment) is made. In such a manner, the rule of law as the supreme legal value is secured. That means that any particularist premise being consisted of facts or certain acts is subject to evaluation whether it is in accordance with universalist premises, i.e., legal provisions. Thereby deductivism in law needs to be defended; however, there appears a question how much of it actually occurs and can be supported. MacCormick argued for the so-called modest deductivism (MacCormick 2005), which is not difficult to agree with.

Deductive syllogism pertains to formal logic in which it holds that if the premises of it are true also the conclusion must be true. Aristotle introduced it in his *Posterior Analytic*, as formal or scientific logic, but also discussed it in the *Topics*, as dialectical syllogism. Although, in the context of law, we need deductive syllogism, it is impossible to claim that the premises created therein are (absolutely) true or logically valid. Even in the clearest case we would rather say that the premises selected are probably valid, which leads us to the criterion of acceptability (by a relevant community of professional lawyers or a relevant audience) as a better term. The acceptability of the premises would point to the fact that a way in which they were created would be accepted for a relevant legal community (in a specific jurisdiction). Even though it is impossible to claim logical validity to legal deductive syllogism, we still need the structure, modest "dialectic" deductivism, in order that the rule of law as the supreme legal value is protected.

As already indicated, quite similar positions seem to have been maintained by MacCormick (1994) and Alexy (1989) in their theories of legal argumentation, where they argued for the first-order or formal/internal criteria or levels of justification, which is typical of clearest cases. According to their approach, any reasoning of a legal decision needs to begin with this level of justification. We could also call the upper and lower premises within such deductive syllogism as the fundamental legal premises, on the basis of which anyone's following the rule of law must be justified. It is the first step that legal practitioners should take in justifying their legal decisions, as well as legal argumentation scholars when reconstructing the same.

The clearest cases in a legal system stop at this point, not calling for additional interpretations and a search for additional evidence to further establish facts. Also, with respect to the lower premise, there is no epistemic problem: we have clear facts because evidence prove them with certainty. Let us see an example of such a case. The so-called procedural issues are usually clear, but not necessarily so. After the service of a first-court judgment there is a 30-day deadline to file an appeal against that judgment. Suppose the service of the judgment was carried out as prescribed: the deadline was respected in terms of time and the recipient signed the proof of service and filed his appeal 15 days from the first-instance judgment's service. Accordingly, in such a case all the premises would be close to being logically "valid." Or in any case, universally acceptable at least.

I call this first level of justification dialectical because what is important is selection of the basic premises as the outer structure of every legal case. However, in legal proceedings even clear cases soon get complicated, and in such a case we need to proceed further from the clearness of the basic premises selected, in order to justify their selection because they are no longer (almost) self-defending or self-justifying as it seems at least in the situation when the case was (still) clear.

This first level of justification to an important extent does not depend on the legal arguers but has been given in advance by the legislature or previous court decisions as well as the facts. We would better understand it when we compare it with another level of justification to follow, namely the rhetorical. Two examples from history are quite illustrative to point to their, not always clear, differences. In *The New Rhetoric*, Perelman and Olbrechts-Tyteca mentioned Quintilian citing Zeno's comparison between dialectic and rhetoric as between a "closed fist," in the case of the former, and an "open hand," in the event of the latter (35–36). One could understand this metaphor that with respect to the premises, the closed fist would signify firm premises that hold the argument together in a strong manner. In order to do that, the premises must be clear, obvious, and relatively independent of the arguer and audiences so that, if you replace the arguers and audience, the case would not be resolved much differently.

Furthermore, in *On Rhetoric*, Aristotle wrote the following:

> Of the modes of persuasion some belong strictly to the art of rhetoric and some do not. By the latter I mean such things as are not supplied by the speaker but are there at the outset – witnesses, evidence given under torture, written contracts, and so on. By the former I mean such as we can ourselves construct by means of the principles of rhetoric. The one kind has merely to be used, the other has to be invented.
>
> (13355b, 36–42)

He mentioned this kind of "atechnical" ("non-artistic")[2] means of persuasion as strictly legal ones in his discussion on forensic rhetoric and supplied the list including five of them: laws, witnesses, contracts, tortures, and oaths (1375a, 26).

What he had in mind in the preceding passage, I believe, is one of distinctions between dialectic and rhetoric, about which he was far from being clear. However, by "the things that are not supplied by the speaker" and "are there at the outset," he seems to have thought about the atechnical means of persuasion – the legal provisions from laws, contracts, etc., as well as facts, evidence, which basically deal with the premises. If they are clear and uncontested, "they just need to be used," in the sense of their relative independence

2 In old Greek, *techne* meant "skill" or "art."

from the arguer, and thus their audience. However, where problems occur with respect to those, they need to be further justified ("constructed" or "invented"), following the principles of rhetoric – the "technical" means of persuasion: logos, ethos, and pathos.

The structure of such a "dialectical argument" from a clear case would be as follows:

Mp (major premise): (Procedural law stipulates that) Appeals must be filed within 30 days from the service of a decision.

mp (minor premise): Appeal A was submitted 15 days from the service of decision B.

c (conclusion): Appeal A was timely.

Methodologically speaking, clear cases end at this point unless they get messy. Honest lawyers would advise their clients that it is worthless to appeal because the case was clearly decided and there is nothing to pick on. However, even in an unclear case the dialectical level of justification would be, methodologically, the first step to take to legally justify the decision. Because this is the unavoidable (thin) line of dialectical (modestly deductive) syllogism, it presents the skeleton legal argument. But the problem in unclear cases is that such a framework remains unclear and cannot play the role of justification, thus it needs to be supplemented by the second level of justification. What follows is an example of such a case, in which the dialectical framework was excavated but needed further justification.

Case No. U-II-1/15, dated 28.9.2015,[3] of the Constitutional Court of the Republic of Slovenia, originated several years ago from the parliament's amendment to the Family Relations and Marriage Act, in which they altered the definition of marriage, from the old one that said marriage had to be entered into by a man and a woman to the new one that such was allowed to be entered into by two different persons. The Slovene citizens opposing to that amendment requested from the parliament to call a referendum so that people would eventually tell whether they agreed with such a change in the statutory definition of marriage, but the parliament refused to do that. Consequently, the petitioners brought the issue to the Slovene Constitutional Court to decide whether parliament's refusal of calling a referendum was in accordance with the Constitution. Following the RS Constitution, any law adopted by the parliament can be subject to subsequent referendum except those concerning taxes and other public finances, national safety . . ., as well as those adopted to eliminate human rights violations. In this case, what was at issue was whether the parliament refused the referendum because the challenged statute was adopted in order to eliminate human rights violations. Finally, the majority of justices held that the parliament's refusal of the referendum was

3 Off. Gaz. RS, No. 80/2015.

unconstitutional and the referendum should have been held, because it is the Constitutional Court that is empowered to establish a violation of human rights, not the parliament.

Let me repeat the following logical structure of the main legal argument, in which the premises and the conclusion are presented:

Mp: Prohibition of referendum if the statute is remedying human rights violations (Art. 90.2.4. of the RS Constitution)
mp: Parliament order prohibiting the referendum concerning the Amendment to the Family Relations and Marriage Act to allow gay marriage[4]
c: Court's decision to allow the referendum (5–4)

This case is only a modest dialectical deductive framework that exists in every legal case due to the mentioned starting points (legal provisions), without which there is no legal argumentation. In such a manner, a reconstruction of the multi-modal legal argumentation begins methodologically with finding the dialectical argument in the case. In routine cases, as already mentioned, it is also the last step because no additional justification is required; however, in unclear ones the premises need to be explained or, better, justified further, which means that we need to proceed to step 2 by applying the rhetorical argument. In the previous Constitutional Court case, the dialectical argument was only a rough framework of what was at issue in it, which was justified by additional means.

Accordingly, the dialectical model of legal argument works in the least field-dependent situations from all the three models. We cannot say that its premises are true or sound, but – in the sense of informal logic being relevant for such an area of practical rationality – that they are generally acceptable by the relevant legal community (the relevant legal audience), so there is no point in their further justification. In extreme cases, we could say that the rules are so clear that there is no need for the audience to be persuaded since it has generally accepted that *a priori*. This level of justification could also be called "legalistic," pointing to its "mechanistic" character of a narrow framework of legal texts and clear facts.

2.2.2 *The Rhetorical Models*

When it comes to unclear cases, as already mentioned, both MacCormick and Alexy claimed that we need second-order (MacCormick 1994) or external criteria (Alexy 1989) of justification, where both premises need to be further

4 In constitutional review, the lower premise of deductive syllogism is not epistemic (with facts) as in the cases of ordinary courts, but also normative where statutory provisions or judicial decisions are evaluated to find their (in)consistency with the constitution.

established due to them being unclear (the upper premise to be further construed by means of the established canons of legal interpretation, and the lower premise further supported by means of additional evidence).[5] To whom are unclear cases unclear? To the relevant legal community as the crucial audience for legal arguers in a specific jurisdiction. In such a situation we deal with premises that are (only) probable. Thus, legal arguers need to justify them further by resorting to various means.

It seems that in such a situation, we no longer deal with a "closed fist" but an "open hand," which from arguers requires the use of "technical" means of persuasion, that is, logos, ethos, and pathos, along with the "atechnical ones," such as the legal provisions of statutes, case law, contracts, and evidence. We are faced with arguments of rhetorical syllogism (i.e., enthymemes),[6] in which their unclarity follows from premises missing, which need to be added by the arguers such that a logical inference is possible. The "external" criteria of justification (Alexy) could mean something that is outside the strict legal premises, such as legal provisions and facts in a specific legal case. Aristotle called the latter "technical" means, while the former "atechnical" means. Thus, the external means could point to some *techne* (or "skill") of the arguer, as skills that have been traditionally typical for the legal profession in order to properly interpret unclear legal provisions.

Regarding the application of the rhetorical approach to legal argumentation (and all its means of persuasion, including logos, ethos, pathos, and physis) to unclear cases, it seems that all unclear cases are not the same. Thus, the mentioned rhetorical means of persuasion are differently applied. The first category of unclear cases includes cases whose unclarity could be sufficiently explained and justified by resorting to so-called legal-systemic arguments, those that are in one or the other manner connected with the legal system in which a case is adjudicated. They do not follow directly from the legal texts, otherwise the case would be clear, but from a broader framework of the legal system. They are used to make systemic connections, fill in gaps, explain ambiguous words, find implicit or hinted purposes, etc. Therefore, they cannot be considered "atechnical" means of persuasion, but "technical," as lawyers' skills or their reasonable argumentation, which have developed in comparable legal traditions. These arguments that we call interpretive as they are used to interpret unclear (normative) legal texts are nowhere explicitly prescribed, nor is the order of precedence of how they should be used determined, but rather they are used according to legal arguers' reasonable judgment of what arguments are to be used to persuade

5 Even in clear cases, facts need to be supported by evidence. This does not apply only to the so-called notorious facts.

6 Walton defined the enthymeme as a way of inference including one or several premises that are not explicitly stated but are necessary so that we are able to derive the entire inference from the text (2001, 93).

their audience. That is why I call them rhetorical and would primarily refer to rhetorical logos.

There is another point that needs to be mentioned in the context of this level of justifying unclear cases and refers – differently than earlier – to the epistemic premise. Unclear facts would usually imply bad or insufficient evidence, a troublesome situation in the legal proceeding, which is as a rule resolved by providing more and better evidence and following the relevant standards of proof. But there is another point that has so far been neglected and refers to a specific type of evidence. (Unclear) legal texts need verbal interpretation, while evidence should enable the epistemic acquisition of appropriate knowledge about the facts they are to prove. However, sometimes words are insufficient to convey the full epistemic scope of some evidence that need to be perceived by the observer in their totality to obtain the full knowledge of them (such as paintings, tastes, and sounds). Their perceiving (also) in the non-verbal form could resolve certain epistemic problems that verbal evidence is not capable of. This will be ensured by visceral arguments.

This book's discussion will emphasize that the multi-modal alternate arguments not only influence the upper (normative) premise, such as ethos (intuitions – kisceral arguments) and pathos (emotions – emotional arguments), which primarily deal with evaluation in one or another manner and are especially important in very unclear cases. But it is especially visceral arguments that deal with the lower (epistemic) premise. Their unclear dimension opens the gate for various rhetorical strategies, not only of "physis" but also of rhetorical logos – such as "strategic maneuvering" with evidence.

Moreover, there seems to be another, second, rhetorical level of justification used to justify the previous one (i.e., the legal-systemic level), which departs even further from the dialectical level. I call it the meta-legal level since it includes values (ethos) and emotions (pathos) of the arguers by which they try to persuade their audience when it is not clear why the legal-systemic arguments were used in a certain manner. It originates from arguers as personalities using the said technical means of persuasion to persuade their audience. However, in order not to only speculate about them but to discuss their actual presence in the reasoning of judicial decisions in the framework of legal argumentation, we need to find their traces, which will usually appear in judges' separate opinions as judges concerns for justice, their background values, emotional involvement, and similar. We will not find them in every unclear case, but mostly in the so-called ideological cases.

But initially, we need to discuss the less "controversial" unclear cases.

2.2.2.1 The Legal-Systemic Level

From Aristotle's technical means of persuasion, there is, first, the rhetorical logos, which seems to include at least two means of persuasion that I discuss here, which stem from both the tradition of classical rhetoric, or were added later based on its understanding. First, there are the so-called standard canons of interpretation or interpretative legal arguments that have been developed in all legal traditions, with no huge differences at least concerning statutory interpretation (MacCormick, Summers 1991). Second, a part of the rhetorical logos, seems to be also what van Eemeren and Houtlosser (1999a) called strategic maneuvering being composed of (i) the selection of topics from those available; (ii) adapting to audience; and (iii) presentational devices, the approach that was followed by a number of legal scholars (especially from the Netherlands, such as Feteris and Plug).

Both of the mentioned rhetorical means of persuasion extend the said atechnical means, such as statutes, when the latter are unclear and somewhat "run out," so the arguers that are skilled in law use such special techniques (Gr. *techne* meaning skills, art, or simply technical means) for their interpretation by not departing too much from the atechnical means, both being part of a legal system. Otherwise, their techniques would be pure discretion that completely abolish the difference between lawyers being skilled and unskilled. These technical means of persuasion in law are part of legal traditions and, although they formally surpass the strictly atechnical means of legal persuasion, they are still in the broader framework of what is reasonable and thus acceptable in law. In such a manner, it seems that with their *Ius est "ars" boni et equi* the Romans did not depart that much from the Old Greek *tecnhe* – also with respect to law.

From the aforementioned, we find logical interpretative arguments, such as *a contrario* and *a simili* as *topoi* already in Aristotle's *Topics* (on dialectical reasoning), but also in *On Rhetoric* (in the chapter on the rhetorical logos), certainly with Greek names that were translated into Latin words by Cicero (Radovčić 2004). Furthermore, linguistic interpretative arguments have also been there, at least in ancient Roman law (Kranjc 2020). In the late Middle Ages, during several centuries of the reception of Roman law in Central Europe, systemic interpretative arguments (such as *lex specialis and lex posterior*) were added, which were followed by historical interpretative legal arguments at the birth of legal history as a scientific discipline by the Historical Legal School in the second part of the 19th century. Von Savigny, who was one of the founders of the mentioned school, dealt with the four types of interpretative legal arguments (von Savigny 1840). Finally, the list of the classical interpretative arguments was joined with purposive (or teleological)[7] interpretation in the first part of the 20th century, to which legal sociology contributed much. Last but not least, in the second part of the 20th century, with the emergence of constitutional courts, human rights, the (new) importance of legal principles, and globalization, some other interpretative arguments joined that list, such as the argument of precedent (in civil law), the argument of principle and the argument of weight, as well as the comparative argument, to name just those predominant.

7 Some of these interpretative arguments are discussed by Perelman and Obrechts-Tyteca in their famous book *The New Rhetoric*.

The second aspect of the rhetorical logos could be what van Eemeren and Houtlosser called strategic maneuvering. Within that, there is, first, the selection of topics from those available or with topical potential, where arguers will select materials from those available in accordance with what they believe best advances their interest (van Eemeren, Houtlosser 1999a, 166), or is simply more reasonable. This corresponds to what in the classical rhetoric was considered as *inventio*. For example, a judge in a minority of the panel may have a different view from their colleagues in the panel and opines that it is perhaps more reasonable to rely on another legal provision from those available and possible in such a case. That forms a circle of available options that are still considered as reasonable in that case.

Furthermore, when it comes to argumentation in a specific legal case, the arguer can find reasonable and effective to organize their arguments in a particular way, which would fall under the rhetorical category of organizing the materials, or *dispositio*. Finally, as presentational devices we can refer to those falling under the framework of rhetorical figures of logos referring to *elocutio*, such as metaphors, antithesis, repetitions, similes, comparisons (Frost 2005, 87), etc.

Let me complete the previous analysis of the dialectical argument with the first rhetorical one.

In the previously mentioned constitutional case about whether to allow or not the referendum on amending the Family Relations and Marriage Act to allow gay people to marry, the following major premise of the basic argument appeared to be unclear. The underlying idea of that provision was that referendums against statutes that are intended to remedy human rights violations were constitutionally prohibited.

> Mp: Prohibition of referendum if the statute is remedying human rights violations

What follows, first, is the analysis of using the rhetorical logos by the Constitutional Court judges. The lack of clarity of that provision, or its enthymematic character, appeared in the dialogue among the judges, the arguers in the case, who were also deciding on the matter of the case. One group of them, who constituted the tight majority in that case (five of nine judges in total), was pro-referendum. In order to clarify the unclear provision, by finding the hidden premise and thus enabling the working of logical syllogism, they relied on (i) the interpretative argument of systemic interpretation. They understood the unclear constitutional provision in light of the overall system of constitutional review applying in the Republic of Slovenia. This is the so-called European model of constitutional review that is – in contradistinction with the (diffused) American model – centralized. This entails that a statute needs to be previously found unconstitutional by either the constitutional court or the European Court of Human Rights. If that was the case and one of these courts required the parliament to amend the statute, such statute cannot be voted on at a referendum. According to them, the parliament was not empowered to remedy an established violation of human rights directly. As a matter of fact, they could do it but that would not prevent holding a referendum on such a statute.

The four remaining judges voted against the majority's decision. In their separate opinions, they found a support for opposing the referendum in (ii) linguistic and historical arguments in order to interpret the mentioned constitutional provision. First, they relied on literal interpretation of the text of that provision which would indicate that no statute that is intended to remedy a human rights violation can be subject to referendum. Second, they backed that view by resorting to a historical argument that nowhere in the preparatory materials of that constitutional provision had been mentioned that, for the purpose of applying this provision, a human rights violation must first be established by either a constitutional court or the European court. That was their strategic maneuvering, by means of which they found or "invented" another interpretative argument to fill in the hidden premise in their version of the syllogism.

2.2.2.2 The Meta-Legal Level

Moreover, the next (rhetorical and) "technical" means of persuasion is the rhetorical ethos. What I focus on here are the following issues: (i) legal maxims or principles that otherwise are part of legal provisions and thus Aristotle's "atechnical" means of persuasion.[8] However, although they are present in legislation and case law, they are usually very abstract and general. In such a manner, it is unclear how to apply them to a specific case. That is why there is a need for the arguers' skills, their *techne* (as the rhetorical ethos), to apply them in specific cases in an appropriate manner. Then, what also seem to apply in here are the arguers' (ii) personal values, as part of broader social values, which are regulated by legal, mostly constitutional, provisions. The choice of a value regulated in a legal provision is usually determined by the pyramid of personal values of the arguer. Finally, the (iii) rhetorical figures of ethos, such as *anamnesis*, *litotes*, *paronomasia*, etc., are also used in this framework.

When it comes to emotions and the rhetorical pathos, it is not easy to find it in the reasoning of court decisions, which at lower levels of adjudication tend to be technical/formal or, at a higher level of adjudication, the result of a collective effort. In order to retain the image of objectivity, judges are reluctant to use emotions in their reasoning. There is a greater chance to find them in separate opinions, where we can find different rhetorical figures of pathos (e.g., *climax*, *energia*, *ominatio*, *perclusio*).

8 Moreover, there are even legal principles that are not specifically written in the legal texts immediately applying in one system but are considered to be part of legal tradition (e.g., the principles of civilized nations).

Concerning the referendum case discussed earlier and the application of the second rhetorical level, the rhetorical ethos was expressed through the judges' values, in which the majority relied on the value of the tradition (a conservative value) of centralized constitutional review in Slovenia, while the minority would depart from that, making an innovation (a liberal value), for reason of remedying the unconstitutionality. Third, and finally, some judges were dissatisfied with their peers in the other camp, so they expressed that eloquently, thereby demonstrating their pathos by using specifically "spicy" words.

2.3 The Dialectical and Rhetorical Dimensions of Multi-Modality in Law

To understand the influence of the alternate modes of argumentation on law, I demonstrate how they interact with, and are relevant for, the logical mode when applied to the legal context. Because law is a special social field that consists mainly of written legal provisions in modern times, the legal argumentation needs to be based on – or at least connected with – the legal provisions. To have multi-modal argumentation present in the context of law, it means that emotions, intuitions, and physicalities as reasons (premises), which are essential for the existence of the alternate multi-modal arguments, must be connected with legal provisions to qualify as legal reasons backing legal standpoints. Thus, they will not appear in law as multi-modal reasons having no relation with the legal provisions whatsoever, which would constitute a formal fallacy.

For the purpose of discussing multi-modality in the domain of legal proceedings, I use a "dialectical" dimension of multi-modal arguments when such arguments or their crucial components become directly part of the legal premises. A typical example of such an argument might be evidence produced to the court when claiming that, for example, the scent of a perfume was copied illegally by the producer of another perfume, thus violating the copyright protection granted to the first perfume.[9] Actually, for such a visceral (multi-modal) argument to qualify as a legal argument, it needs to be incorporated into a standard legal argument, such as the following one: Mp (major premise): Whoever produces a same artistic or literary work as the one protected by copyright law under another name violates copyright law. mp (minor premise): Perfumes 1 and 2 under their different names are in fact the same (Evidence: The smelling-of-the-scent experiment). C: Perfume 2 violated the copyright of Perfume 1.

The crucial part of the legal argument was the scent evidence, which was the most important epistemic condition fulfilled so that the minor premise was established, and the deductive syllogistic argument carried out. Thus, it can be deemed that that kind of multi-modal argument, appearing in the

9 This was actually a real case before a court, and it is described in the continuation.

framework of a legal argument, had a dialectical dimension. A dialectical connection between the scent of the perfume and the lower premise will be established only if the evidence was clear, to establish the existence of facts matching the legal facts in that case. Considering that the legal text to be applied was also clear.

The other type of dimension of alternate multi-modal arguments in the legal context is rhetorical,[10] whereby an indirect connection with the premises is constituted. Rhetorical means of persuasion, even if used merely as a rhetorical device, have argumentative value (Tindale 2004, 19) because they could make a difference and bring a change of perspective (Perelman, Olbrechts-Tyteca 1969, 169). In the event of clear evidence that a defendant had committed the crime for which he was accused, an emotional closing speech by the attorney in favor of his client (e.g., an appeal to pity (*pathos*)), addressing the panel of professional judges before they retreat to deliberation, will not impact the verdict. However, when it comes to, e.g., sentencing and balancing or aggravating and mitigating circumstances, it becomes more important the less clear a case is.[11] Accordingly, judges must be aware that in law the "rhetoric of any case – how it can be presented most persuasively – in no way conflicts with its merits – that is, the rational strength of the relevant arguments" (Posner 1995, 512). Or, going back to the evidence of scent: its elusive character and the consequent diminished ability of arguers to capture it in words, will give it rhetorical potential.

2.4 Models and Types of Legal Argumentation and Multi-Modality

Groarke argues that any comprehensive theory of legal argumentation should accommodate multimodality and recognizes the role that non-verbal elements play in legal reasoning (Groarke 2017, 7). He claims that multimodal arguing must be recognized and accepted as an integral element of legal reasoning, as a form of arguing that is even superior to purely verbal arguing that the law traditionally has assumed to be a paradigm (Groarke 2017, 12–13). We will see next that both the dialectical, as well as rhetorical, dimensions of such arguments are possible.

Due to the development of new technologies in communication (and most often in argumentation), and new findings by neuroscience and cognitive psychology about our brain activity, it is necessary to evaluate what multimodality can bring to legal argumentation and how its traditional role has been affected. To do so, we need to consider legal argumentation in the most comprehensive way possible, focusing not only on legal arguments in their

10 According to Tseronis and Forceville, any means of communication can be analyzed as an argument if it functions to gain assent from an audience (Tseronis, Forceville 2017, 4).

11 "It is true that in a modern trial the grosser forms of appeal to emotion . . . can be kept out by rules of evidence. But subtler yet perhaps equally misleading forms of emotional appeal cannot be" (Posner 1995, 510–511).

static (or logical) way as legal conclusions (e.g., legal briefs and motions, decisions, and judgments) based on legal premises (legal provisions and facts).[12] We should also cast our net wider, to encompass the process of making and exchanging legal arguments before courts – the most important legal forum in which judges decide and justify decisions on the basis of rules for a reasonable discussion (the dialectical aspect).[13]

As already mentioned, I base my idea that the dialectical model of legal argumentation might be found in the first model on a formal relation between the premises and the conclusion – and particularly clear cases that can be justified on the basis of the so-called internal (or first-order) justification. In the rhetorical models, unclear legal cases are justified externally, or as part of the second-order justification, by using additional canons of interpretation (e.g., the triplet of linguistic, systematic, and evaluative canons of interpretation) to establish an unclear major premise containing legal provisions, and specific evidence to meet certain standards of proof to additionally establish the minor premise consisting of concrete facts (Alexy 1989; MacCormick 1994). And there is also the third-order justification with values backing (purely) legal choices. Finally, we should not forget the audience in front of which legal arguers try to accommodate the dialectical framework of a legal system in which they defend their positions by means of the effective presentation of legal arguments, as well as their views and positions (the rhetorical view). Only a broader context of legal argumentation will allow multi-modal arguments to be accommodated along with traditional legal arguments in the legal discourse. In light of this, there is a pressing need to understand their dialectical and rhetorical dimension.

Legal argumentation thus broadly conceived is not monolithic in its socio-legal dimension. There is a difference, in terms of a dialectical and rhetorical dimension, whether multi-modal arguments are presented: (i) from lawyers to professional judges; (ii) from lawyers to juries; and (iii) from judges to senior judges.[14] In connection with this, we can have different types of legal argumentation because we have different arguers and audiences. The professional framework of argumentation between lawyers and judges, as legal professionals who basically argue on the basis of legal provisions, is relatively closed dialectically, so there is less room for the use of multi-modal arguments as rhetorical devices.[15] The legal context is certainly different than our everyday situations.

12 This could refer to the requirements of correct substantive law applied and correct and complete states of facts established.

13 This could be related to the requirements of specific rules of legal procedure to be followed.

14 Furthermore, legal arguments could also be presented from lay parties to either juries or professional judges, or from judges to the audiences of either lay parties, and lawyers, and the universal audience as a community of reasonable persons (Perelman, Olbrechts-Tyteca 1969).

15 We could even say that, due to formal constraints imposed in the legal context, the dialectical dimension is, at least as a starting point, more important than the rhetorical one so that we may use van Eemeren's conception of the "rhetorical inside the dialectical" (van Eemeren 2015). However, there is also an extensive space for rhetoric and not only in the direction of

However, to some extent, room exists for rhetoric and multi-modality in courts, despite the fact that the majority of legal activities are conducted in a written form – the paradigm semiotic resource of the logical mode. This was not the case when Aristotle (2004) wrote his *Rhetoric*, when oral advocacy before lay juries predominated in popular courts (Lanni 2008).

The use of multi-modal arguments in a dialectical or rhetorical manner can be reconstructed from oral presentations and briefs by lawyers and the written opinions of judges. Lawyers' briefs and presentations, as well as the opinions of judges, provide more materials for a reconstruction than the majority opinions of courts, which need to be more official and "logical." This obviously follows from their different institutional roles: the latter need to be convincing (or "strongly persuasive"), while the former may merely be persuasive – if such an idealized distinction is ever possible to withstand its realist application.

2.5 The Four Modes and Traces of Multi-Modality in Court Cases

2.5.1 The Dialectical and Rhetorical Dimensions of the Legal Logical Mode (Legal Logos)

Concerning the potential to discern traces of multi-modality in judicial decisions, from the outset we should differentiate between majority court decisions and the separate (*seriatim*) opinions of judges. Concurring and dissenting opinions have become more frequent not only in common law jurisdictions, where they are commonplace, but also in civil law systems, being found in constitutional courts and also in an increasing number of supreme courts. They have better potential for multi-modal research than the majority decisions that are the result of a collective effort, are more official in terms of style, and, as such, are dialectically "polished out" and "dry" concerning multi-modality arguments. However, when majority decisions are not logically coherent (inconclusive, wrong, or fallacious), which can sometimes occur even at the level of the highest courts, then we might have an indication that the alternate modes had some relevance in the case. However, to prove this hypothesis, we need to find traces of such judicial multi-modal rhetoric in the legal text – otherwise we would be forced to merely conclude that the dialectic was used in a sloppy manner in that particular case.

According to Aristotle, truth was often hidden, and probabilistic approximations were all that were feasible in many cases, facilitated by the rhetorical techniques he catalogued (Posner 1995, 513). Aristotle wrote, "We believe good men more fully and more readily than others: this is true generally whatever the question is, and absolutely true where exact certainty is impossible and

steering the discussion in the framework of the logical mode (*logos*), but also concerning the use of *pathos* and *ethos* (cf. van Eemeren 2010).

opinions are divided" (Rhetoric 1356a, 6–9). According to Posner, "Rhetoric comes into its own not, as Aristotle thought, when there is radical uncertainty but when the facts are known and the question is how to bring an audience to understand and be moved by them" (Posner 1995, 529). Nevertheless, Aristotle highlighted situations with a deficient logical mode, when probabilistic approximations are all that are feasible, and which are facilitated by rhetorical techniques. In unclear cases, we begin to realize that the rhetorical dimension eventually is more important than the dialectical as the discussion is steered in a particular direction, based on the values of those arguing.

For obvious reasons, the logical mode will serve dialectical purposes with respect to law; however, it is also necessary to emphasize a possible rhetorical dimension concerning the logical mode. For an example of this, consider Feteris's analysis of the Dutch unworthy spouse case, where she analyzes the strategic maneuvering (van Eemeren 2015) of the Dutch Supreme Court when resolving the case in a dialectic manner, steering the discussion in the direction it wanted (Feteris 2015). Accordingly, (even) in the framework of the legal logical mode itself possibilities exist for various rhetorical strategies, used not only by lawyers but also judges.

Lawyers' dialectical commitments are obvious. They stem from the central argument of their *ars operandi*, which is the logical argument of deductive syllogism,[16] which makes it possible for facts and legal norms to meet at some point in order for us to designate something as legal (or not legal). The deductive syllogistic argument is composed of a major premise, where lawyers place legal norms, and a minor premise, including facts, the evaluation of whether facts and norms meet being the conclusion. At least at the level of framework, this argument is indispensable for any procedure that wants to be in conformity with the rule of law. Legal argumentation theory understands it to be crucial for justifying the so-called clear (or easy) cases in the internal context of justification (Alexy 1989).

However, in unclear cases at the major premise we can have ambiguous, vague, or gapful legal norms, or at the minor premise an uncertainty whether facts do correspond to selected legal norms. This is the point where the rhetorical dimension steps in to the reasoning of legal decisions. Thus, we need to go through a process of external justification (Alexy 1989) and either interpret legal norms or additionally establish facts to meet legal facts on the basis of evidence meeting specific standards of proof. Further, in legal interpretation, which is closely related to legal argumentation, as most often legal norms need to be interpreted first before legal decisions are made and then argued in the reasoning, canons of interpretation or interpretative arguments are used, the role of which is to help establish the legal meaning of specific legal provisions.

Some of these canons are sometimes named as *quasi* logical interpretative arguments, such as: *a contrario*, *a simili*, *a fortiori*. Their Latin names

16 Which is often accompanied by induction.

were given by Cicero, although they already appear in Aristotle's *Rhetoric*, where he treats *logos*. Their role is to prove the relevance of legal norms as major premises. Additionally, there are other canons of interpretation, including intentional, linguistic, historic, systematic or systemic, and logical canons, better known as Savigny's interpretative canons (von Savigny 1840, 212–216). It is interesting that in subsequent lists of interpretative canons, such as those composed by MacCormick and Summers (1991) and Feteris (2017), the explicit adjective logical was left out. It seems that the authors understood the self-obvious connected of such arguments with informal logic or dialectic, to the effect of that very word "logic" no longer being necessary to be explicitly mentioned, rather than they would think that logic no longer plays a role.

Later, teleological or purposive interpretative arguments were added to the list. They serve the same purpose as the first-mentioned arguments: to establish the meaning of and prove the relevance of the legal norms to apply. When it comes to establishing relevant facts as legal facts, we have other means to rely on: evidence and standards of proof, as specific categories to prove the necessary existence of facts matching the legal facts so that the legal norms may be applied.

Furthermore, the principles of coherence and consistency being the most fundamental pillars of any rational system such as law strives to be, are very important for the functioning of the rule of law (MacCormick 1994). There, one can find arguments of principles, arguments of precedents, and arguments of weight when balancing legal principles or fundamental rights. Closely linked with the principle of coherence is argument *a pari* and so forth.

Then, conceptual logic is important for linguistic interpretation as well as for any understanding of law that wants to be logical. Even historical interpretation and analysis in law, indicating legal purposes to establish a connection between certain means and ends, as well as economic analysis in law dealing with costs and benefits, designate reasoning that is a kind of informal logical reasoning. Moreover, avoiding formal and informal fallacies stresses the importance to reason rationally.

The ancient idea that legal *logos* can also be treated from a rhetorical perspective is further supported by the idea of strategic maneuvering. In the last decade that van Eemeren's and Houtloser's concept has been used by some Continental legal scholars (e.g., Feteris, Plug) in analyzing court decisions to emphasize the ability, and in fact lawyers' practice, to use *logos* effectively. By referring to "topical selection, organization of materials, and presentational devices" (van Eemeren 2010), traditional rhetorical elements such as *inventio*, *dispositio*, and *elocutio* were refurnished to point that modern lawyers have not changed much from their ancient predecessors in their ambition to win an argument. Among the tasks to be mastered by an orator, *inventio*, *disposition*, and *elocutio* are to be used in written argumentation, while *memoria* and *action* are more appropriate for oral advocacy (Frost 2005, 4–5).

In the US especially, in the last decades, there have been hundreds of different books and manuals on how to analyze legal authority, write a legal document, organize a legal discussion, write effective paragraphs and sentence structure, write to the court and make appellate briefs (see, e.g., Shapo, Walter, Fajans 1991). There have been materials on how to frame thoughts, phrase sentences, choose words, and what to consider in analytical and persuasive writing, legal drafting, and document design (e.g., Garner 2001).

Last but not least, there have been concerns expressed about the elements of legal style, especially when rhetorical figures are dealt with. This is especially important when legal opinions are studied of the highest courts' judges, of which particularly concurring opinions are of particular interest. In relation to *logos*, there exist the figures of comparison (such as metaphor, *simile*), syntactic arrangement (*parallelism, climax, or antithesis*), or repetition (Garner 2002). The role of rhetorical figures in the context of logos is that they work subtly, indirectly, and express what cannot be literally asserted in a formal language. They "steal their way secretly into the minds of the judges" (Frost 2005, 89). Another rhetorical figure that has a clear rhetorical legal function is metaphor, which is used to crystalize analyses or arguments. In its rhetorical dimension, it is a figure of thought having a logical value. Metaphor is a comparison and analogy, which gives the audience cognitive insight not usually achievable by lingering syllogistic reasoning (Frost 2005, 87–89).

To that, one can surely add *antithesis* ("placing opposites" being a choice or arrangement of words, often in parallel structure that emphasizes a contrast) and *parallelism* ("alongside one another"; constructions in adjacent syntactic units often giving an equivalent, complementary, or antithetic sense), as figures of *similitudo* (comparison), which have a rhetorical logical value in law (Garner 2002, 160, 163; Frost 2005, 109–116).

2.5.2 *The Dialectical and Rhetorical Dimensions of the Kisceral Mode (Values and Legal Ethos)*

Gilbert's kisceral mode is centered around intuition. For an argument in the (genuine) kisceral mode, the reason(s) (premise(s)) for a standpoint must be intuitive. Concerning the kisceral mode of arguing, what would be of particular interest is the intuitive aspect of values.[17] There are different kinds of values, including moral values, which are very important in the context of law. However, more than moral values appear in the framework of legal argumentation. But how are values connected with intuition?

> Values guide choices by evoking a sense of basic principles of right and wrong (e.g., moral values), a sense of priorities (e.g., personal

17 According to Groarke, the consideration of values forces us to "rely on language in a way which is connected to human experience in a notoriously vague way" (Groarke 2017, 24).

> achievement v. group good), and create a willingness to make meaning and see patterns (e.g., trust v. distrust).
>
> (Oyserman 2015, 36)

They have intuitive appeal as an explanatory construct and "are embodied in seeming gut reactions that something is right, moral, or natural versus wrong, immoral, or unnatural" (Oyserman, ibid.). Furthermore, they "can be thought of as priorities, internal compasses, spring-boards for action – moral imperatives." Also, they contain cognitive (thinking) and affective (feeling) elements, having a selective or directional quality, and are internalized (Oyserman 2015, 47).

We follow one set of values rather than another due to a very complex net of different influences on our cognitions. In this context, it is interesting to examine how an intuitive (internal) perception could be argued externally. Because we cannot argue intuitively, we are compelled to argue about what we have perceived intuitively. We need words or other semiotic resources (e.g., gestures, pictures, sounds) to describe and assert our intuitions. By expressing our values through how we interpret legal provisions, we apply the ideas most important from our intuition to our understanding of legal provisions – leaving discursive traces of our values behind.

Arguing on the basis of values might bring a personal element to legal discourse, one that was not generally envisaged when the relevant legal provisions were enacted and which are to be applied generally. Thus, vague or ambiguous legal provisions are the so-called Trojan horses for the entry of value judgments into legal provisions (Kennedy 1996).

If a legal text is unclear, it permits several legally acceptable, and possibly conflicting, outcomes within the framework of the legal text. If several legally possible solutions exist, the choice of one of them can be made on the basis of logic, as well as by means of other modes. Of these, the kisceral mode with supplementary argumentation based on values, is a very frequent one – especially in socially controversial cases. Vague legal norms, such as constitutional norms, permit interpretation in different directions. Interpretation also depends on different values that are loosely linked to specific legal provisions.

To discern this from judicial decisions is not the easiest task, since judges tend to be official, legalistic, and value neutral in their decisions. However, traces of argumentation by means of values to fill in gaps in the legal logical mode sometimes exist. Discerning these types of arguments is easier in oral arguments because lawyers are freer than judges to argue in such a manner.

People understand phenomena (un)consciously, using unstated values that determine our thinking across all activities. For example, if freedom and liberty have priority over responsibility in a person's value system, then regarding abortion, a person would tend to prefer pro-choice rather than pro-life interpretations – whether they are a lay person or judge. The judge as a professional may be more cautious to take into account his or her institutional constraints. Thus, people tend to understand such cases and vague legal norms connected with them (which are, as a rule, loose), which leads us to consider these cases unclear – at least from the position of predominant values.[18] Accordingly, we can find traces of values (or arguments of values) from either open statements about background values (that more or less are linked with legal texts) or rhetorical devices used by arguers to try to make their logical arguments more effective – especially in situations in which the premises and possible outcomes are not very clear.

Aristotle understood ethos as the character of a speaker. Today we can extend ethos to the character of a culture, community, nation, or a group to understand the fundamental values of a specific person, people, corporation, or movement. What is important is not the individual character of ethos but also its community and public significance. According to Halloran, it became a cultural phenomenon so that the "interdependence between ethos and cultural context to manifest the virtues most valued by the culture for which it speaks" is considered (Halloran 1982, 58, 63).

It is in unclear cases (such as euthanasia, cloning, the death penalty, gay marriage, abortion), when no precedent exists, that intuition and values based on intuitions are important[19] since logic cannot be used when precise demonstration is impossible (Posner 2010). In such cases, we have a clash of values that courts need to resolve.

Values are connected with legal provisions in two ways: they appear in the legal system as (general) legal principles: e.g., the value of equality is encoded in the Equal Protection Clause of the Constitution. This would be their dialectical dimension, in which they are immediately part of legal norms and enter legal discourse in a direct manner, as major premises. As such, they result from a collective effort on the part of the legislature (and courts) to form a constitutive part of a legal system. However, another dimension of values exists when used in legal argumentation. I term it "rhetorical," and it refers to personal (or subjective) values that judges read in the objective values when trying to steer the discussion in a certain direction with regard to interpreting a certain objective value. Next I present some examples of that.

We deal with ethos in a dialectical sense when we find a connection between law and morality or ethics. It means that a legal norm, a necessary premise in the argument of logical deductive syllogism, is also a moral norm. There are a number of legal principles that embrace these two dimensions, legal and ethical norms, such as equality before the law, the principle of equal protection of rights, the proportionality principle, the principle of social justice, the principle

18 When in unclear cases, in the external context of justification, no normative requirement exists regarding the proper canon of interpretation (e.g., either linguistic, systematic, historical, or purposive) is to be used, whether interpretation is to be formalist or purposive, or which result of interpretation is to follow (e.g., either literal, restrictive, or extensive); the choice made by the judge is based on values (of judges' legal "philosophy").

19 Since the law is not exhausted in legalism, "(T)he first decision in a line of cases may be the product of inarticulable emotion or hunch" (Posner 2010, 111).

of conscientiousness and fairness, the equivalence principle, the adversarial principle, and many others.

Moreover, there are a number of especially fundamental rights that are both legal and ethical norms, such as the inviolability of human life, prohibition of torture, protection or personal liberty, protection of human personality and dignity, etc. They are part of so-called negative human rights, which are a reflection of the protection of individual morality in relation to the state. However, there are also a number of positive human rights, such as the right to health care, right to social welfare, rights of disabled persons, etc., as expressions of social justice.

These belong to the so-called dialectical ethos because of their dual nature: on one hand the have an explicit moral dimension, and on the other hand, as legal norms, they are necessary premises of logical inference, which is as a rule informal because these legal norms have a broad meaning and can be applied in different directions, thus it is almost impossible to deal with formal rationality. Furthermore, the dialectical dimension of kisceral arguments related to legal principles, and values embedded in them, is quite different from the dialectical dimension of legal rules. The latter are much more narrowly tailored than the first so the arguers' argumentation "fist" can be much firmer in the event of rules than principles. Accordingly, the legal principles' dialectical dimension is much thinner than the one of the legal rules'.

In *Plessy* (discussed in the previous chapter) the dialectical dimension of a legal principle was the Equal Protection Clause determined in the Constitution. From the previous accounts we can see how the dissenting Justice Harlan's private system of values and moral intuitions, taken in conjunction with his family members' views and changed social circumstances, proceeded to alter his earlier public positions. Consequently, by the time he penned his *Plessy* dissent, he viewed the Equal Protection Clause differently than the other seven justices who decided the case. His intuitive (moral and (ir)rational) reasons must have played an important part in his dissenting opinion.

If we take the constitutional amendments as embodying the (objective) value of equality as a dialectical dimension of such a value, Harlan's reading of the constitutional clause imparts a rhetorical message. His rhetoric of values suggests a different reading of the US Constitution than the majority's reading, which eventually led to the Court's rejection of the "separate but equal" doctrine. It might thus seem to be a pretty ordinary claim that moral factors influence judicial decision-making. However, by pointing to a specific kisceral mode within a multi-modality theory of legal argumentation, I show its distinct character in comparison with the logical mode. This contributes to greater transparency in decision-making and its justification, since on one hand it stresses the importance of judges' creativity, and on the other hand it reveals that judges may potentially hide behind the letter of the law in unclear cases.[20]

20 A similar study to identify the role of superior judges' personal values in written legal opinions was made by Cahill-O'Callaghan (2013). She analyzed a UK Supreme Court case, *R v. JFS*

Moreover, there is a further possibility of using *ethos* in a rhetorical manner. Here I refer to the use of rhetorical figures in law such that they promote the authority and credibility of the speaker. Although nearly every figure of speech may be employed in such a manner, many figures are specifically designed to do so, or else are likely to build the speaker's ethos in addition to any other effects.

For example, *litotes* as a figure, which was used in Ad Herennium, suggests frugality and modesty and can be used to establish credibility by downplaying one's accomplishment in order to gain the audience's favor. It is a figure that takes the form of negating an opposite (not bad = good, not guilty = innocent). Justice Frankfurter used in his dissent in *West Va. Bd of Educ. v. Barnette* (319 U.S. 624, 646) (1943) the following litotes: "One who belongs to the most vilified and persecuted minority in history is not likely to be insensible to the freedoms guaranteed by our Constitution" (Garner 2002, 157).

Paronomasia is a figure of wordplay that can be used to damage credibility. It is about the suggestive use of similarity between words or of a word's different senses. It is the figure of punning or word-shunting. In the title of Dworkin's famous book *Taking Rights Seriously*, the author played effectively on two English idioms, *to take rights* and *to take (something) seriously* (Garner 2002, 157–158).

Finally, *metaphor* is a figure of an implicit comparison between two things of unlike nature that nevertheless have something in common. A metaphor says not that a thing is like something else, but that it is that something else. Consider, for example, Dworkin's metaphor of Hercules for a judge that is able to find a moral principle for any hard case. Furthermore, metaphors are closely linked to the credibility of the person who makes them, such that the advocate's character is also revealed by his or her stylistic choices, one of them being the rhetorical figure of metaphor (Frost 2005, 92–94).

***

Governing Body, as an example of a divided judicial opinion in the United Kingdom Supreme Court. In that case, the (JFS) school's admissions policy gave preference to children who were recognized as Orthodox Jewish through the application of the matrilineal test. This test requires that the mother of the child is Jewish by birth or by Orthodox conversion. In that case, M's mother was not born Jewish and her conversion was not Orthodox but Masorti, a non-orthodox form of Judaism. On this basis, Boy M, who was a practicing Orthodox Jew, failed to meet the criteria of the matrilineal test and was refused admission. By relying on their personal values, of either universalism or tradition, the Supreme Court judges diverged in their opinion. The first group of them supporting universalist values argued that the school's policy was racist, while the second group of judges, the traditionalists, supported its discrimination as still admissible. To prove the existence of their personal values as extra-legal factors in the judgment, the author carried out both a qualitative and quantitative analysis. A similar argument was also made by Beck (2012) from analyzing judgments of the Court of Justice of the EU.

By the following, Aristotle certainly highlighted situations with a deficient logical mode, when probabilistic approximations are all that are feasible and which are facilitated by rhetorical techniques: "We believe good men more fully and more readily than others: this is true generally whatever the question is, and absolutely true where exact certainty is impossible and opinions are divided" (Rhetoric 1356a, 6–9). In unclear cases, we begin to realize that the rhetorical dimension is eventually more important than the dialectical as the discussion is steered in a particular direction based on the values of those arguing.

2.5.3 The Dialectic and Rhetoric of Emotions in Law (Legal Pathos)

A traditional portrait of judicial proceedings and judges shows them as non-emotional, to meet the requirements of impartiality and objectivity in dispensing justice. A typical example was of a Slovene Supreme Court judge who asserted that while he forgot about emotions in the courtroom, when outside he began to enjoy all their colorfulness (Ogrizek 2002). In recent years, this view has become outdated, as emotions now are welcome to be present in the adjudication of judges (Maroney, Gross 2014). Emotions, moreover, influence judicial decision-making (Bandes 2016). Even prominent judges have admitted that they use emotions in their decision-making now (Brennan 1988;[21] Posner 2010[22]). It is not surprising that, from the birth of judicial rhetoric in Ancient Greece, lawyers (or those litigating cases in court) have tried to appeal to judges' emotions (*pathos*) when addressing them. However, judicial reasonings traditionally have tried to remain as dispassionate as possible (in the logical mode) (Sandler, Epps, Waicukauski 2010; Scalia, Garner 2008).

Traditionally, it was safer for judges not to show their emotions in their judgments because of the professional requirement for them to be objective and impartial. At a certain point in history, especially in Continental Europe after the French Revolution, they were even required to be logomachists (or "subsumption machines").[23] Frankly, emotions are not only able to back a reasonable and legitimate judgment but also can be harmful and distracting when reasonableness does not prevail.

In the dialectical sense, which is concerned with structural issues of arguments, certain emotions are already part of the enacted legal norms as premises of legal deductive syllogism. Such emotions can be called "institutionalized emotions" because they exist in legal provisions at an abstract and general level, as they were put in place by the legislature when passing that law. For

21 By proclaiming that judges must embrace passion as "the range of emotional and intuitive responses to a given set of facts or arguments, responses which often speed into our consciousness far ahead of the lumbering syllogism or reason."

22 Admitting that judges' decisions are also based on "temperament, emotion, experience, personal background, and ideology."

23 Montesquieu required that judges be the "mouthpieces" of the law (Montesquieu 2011).

example, in the criminal offense of "Insult,"[24] there needs to pre-exist, at a general and abstract level, a certain negative emotion as a constitutive element of that criminal offense, which is concretized when a certain person in fact commits such a criminal offense. In the situation of such pre-existing emotions, the emotional mode overlaps with the logical mode.

When the emotional arguments used by judges are not with legal premises (the logical mode), then they are fallacious.[25] However, it is not only lawyers who use rhetorical devices when trying to persuade their audience (i.e., judges and/or juries); the rhetorical devices of judges might be used to persuade their audiences (i.e., superior judges, other lawyers, parties, the general public). To some extent, judges also act as rhetoricians to make their legal arguments more effective. Because majority judgments tend to be more dialectical, we find some emotional elements that are rhetorical in their use of devices, mainly in separate opinions. These may also be of a persuasive character for future courts and their decisions, contributing to legal development as a result.

Emotional elements within the rhetorical model are used: (i) to back a reasonable judgment; (ii) in a clearly fallacious manner; or (iii) to steer a discussion in a certain direction. For example, lawyers try to influence judges to disqualify expert witnesses. Certain videos can have emotional impact as well. Lawyers' audiences are either jurors or judges. Because judges are trained to use legal knowledge, and are aware of the potential influence of emotions on their logical judgments, it is easier for lawyers to use emotional devices with respect to juries, despite the fact that they are instructed about the appropriate legal rules they need to consider before giving a verdict. Another possible use of emotional devices is judges trying to influence other judges in other courts or in future cases, examples of which I give next. For example, in recent years, Supreme Court opinions have employed controversial emotional language. One Court watcher recently called Justice Kennedy's majority opinion in *Obergefell v. Hodges* "gorgeous, heartfelt, and a little mystifying," whereas another called Justice Antonin Scalia's dissent in the case a "temper tantrum on paper." One commenter referred to Scalia's 21-page dissent in *King v. Burwell* "one of the most scathing and linguistically creative dissents in recent memory." Court commentators also have remarked

24 Which would read, e.g., "Whoever insults another person, is fined in the amount of. . . ."

25 The so-called fallacies of emotion use emotion in place of reason in order to attempt to win the argument. The problem is that as "emotional creatures" people often erroneously make decisions based on emotions when reason and logic tell them otherwise. However, using appeals to emotion as a backup to rational and logical arguments is not fallacious (Brinton 1988). In discussing ***argument ad populum*** (appeal to popular sentiments), ***argument ad misericordiam*** (appeal to pity), ***argument ad baculum*** (appeal to a threat, force, fear), and ***argument ad hominem*** (personal attack) as emotional arguments, Walton points to their important role in persuasion but warns against their potential fallacious use (Walton 2002).

that Justice Sonia Sotomayor wrote a "blistering" dissent in *Glossip v. Gross* (Escalante et al. 2015).

In the aforementioned case dealing with the Slovene Constitutional Court's decision concerning a referendum against the statutory "legalization" of same-sex marriage, Judge Mozetič concurred with the majority opinion. In his concurring opinion, he responded to an argument that that referendum should have been constitutionally prohibited as it was inadmissible that a majority decides on the issues of a minority (thus violating human rights). He became somewhat emotional (angry) when emphasizing:

> Here we hear another argument that people are not capable of deciding on all issues regulated by statutes, that they can be manipulated, misled, are conservative, do not want changes, etc. I refuse such positions because that would mean that they are not able to vote (voters are people). Should we then prescribe that only smart, advanced people, such that do not succumb to manipulation, are entitled to vote (also at a referendum), but in no manner conservatives and Catholics.[26]

Judges, however, advise lawyers to avoid such emotional language. Scalia, in his legal-writing primer with Bryan Garner, recommended attorneys not to "make an overt, passionate attempt to play upon the judicial heartstring" as "[i]t can have a nasty backlash" (Scalia, Garner 2008). There is also a procedural rule (e.g., Supreme Court Rule 24.6, but other courts have similar rules) directing lawyers that a brief shall be "free of irrelevant, immaterial, or scandalous matter" (Escalante et al. 2015). Nevertheless, the language of such rules is vague, thus giving room for lawyers to be emotional to some extent, especially if the case is decided by a jury. Thus, for example, in the Moussaoui (9/11) trial, the government prosecutors appealed to the jury's emotions by presenting a cockpit tape from United 93, photographs of burned bodies from the wreckage of the Pentagon, a recording of a man's final phone call made in his WTC office (complete with a "synchronized video" of the towers collapsing), and the testimony of former NYC Mayor Rudy Giuliani about what he witnessed during the day of the attacks (Linder 2006).

Because legal language cannot directly use appeals to emotions, they are usually expressed in an indirect manner. Thus, opportunities exist for using rhetorical figures of an emotional value that influence the audience in an indirect way, interwoven in the logical structure of argument. This seems to be a position of Aristotle regarding *pathos.* According to Quintilian, a metaphor is inherently emotional through producing emotional pleasure in the audience. There is also an aesthetic component of language in metaphors, providing an important emotional complement to their purely logical components (Frost 2005, 92).

26 That judge has been a long-time member, at some point even a member of parliament, of the Christian-Democratic political party.

Another figure of speech that propels emotion or pathos in the audience is *climax* or "ladder," a figure of syntactic arrangement, being arrangement of a series of notions in such an order that each is more important or impressive than the preceding (Garner 2002, 162–163). Moreover, *antithesis* and *parallelism* also have a potential emotional effect in legal language (Frost 2005, 109–116).

2.5.4 The Power of Visceral Argumentation (Legal "Physis")[27]

Various sensory arguments, such as visuals, sounds, etc., can have both dialectical as well as rhetorical relevance in legal proceedings. They are important in legal argumentation from the position of the evidence that is needed to establish the minor premise of the deductive syllogism. Specific evidence is needed in order to prove that the facts of a case do, indeed, match the legal facts of a relevant legal provision such that it can be applied. Many pieces of evidence are sensory in character, which follows next in their presentation. There are two ways they are applied in the legal context.

2.5.4.1 The Dialectical Dimension

First, visceral (or "sensory") evidence is used in the dialectical sense to prove the existence of the minor premise. This is especially true in criminal cases that use clear direct evidence to prove, for example, with certainty (or beyond a reasonable doubt), that a defendant has committed a criminal offense. This is the approach taken by prosecutors in the reasoning of indictments as well as judges in the reasoning of judgments. This is not generally the case for lawyers because they need to develop a different strategy (or make their client plead guilty to get a lower sentence) if they want to help their clients. In the situation of clear evidence, a dialectical relation is established between the evidence and the legal premise because it is the evidence that enables the establishment of that premise. The relation between evidence and facts enables the application of the legal deductive syllogistic argument.

The Rodney King case presents an example of clear multi-modal (visual) evidence (Groarke 2017, 12). King was beaten violently by LA police officers during his arrest for fleeing and evading police on an LA road. A bystander filmed the incident from his nearby balcony and sent the film to a local news station. The film showed King being beaten by the police. The four officers were tried on charges of use of excessive force, yet three were acquitted by a jury composed of only white jurors. Within hours of the acquittals, the

27 The broadest meaning of the old Greek word *physis* was nature. According to Kelly, this meant "the natural physical universe and the instinctual nature of its human inhabitants, which were unvarying everywhere" (Kelly 2007, 14). In this sense, we could understand it to refer to the visceral mode.

1992 Los Angeles riots started, sparked by outrage among African Americans over the verdicts in face of such clear evidence of police violence. The federal government prosecuted a separate civil rights case, in which two of the police officers were found guilty and sentenced to prison.

2.5.4.2 *The Rhetorical Dimension*

There is, however, another way of using such arguments – namely the rhetorical. This is especially true in cases from the domain of intellectual property law (copyright law and industrial property law), where different artistic works and industrial products expressed in pictures, sounds, scents, etc. need to be compared so that their distinct individuality is legally protected. This is a complex procedure because such viscerals often resemble one another to some extent, so a very detailed analysis needs to follow to establish their (dis)similarity. From a first glance, it is far from being clear whether there is too much similarity between them, or not. In particular, the impossibility of the exact "translation" of such multi-modal arguments into words opens up avenues for various interpretations or "strategic manoeuvring" (van Eemeren 2010) by different legal arguers, such as lawyers and judges, with the former having more room for doing so than the latter, who are bound institutionally much more by the requirements of reasonableness. Here, too, we have more and less ambiguous situations concerning the evidence used. Next I present some examples from different areas of sensory argumentation.

Moreover, in criminal cases we can also apply the rhetorical model when unclear circumstantial[28] evidence exists. We might have pictures, sounds, etc. but not know how many we would need for a "logical circle (of reasonableness) to close."[29] In such a situation, room exists for steering the discussion in one direction or another.

2.5.4.3 *Visual Arguments*

The *Rodney King* case is an example of using visual argumentation in a dialectical manner. This is a case with clear evidence, but if evidence is ambiguous

28 Circumstantial evidence can also be very clear like forensic evidence (as evidence obtained by scientific methods such as ballistics, blood tests, and DNA tests).

29 In Case No. Kp 4/2006 of July 17, 2006 (the Perić case), the Slovene Supreme Court developed the "logic-circle-closes" test to evaluate when there is enough circumstantial evidence to reach the standard of beyond reasonable doubt necessary for a criminal judgment of conviction. In that case a young man was convicted of having murdered his family. The circumstantial evidence used in that case was a socket of the bullet that was found at the crime scene and compared with those he otherwise used for his pistol, a watch that was supposed to have been used by his father but was found with the defendant, and a video of his car filmed at a gas station on the way between the place he lived and the crime scene. Relevant for our case would be the last (visual) circumstantial evidence because there might be several photographs of a defendant's car on the way to the crime scene. These photographs depend on the entire context of other circumstantial evidence but give grounds for rhetorical strategic maneuvering in different directions of the case.

room exists for steering the discussion in a certain direction. A selection of such cases is presented next.

Concerning visual argumentation in the legal context, Murray focused on visual legal rhetoric, stressing the powerfulness of arguing by means of visuals in court. He not only argues that visual imaging is faster than words but also better than words, since the brain processes images in such a way as to allow greater perception, comprehension, and the retention of certain kinds of information. In his opinion, visual modes of persuasion (visual tools) can construct meaning and improve the persuasiveness of legal writing discourse (verbal tools) regarding content, arrangement, and style. He calls for attention concerning the potential misleading and prejudicing of the audience's reception or understanding of communication (Murray 2016, 121–122, 155).

In his essay, Murray discusses several legal cases in which visual legal arguments were used. An exemplary one is *Apple v. Samsung*, an intellectual property case in which Apple claimed that Samsung copied the look, feel, operation, and functionality of its iPhone to produce smartphones that infringed upon its trademark, industrial design, and patent rights. To support its claim, Apple's counsel used two photographs as visual arguments. In the first one, several of Samsung's products from 2004 to 2006 were exhibited that looked completely different from the iPhone, which was released in 2007. In the second photograph, Samsung smartphones from post-2010 were depicted that looked similar to the iPhone. The claim was that all of Samsung's smartphones were copied from Apple's iPhone.[30] However, Samsung defended itself by means of two photographs, the first showing that some of its phones before the iPhone looked similar and, on the second, that some of the smartphones introduced after the iPhone looked different from the iPhone (Murray 2016, 133–134).

The strategy of both counsels was to show the part of the story that was advantageous to their client's position. What is important for visual legal argumentation, however, is why the counsels decided to use such a tactic. Obviously because the "visuals were better at telling the specific part of the story the clients wanted to tell than verbal means would have been" (Murray 2016, 136).

Furthermore, Groarke reports on a case in which two painters claimed authorship of "big eyed" paintings of children. Thus, in an attempt to determine who was the real artist, the judge asked the two alleged painters to paint a big-eyed child before the court. While the male painter excused himself due to a sore shoulder, the female painter successfully passed the "test" and was awarded the authorship of those paintings (Groarke 2017, 17–18).

30 Apple's evidence submitted to the court included side-by-side image comparisons of iPhone 3GS and i9000 Galaxy S to illustrate the alleged similarities in packaging and icons for applications. However, the images were later found to have been tampered with in order to make the dimensions and features of the two different products seem more similar, and counsel for Samsung accused Apple of submitting misleading evidence to the court (Kane, Sherr 2011; Victor 2012).

2.5.4.4 *Arguments of Sounds*

Concerning the sense of hearing and auditive arguments, remember the previously mentioned case of Stanley "Tookie" Williams, the gang leader executed in 2005, reported by van den Hoven and Kišiček. They analyzed a video clip as part of a 2005 campaign to urge the then governor of California, Arnold Schwarzenegger, to grant clemency to Williams. Convinced that he should have been pardoned by the governor, they claimed that the prosodic information, such as "pitch, pitch range, voice quality, intonation, tempo, loudness, emphasis, accentuation, and (non-)fluencies of the speaker (i.e. Williams)," which cannot be translated into words, showed that Williams had become "re-socialized" and thus a better person from being in prison for such a long time. They mainly associated such prosodic features with emotions (*pathos*) and ethics (*ethos*) (van den Hoven, Kišiček 2017).

Furthermore, in the Moor murder trials, one of the key pieces of evidence used to convict Ian Brady and Myra Hindley was a 13-minute tape recording of one of their victims screaming and sobbing to present how they suffered before their death (Groarke 2018, 318).

Finally, in pop music history a number of copyright infringement cases exist relating to lyrical lifts and unlicensed sampling – melodies that sound "just a tad too similar." Some of these cases were settled out of court, others resolved by the courts. For example, George Harrison was found guilty of "subconscious plagiarism" for his song "My Sweet Lord" with regard to The Chiffons' song "He's So Fine" and ordered to pay a significant amount of compensation. Moreover, in the case of *Fogerty v. CCR*, Fogerty brought his guitar to the courtroom witness stand to play his song to demonstrate that the two songs were, in fact, different, and the case subsequently was found in his favor (Runtagh 2016).

The problem is similar to that in other "visceral cases," where it is hard to argue only with words. One also needs to reason with physicalities to present the full range of such a case and demonstrate certain differences that cannot be (fully) verbalized.

2.5.4.5 *Arguments of Scents and Tastes*

Furthermore, argumentation on the basis of scents and tastes also has entered the legal arena in cases regarding copyright protection. In *Lancôme v. Kecofa* decided in 2006, the Dutch Supreme Court held that, under Dutch copyright law, with its open and non-exhaustive description of the types of works, a scent (such as a perfume) can be a work protected by copyright. The court considered a scent susceptible to human perception, capable of having its own original character and capable of carrying the personal mark of its creator. Thus, according to the court, the scent itself is the subject of copyright protection, not the recipe or the substances (Jonkhout 2017).[31]

31 Cf. the situation in France where, in several cases from 2006 to 2013, the French *Cour de cassation* refused to grant copyright protection, holding that copyright protects creations in their tangible form, in so far as these are identified with sufficient precision to allow their

Taste also has been protected under copyright law. In 2012, the producer of Heks'nkaas ("witches cheese") requested an ex-parte order from the District Court of The Hague to protect the cheese against a competitor who had created their own "Magic Cheese." By relying on *Lancôme v. Kecofa*, the court decided that taste could be protected under copyright law. After tasting both cheese products, the court held that the taste of Heks'nkaas's cheese would fulfill the criteria for copyright protection and would meet the threshold of having an original character and taste carrying the personal mark of its creator (Jonkhout 2017).

In another case, in 2015, the producer of Heks'nkaas launched court proceedings before the District Court of Gelderland against another producer of cheese. This time, the court requested the producer of Heks'nkaas substantiate the elements of the taste of their cheese that merited copyright protection. However, the court held that both the producer and its expert witness failed to describe these specific elements sufficiently. The producer of Heks'nkaas argued that it was impossible to describe these elements because one should experience the taste personally. Finally, the court refused this argument and declined to taste Heks'nkaas to find the grounds of protecting that cheese by copyright law. The court added that the taste of a product may vary with the age of the product, the air exposure of the product, the temperature, and also the subjectivity of how the taste of such a product is experienced (Jonkhout 2017).

The producer of Heks'nkaas appealed, and the Dutch Regional Court of Appeal stayed the proceedings and referred the question for a preliminary ruling to the European Court of Justice, since the copyright legislations of the member states have to a certain extent been harmonized by an EU directive. The referral asked whether Directive 2001/29 must be interpreted as precluding (i) the taste of a food product from being protected by copyright under that directive and (ii) national legislation from being interpreted in such a way that it grants copyright protection to such a taste (Jonkhout 2017).

The ECJ judgment included two different positions taken by opposing parties concerning the copyright protection of taste. According to Levola, who sought copyright protection of their cheese, the taste of a food product may be classified as a work of literature, science, or art that is eligible for copyright protection. Levola relied by analogy, inter alia, on the judgment of June 16, 2006, of the Supreme Court of the Netherlands, in *Lancôme*, in which that court accepted in principle the possibility of recognizing copyright of the scent of a perfume. Conversely, Smilde, who had allegedly violated the copyright protection, submitted that the protection of tastes is not consistent with the copyright system, as the latter is intended purely for visual and auditory creations. Moreover, the instability of a food product and the subjective nature of the taste experience precluded the taste of a food product from qualifying as

communication. The fragrance of a perfume is not in itself a work of the mind, apart from its development process. It does not have a form with the characteristics of a work of the mind itself (Jonkhout 2017).

a work for copyright protection. Smilde further submitted that the exclusive rights of the author of a work of intellectual property and the restrictions to which those rights were subject were, in practical terms, inapplicable in the case of tastes. The referring court noted that the French *Cour de cassation* had categorically rejected the possibility of granting copyright protection to a scent, in particular in its judgment of December 10, 2013. There was, therefore, divergence in the case law of the national supreme courts of the European Union when it comes to the question as to whether a scent may be protected by copyright.

Finally, the ECJ decision[32] was that the

> taste of a food product cannot, however, be pinned down with precision and objectivity. Unlike, for example, a literary, pictorial, cinematographic or musical work, which is a precise and objective form of expression, the taste of a food product will be identified essentially on the basis of taste sensations and experiences, which are subjective and variable since they depend, inter alia, on factors particular to the person tasting the product concerned, such as age, food preferences and consumption habits, as well as on the environment or context in which the product is consumed. Moreover, it is not possible in the current state of scientific development to achieve by technical means a precise and objective identification of the taste of a food product which enables it to be distinguished from the taste of other products of the same kind.

Accordingly, the Court concluded that Directive 2001/29 prevented the national legislation from being interpreted in such a way that it granted copyright protection to the taste of a food product.

2.6 Multi-Modal Arguments and Arguments About Multi-Modality

Groarke highlights that we should distinguish between "multimodal arguments" and "arguments about multimodality" (Groarke 2018, 325). He refers to auditory arguments, but his claim can be extended to visual and taste arguments, as well as other visceral arguments.[33] In his opinion, the difference resides in the character of their being in a non-verbal or verbal form. For his multimodal theory, this kind of distinction is of crucial importance because what he views as multimodal are non-verbal arguments. This is not the case for Gilbert, who does not make such a difference and for whom

32 Case C-310/17, November 13, 2018, *Levola Hengelo BV v. Smilde Foods BV.*

33 Based on Jung's cognitive functions, and that of sensation, I list all the arguments under Gilbert's visceral mode as sensory arguments. All those are based on physicalities from our five senses.

multi-modal arguments can be in verbal form. What is important for multi-modal arguments to exist as such, according to Duran, is that the thrust of an argument is in the multi-modal form (2022). This is to say that, for example, if a visceral argument is verbalized this semiotic change does not change its independent visceral quality. However, the process of verbalization may still open room for various interpretative strategies.

Due to the explicit substantive and procedural requirements that subsume the facts of a case under the relevant legal provisions, genuine multimodal arguments in judicial proceedings are turned ("translated")[34] into arguments about multimodality (Groarke 2018). Genuine multi-modal arguments, including visuals or sounds as crucial evidence that have (not) persuaded or convinced the judges, need to be verbalized ("translated") and described so that a deductive syllogistic "test"[35] is carried out in the reasoning of a judgment. Certainly, the verbal interpretation of certain multi-modal arguments, such as the visceral (visual, auditory, etc.) arguments presented to establish that certain facts qualify as legal facts in the deductive argument, is only an approximation to the full power of such arguments (consider the English idiom "A picture is worth a thousand words"). Yet in legal proceedings, it is necessary for the case to be legally resolved. Although any verbal description of such multi-modal arguments reduces the aforementioned power of such arguments by restricting their non-verbal message, we cannot assert that multi-modality had no role in such argumentation if that particular multi-modal argument actually decided the case. The fact that such an argument was put into words in order to be described and analyzed does not change its importance for the legal case. The need for the "translation" of (genuine) multi-modal arguments into arguments about multi-modality, especially when their verbalization is difficult or only approximately possible, in order for multi-modal arguments to be connected with legal provisions, opens up room for different rhetorical approaches and strategies that can be taken. In the framework of such, possibilities for strategic maneuvering exist, in the manner of being effective within a dialectical framework (van Eemeren 2015), by those that are supposed to do such a "translation."

A distinction between the two categories should be made because when we try to describe or interpret "genuine" multi-modal arguments by means of words, we reduce their communicative as well as their rhetorical power. In the legal context, genuine multi-modal arguments, at least in the visceral mode, are used mostly by lawyers presenting various pieces of evidence, as described earlier, in a genuine multi-modal way. However, courts (with professional judges) who evaluate such (genuine) multi-modal arguments and keep records

34 I use parentheses before and after the word translation because I agree with multi(-)modality theorists that some kind of literal or "faithful" translation is impossible, at least when it comes to physicalities within the visceral mode.

35 A kind of a typical legal "experiment" in order to come to a legal decision.

of such evaluations in the reasoning of their decision, use arguments about multi-modality in the sense that they verbally explain how they evaluated those genuine multi-modal arguments. Their use of multi-modal arguments in such a manner reduces their power.

However, judges write reasonings of judgments for their audiences, whether a particular or general one. Their verbal evaluation of genuine multi-modal arguments also has a rhetorical value in that they want to persuade their audience; most frequently in the event of appeals, senior judges might make a recommendation about the direction in which the evaluation of particular genuine multi-modal arguments should proceed. The strategy they resort to makes their arguments effective within the overall structure of reasonable (dialectical) argumentation. That normally depends on how much room they have for such strategic maneuvering in terms of the types of evidence, its ambiguity, and the legal field in which it is used (i.e., what standard of proof it needs to satisfy).

2.7 Conclusion

The predominant reliance of courts is on critical thinking, (informal) logic, and rational reasons. This is chiefly for two purposes: (i) logic and *ratio* are the best social means for keeping social relations regulated, predictable, stable, and to resolve social disputes in a peaceful and controlled manner, and (ii) from the normative perspective, the justification of a decision in a successful logical way is the strongest possible justification since it shows that a legal conclusion truly follows the "meeting" of the upper and the lower premises of the deductive syllogistic argument. That is, so to say, an ideal from the rule-of-law point of view.

Courts are also the most important audience for lawyers and other parties. Thus, they try to follow their expectations when preparing cases in terms of the dialectical mode of deciding upon and justifying legal decisions. However, even with courts, which is even more the case with lawyers whose commitments are legally speaking not as entrenched with reasonableness as those of judges, there is room for their rhetorical strategies. Thus, multi-modal argumentation can be seen in most situations as an invitation to understand or re-emphasize the use of legal rhetoric.

Although it seems that the legal domain with its formal requirements is more of a dialectical "enterprise," room exists for rhetorical arguments (van Eemeren, Houtlosser 1999b, 493). Arguers try to "exploit the opportunities afforded by the dialectical situation for steering the discourse rhetorically in the direction that best serves their interests" (van Eemeren, Houtlosser 2000, 295). This not only refers to *logos*, but also to *ethos*, *pathos*, and *physis* as modes of argument alternative to the logical mode. In addition to their dialectical goals, legal arguers seek rhetorical moves. This can be established by analyzing the reasoning of decisions in unclear legal cases, whereas in clear cases this potential is limited because of the predominance of the logical mode. A descriptive component to my project exists – namely, how lawyers who argue multi-modally extend the prevailing dialectical mode. Moreover, toward the end of this book, I also explore normative components in studying the boundaries of legal rhetoric within the general dialectical framework of law.

References

Alexy, Robert. 1989. *A Theory of Legal Argumentation*. Oxford: Clarendon Press.

Aristotle. 2004. *Rhetoric* (Transl. by W. Rhys Roberts). Mineola, New York: Dover Publications, Inc.

Bandes, Susan A. 2016. "What Roles Do Emotions Play in the Law?" www.emotionresearcher.com/what-roles-do-emotions-play-in-the-law/ (29.3.2019).

Beck, Günther. 2012. *The Legal Reasoning of the Court of Justice of the EU*. Oxford, Portland, Oregon: Hart Publishing.

Brennan, William J. 1988. "Reason, Passion, and the 'Progress of the Law'." *Cardozo Law Review*, 10: 3–23.

Brinton, Alan. 1988. "Pathos and the 'Appeal to Emotion': An Aristotelian Analysis." *History of Philosophy Quarterly*, 5 (3): 207–219.

Cahill-O'Callaghan, Rachel J. 2013. "The Influence of Personal Values on Legal Judgments." *Journal of Law and Society*, 40: 596–623.

Duran, Claudio. 2022. "Reflections on the Physical or Visceral Mode of Argumentation in Michael Gilbert's Theory of Multi-Modal Argumentation and its Relation to Gesture Studies and the Embodied Mind." *Informal Logic*, 42 (3): 583–601.

Escalante, Sarah et al. 2015. "An Empirical Analysis of Emotional Language in Legal Briefs before the Supreme Court." www.scotusblog.com/2015/12/an-empirical-analysis-of-emotional-language-in-legal-briefs-before-the-supreme-court/ (15.5.2019).

Feteris, Eveline T. 2015. "Strategic Manoeuvring in the Case of the 'Unworthy Spouse'." In Manzin, Maurizio, Puppo, Federico, Tomasi, Serena (Eds.). *Further Steps Towards a Pluralistic Approach*. Studies on Argumentation & Legal Philosophy/10. Trento: Università degli studi di Trento, Quaderni della Facoltà di giurisprudenza.

Feteris, Eveline T. 2017. *Fundamentals of Legal Argumentation*. Dordrecht: Springer.

Frost, Michael H. 2005. *Introduction to Classical Legal Rhetoric: A Lost Heritage*. Aldershot, Burlington: Ashgate.

Garner, Bryan A. 2001. *Legal Writing in Plain English*. Chicago: The University of Chicago Press.

Garner, Bryan A. 2002. *The Elements of Legal Style*. Oxford: Oxford University Press.

Groarke, Leo. 2017. "Multimodality and the Law." In Manzin, Maurizio, Puppo, Federico, Tomasi, Serena (Eds.). *Multimodality and Reasonableness in Judicial Rhetoric*. Studies on Argumentation & Legal Philosophy/2. Trento: Università degli studi di Trento, Quaderni della Facoltà di giurisprudenza.

Groarke, Leo. 2018. "Auditory Arguments: The Logic of 'Sound' Arguments." *Informal Logic*, 38 (3): 312–340.

Halloran, Michael S. 1982. "Aristotle's Concepts of Ethos, or if not His, Someone Else's." *Rhetoric Review*, 1 (1).

Jonkhout, Hans. 2017. "The Scent and the Taste of Copyright Law." *Eurojuris International*. www.eurojuris.net/en/node/44283 (15.4.2019).

Kane, Yukari I., Sherr, Ian. 2011. "Apple: Samsung Copied Design." *The Wall Street Journal*. Dow Jones & Company (11.8.2012).

Kelly, John M. 2007. *A Short History of Western Legal Theory*. Oxford: Clarendon Press.

Kennedy, Duncan. 1996. *A Critique of Adjudication*. Cambridge: Harvard University Press.

Kranjc, Janez. 2020. *Rimsko pravo*. Ljubljana: GV Založba.

Lanni, Adriaan. 2008. *Law and Justice in the Courts of Classical Athens*. Cambridge: Cambridge University Press.

Linder, Douglas. 2006. "Moussaoui (9/11) Trial." https://famous-trials.com/moussaoui (15.5.2019).

MacCormick, Neil. 1994. *Legal Theory and Legal Reasoning*. Oxford: Clarendon Press.

MacCormick, Neil. 2005. *Rhetoric and the Rule of Law*. Oxford: Oxford University Press.

MacCormick, Neil, Summers, Robert. 1991. *Interpreting Statutes*. Aldershot: Dartmouth.

Maroney, Terry A., Gross, James. 2014. "The Ideal of the Dispassionate Judge: An Emotion Regulation Perspective." *Emotion Review*, 6: 142–151.

Montesquieu, Charles de. 2011. *The Spirit of the Laws*. New York: Cosimo Classics.

Murray, Michael D. 2016. "The Ethics of Visual Legal Rhetoric." *Legal Communication & Rhetoric*, 13: 107–155.

Ogrizek, Dušan. 2002. "Sodnikov pogled na jezik (in pravo)." *Podjetje in delo*, XXVIII (6–7): 1078–1085.

Oyserman, Daphna. 2015. "Values, Psychology of." *International Encyclopedia of the Social & Behavioral Sciences*, 25: 36–40. 2nd ed., Elsevier Ltd.

Perelman, Chaïm, Olbrechts-Tyteca, Lucie. 1969. *The New Rhetoric: A Treaties on Argumentation*. Notre Dame: University of Notre Dame Press.

Posner, Richard A. 1995. *Overcoming Law*. Cambridge, London: Harvard University Press.

Posner, Richard A. 2010. *How Judges Think*. Cambridge: Harvard University Press.

Radovčić, Vesna. 2004. *Pravni aspekti u učenjima antičke retorike*. Zagreb: Pravni fakultet Sveučilišta u Zagrebu.

Runtagh, Jordan. 2016. "Songs on Trial: 12 Landmark Music Copyright Cases." www.rollingstone.com/politics/politics-lists/songs-on-trial-12-landmark-music-copyright-cases-166396/the-beach-boys-vs-chuck-berry-1963–65098/ (8.10.2019).

Sandler, Paul M., Epps, JoAnne A., Waicukauski, Ronald J. 2010. "Classical Rhetoric and the Modern Trial Lawyer." *Litigation*, 36 (2).

Scalia, Antonin, Garner, Bryan A. 2008. *Making Your Case: The Art of Persuading Judges*. St. Paul, MN: Thompson West Publishing.

Shapo, Helene S., Walter, Marilyn R., Fajans, Elizabeth. 1991. *Writing and Analysis in the Law*. Westbury: Foundation Press.

Tindale, Christopher W. 2004. *Rhetorical Argumentation. Principles of Theory and Practice*. Thousand Oaks, London, New Delhi: SAGE Publications.

Tseronis, Assimakis, Forceville, Charles (Eds.). 2017. *Multimodal Argumentation and Rhetoric in Media Genres*. Amsterdam: John Benjamins Publishing Company.

van den Hoven, Paul, Kišiček, Gabrijela. 2017. "Processing Multimodal Legal Discourse; The Case of Stanley 'Tookie' Williams." In Manzin, Maurizio, Puppo, Federico, Tomasi, Serena (Eds.). *Multimodality and Reasonableness in Judicial Rhetoric*. Studies on Argumentation & Legal Philosophy/2. Trento: Università degli studi di Trento, Quaderni della Facoltà di giurisprudenza.

van Eemeren, Frans H. 2010. *Strategic Maneuvering in Argumentative Discourse: Extending the Pragma-Dialectical Theory of Argumentation.* Amsterdam: John Benjamins Publishing Company.

van Eemeren, Frans H. 2015. "The Indispensable Connection between the Dialectical and the Rhetorical Perspective on Argumentation." In Manzin, Maurizio, Puppo, Federico, Tomasi, Serena (Eds.). *Further Steps Towards a Pluralistic Approach.* Studies on Argumentation & Legal Philosophy/10. Trento: Università degli studi di Trento, Quaderni della Facoltà di giurisprudenza.

van Eemeren, Frans H., Houtlosser, Peter. 1999a. "William the Silent's Argumentative Discourse." In van Eemeren, Frans H. et al. (Eds.). *Proceedings of the Fourth International Conference of the International Society for the Study of Argumentation.* Amsterdam: Sic Sat.

van Eemeren, Frans H., Houtlosser, Peter. 1999b. "Strategic Maneuvering in Argumentative Discourse." *Discourse Studies*, 1 (4): 479–497.

van Eemeren, Frans H., Houtlosser, Peter. 2000. "Rhetorical Analysis within a Pragma-Dialectical Framework: The Case of R. J. Reynolds." *Argumentation*, 14: 293–305.

Victor. 2012. "Apple Back to Manipulate the Evidence in a Lawsuit Against Samsung?" AndroidShine.com (11.8.2012).

von Savigny, Friedrich C. 1840. *System des heutigen römischen Rechts.* Band 1. Berlin: VEIT.

Walton, Douglas. 2001. "Enthymemes, Common Knowledge and Plausible Inference." *Philosophy and Rhetoric*, 34 (2): 93–112.

Walton, Douglas. 2002. *The Place of Emotion in Argument.* University Park: Penn State University Press.

Wenzel, Joseph. 1990. "Three Perspectives on Argument." In Trapp, Robert, Schuertz, Janice (Eds.). *Perspectives on Argumentation: Essays in Honor of Wayne Brockriede.* Prospect Eleights, IT: Waveland Press.

West Virginia State Board of Education v. Barnette. 1943. 319 U.S. 624.

3 Visual as Multi-Modal Argumentation in Law

3.1 Introduction

Apart from the logical mode, Gilbert also discusses the emotional mode, the kisceral (intuitive) mode, and the visceral (physical) mode[1] of which visual argument is a typical example. Within that theory, it is important that at least one premise (preferably reasons) is in an alternate (in this case, visceral) mode. This chapter deals with visual argumentation following Gilbert's theory of multi-modal argumentation. Therefore, a visual argument will be one in which at least one premise is visual.[2] However, in my analysis of visual argumentation in law, I also borrow certain findings from another similar approach to the topic called multimodality (without a hyphen).[3] Both claim their origin in social semiotics, which had invented the term multimodality that Gilbert extended to argumentation theory. Both approaches would agree that if argumentation is only in one mode, it is called monomodal, while a combination of more than one mode constitutes multi-modal argumentation (see, e.g., for the multimodal approach, Forceville 2020, 65). With respect to real-life arguments, it is very rare to find them in one pure mode only. When combined, they are designated as "multimodal ensembles" (Kress, Van Leeuwen 2001).

What was previously mentioned as an example of such a visual argument, used in the legal context, was the video of the beating of Rodney King by the police. A bystander filmed the incident from his nearby balcony and sent the film to a local news station (Koon, Deitz 1992; King, Spagnola 2012). The

1 According to Gilbert, "these arguments are primarily physical and can range from a touch to classical nonverbal communication, i.e. body language, to force" (1997, 84).

2 If there is some verbal text accompanying the visual, it may not change the point that the visual plays an important part in the argument. What is important is the view that the visual brings an additional dimension to merely verbal argumentation.

3 A major difference between the two approaches is that, unlike Gilbert's approach to multimodality that dicusses the four modes, multimodal theory of argumentation generally takes into account the following modes: visuals, written language, spoken language, bodily movement, sound, music, olfaction, taste, and touch (see, e.g., Forceville 2020, 67). This approach generally falls within what Gilbert would call the visceral mode.

DOI: 10.4324/9781003433767-4

film clearly showed King being beaten repeatedly by the police. The structure of that quite clear visual argument (P → C) could be as follows: the conclusion (C): "King is being beaten brutally by the police" is supported by the premise (P): "Many harsh movements by the police officers hitting his body," where P is in a purely visual (thus non-verbal) form. Thus, quite clear visual evidence was appropriately interpreted (or "translated" from the visual mode) to form a verbal antecedent.

Yet the relevance of visual arguments for legal procedures and legal argumentation has not generally been discussed until relatively recently (Groarke 2017). Visuals (such as photos, videos, etc.) have indeed been part of legal proceedings since their technological invention, and paintings, drawings, sketches, etc. had even featured before. They are mostly used in such proceedings in the form of evidence – because we do not have visual legal provisions but have not been discussed as separate arguments, where their non-verbal form would be analyzed in the face of general legal arguments that are verbal. They have been more or less taken for granted in the frame of legal syllogism. Why this traditional neglect for them? Perhaps because logic has dominated the field and such visuals have simply been taken as evidence, which is part of the lower premise of a legal deductive syllogism, where the only question was whether such evidence meets a certain standard of proof prescribed for the specific legal proceedings.

With the advent of information technologies, the internet, social networks, etc., visuals have become more important in human communication than ever before. It also became obvious that they cannot be just "automatically" used in the logical skeleton of typical legal argument, especially because of their different semiotic resources than words. Thus, problems have appeared that need to be addressed additionally to examine the possibility of traditional (i.e., logical) legal arguments being influenced by multi-modality. From multi-modality, the so-called alternate modes (i.e., emotional, kisceral, and visceral) are especially interesting, particularly in terms of seeing how they interact with the predominant logical mode in law, and what kind of dynamics they bring to the static character of traditional legal arguments.

However, before any discussion on multi-modality and law begins, it should be stressed that the legal context is a special social context in which a greater level of formality applies than in other social situations. Thus, special rules of substantive and procedural law are enacted in order for courts with mostly professional judges to decide upon the most important social disputes, so their decisions have very important consequences for the whole of society. Hence there is a need for these decisions to be properly made and reasoned and, therefore, the basic rule of the legal context emphasizes its strong institutional and normative constraints. If a legal dialogue is about communicating on the basis of legal norms, legal argumentation cannot be free from using them. Nevertheless, legal systems are not immune to interpretative problems such as gaps, vagueness, and ambiguity. The findings from visual (and multi-modal) argumentation theory only contribute to the notion of legal indeterminacy.

Or proves, once again, its argumentative not demonstrative agenda (Perelman, Olbrechts-Tyteca 1969, 13).

In this chapter I initially analyze the importance of multi-modal visual arguments in the framework of legal argumentation, whereby I emphasize the role of visuals as evidence in the legal context, discuss the necessary semiotic "translation" of visuals into their verbal dimension, and point to a difference between thick and thin visuals. Based on the theoretical model of the use of visuals in the legal context presented in the first part, in the second I reconstruct a real legal case in a multi-modal manner and present some final thoughts about the problem in the conclusion.

3.2 Visual Arguments in Legal Argumentation

3.2.1 Visual Arguments as Legal Evidence

As already mentioned, if a visual argument is to be part of an acceptable line of legal argumentation from a legal point of view, it needs to be connected to relevant legal provisions and their application to relevant facts. When dealing with visuals as facts or evidence to be used in legal proceedings, visual argumentation becomes an inseparable part of legal argumentation. Let me refer next to the example of visual argument reported by Groarke (2017, 17–18) and see how it was applied as legal evidence used by the court in that case.

Remember the so-called Keane controversy about

> the question whether Walter or Margaret Keane was the American artist who painted "big eyed" paintings of children, women and animals that were popular in the United States in the 1960s. The court determined Margaret was the right painter and produced a judgment awarding her damages. Margaret's act of painting was submitted as [non-verbal] evidence for the conclusion that she was the artist who painted the well-known big eyed paintings.
>
> (Groarke 2017, ibid.)

The visual argument in that case reads as follows: Claim – Margaret's painting painted before the court is (almost) the same as the previous "big eyed" paintings; Reason – [the painting itself] is an example of the non-verbal visceral mode.

This is not exactly the same as the legal argument in the logical mode, which was made previously in the lawsuit, and went in the following manner: *Mp* (the major premise consisting of legal norms): "Anyone whose copyright is violated, is to be redressed concerning their moral (recognizing authorship) or material rights (awarding compensation) respectively." In the *Mp*, copyright holders could be defined to include (i) painters as well (ii) copyright violations to include false authors pretending to be original ones. At the level of the factual premise of the legal argument we have *mp* (the minor premise consisting of relevant facts), which reads in the following manner: "Margaret's copyright was violated since she was proved (by the evidence taken in the form of Margaret's painting before the court – the visual argument in that case!) to be the original author whose authorship had been stolen." Finally, what follows is *c* (the conclusion inferred on the basis of the minor premise subsumed under the major premise): "Margaret's copyright is to be redressed."

Thus, the aforementioned visual argument (of Margaret's painting before the court) was used as legal evidence to prove the existence of the minor premise in that case so that the deductive syllogistic inference was possible by applying the relevant copyright provision to the described facts. By means of this evidence it was proved that Margaret was the original author, which meant that her ex-husband stole the authorship of big-eyed paintings from her.

The use of visual arguments as legal evidence in legal cases has been commonplace for quite some time. With technological development, our societies have very much become visual, which means that the use of visual arguments will only increase. However, their use in legal proceedings to date to prove the existence of certain facts so that specific legal provisions are applied has been taken for granted somewhat. Here I try to show that this should not be the case, as there are different visuals, some with multiple meanings discovered not until they try to be interpreted. And what is important, we do not face exactly the same problems as when words are interpreted. As semiotic resources, visuals are different from words and never completely (or literally) translatable by them. Both visual and verbal arguments in their monomodal forms might be already complex, not to mention their multi-modal (visual-verbal) combinations. Thus, in the process of their use in legal proceedings in such a case, there seems to be plenty of room for different strategies that lawyers might use in order to persuade their audience about their positions.

3.2.2 Semiotic "Translation"

To qualify arguments that are constructed in everyday life as visual, they need to be made in a visual mode, where their reasons/premises are (non-verbal) visual, such as pictures, paintings, photographs, videos, drawings, sketches. As a matter of fact, it would be quite unusual if not impossible to find pure visual arguments. They are usually accompanied with some (verbal) text (in a premise or conclusion) and are in fact already as such multi-modal. In semiotics, it is held that every image (or visual) is polysemious (has multiple related meanings). Thus, the role of the verbal text accompanying a visual is to anchor and relay it. Anchoring helps to control it by avoiding other meanings and keeping it away from any emerging connotations, while relaying is to fill the gap that the images cannot (Barthes 1967).

However, in order to be used in a legal argument, in the case of evidence to enter the minor premise of a legal deductive syllogism, they need at some point to be verbalized. There are several reasons for this: legal provisions with possible sanctions for their violations are in a verbal form, the evaluation of evidence with all discussions in the courtroom is verbal. Such is the verbal justification of their application with a proper analysis in the reasoning of a judgment in such a form. Before such an inference is made, a legal norm has to be extracted from a relevant legal provision in view of the applicable facts as well as concrete facts extracted from brute, in this case visual, facts (supported by evidence) on the basis of the legal norm. Engisch illustrated the interdependence between the normative legal text and the description of the case with his metaphor of "looking back and forth" ("*Hin- und Herwandern des Blicks*") (von Engisch 1943, 15).

Therefore, a visual (e.g., evidence) needs to be translated into a verbal form to be subsumed under a verbal legal norm. However, as Kjeldsen notes, literal translation between different multi modes is impossible (2015).[4] The verbal means do not actually suffice to capture the rich information communicated by images to an audience (Kjeldsen 2016). However, some kind of semiotic translation of visuals into words is therefore necessary in the legal context, despite the fact that it constitutes something of a "leap." Translations across modes, for example from image to speech, are both possible and difficult and always achieved with enormously difficult selection, at a considerable level of generality (and in inevitably significant changes in meaning) (Kress 2010, 10). Blair claims that the verbal is to be understood as a placeholder for the visual, not a "translation" of it: verbal reconstruction rarely captures all that was expressed in the visual argument, but rather is a placeholder for it and provides us with a reference for use in evaluating the cogency of the visual argument (2015, 220). Therefore, there is a risk of overemphasizing the role of the verbal over the visual by using merely linguistic properties to assess the visual because some important features of images may remain outside of the linguistic perspective (Tseronis, Forceville 2017, 15).

When the verbal mode is combined with the visual mode, it is wrong to assume that the verbal mode conveys the standpoint while the visual mode is only the reasons in support of it so that it is simply used to appeal to the audience's emotions (Tseronis and Forceville, ibid.). The meaning conveyed by texts in which more than one semiotic mode is at play is never the sum of a distinct part of a multi-modal text (Jewitt 2014). The meanings of one mode and the meanings of others resonate so as to produce more than the sum of the parts (Bateman 2014, 6).

But the "translation," whatever it may be, from the visual into the verbal logical mode is necessary in the context of legal argumentation. Otherwise, there is no way of confronting legal evidence in the visual form with facts that

4 Which Jung also claimed for his four cognitive functions (Jung 1971).

need to be in the verbal form so that a relevant legal provision is applied in a verbal form. Legal arguers need to "translate" their alternate arguments into the logical mode, the "language of legal norms and legal systems," to pass muster in terms of the rule of law.

In this case, a "semiotic translation" implies that various non-verbal "semiotic resources" (or speech acts (Groarke, Tindale 2004)) need to be "translated" in the verbal mode in order to play some role in legal proceedings. This not only applies to visuals, such as pictures, photos, etc., but also to other physicalities from the visceral mode, including sounds, tastes, and smells, although in this chapter I limit myself to visuals. In certain cases, there is no problem with this since visual "reasons" can be more or less easily "translated" into (legal) words, about which there would be no major disagreements in the relevant legal community because the premises would be considered as clear. In such clear cases, the "translation" is unproblematic. As such, I refer next to semantically thin visuals (see also Kjeldsen 2015). There are also other types of cases, where such a "translation" is far from smooth. In such cases, bridging a gap between the alternate modes and the legal logical mode is controversial due to various reasons, both visual and verbal. I call such visuals semantically thick ones (see also Kjeldsen 2015). Kjeldsen calls the enthymemes, referring to rhetorical syllogism in which either the premise(s) or the conclusion is left to be completed by the audience that has the task of "filling in the blank" by having recourse to contextual information (2017).

3.2.3 Semantically Thin and Thick Visuals Inviting Alternate Arguments

The difference between semantically thin and thick visuals is reminiscent of the distinction between a figurative and abstract painting. When you sit in a gallery in front of a still-life painting, your thoughts would perhaps travel less far than in the case of an expressionist painting, although one would expect that figurative paintings, as works of art, would be still stronger in their messages than unclear legal texts, which have an institutional tendency to be as precise as possible.

Clearly understood visuals are semantically thin, which means that they do not invite different interpretations ("translations") from those that interpret them. In such cases, we can expect quite easy "translation" from their visual to the verbal mode. This means that there would be no substantial gap between the two modes. Recall that the example of the video of the Rodney King beating from the very beginning of this paper. Also, I mentioned that the prosecution and defense could have argued about the "translation" of the video. In fact, it was not very much disputed because the filmed beating of Rodney was quite clear. In such a non-problematic case, the visual mode and its reasons were easily "translated" into the verbal mode of the minor premise, thus producing the following figure:

Figure 1: Easy "Translation" of Thin Visuals

Vr eT mp

Legend:

Vr = visual reasons
mp = minor premise
eT = easy translation

However, when it comes to unclear cases, one possibility is that legal premises are indeterminate, e.g., ambiguous[5] or vague,[6] and need to be interpreted (in the narrow sense)[7] in order to be properly applied. But the problem can also be with the unclear factual premise. In our situation, this would apply to unclear visuals as evidence in the legal context, which are semantically thick. Consequently, the interpreters ("translators") of such evidence, arguers and audiences, would evaluate them differently, based on what meaning they glean from them. Therefore, because of unclear visuals, problems occur with their verbalization, i.e., "translating" them into the verbal mode. Thus, the following figure of a hard "translation" might apply:

Figure 2: Hard "Translation" of Thick Visuals

Vr hT mp

Legend:

Vr = visual reasons
mp = minor premise
hT = hard translation

5 By ambiguity in law I mean that a legal provision has several, at least two, meanings. For example, in *Smith v. United States*, 508 U.S. 223 (1993), the provision of Title 18 U.S.C. 924(c)(1) requires the imposition of specified penalties if the defendant, "during and in relation to . . . [a] drug trafficking crime [,] uses . . . a firearm." In that case the defendant offered to trade an automatic weapon to an undercover officer for cocaine, and the mentioned provision could have been understood in two possible ways: (i) the use of the firearm for the purpose of exerting force or violence concerning sellers of drugs or third parties who would prevent the deal; or (ii) the use of the same as a good or payment method.

6 I consider a legal provision "vague" when it is very general. An example of such would be general legal principles ("rule of law") and general legal standards such as "public interest," "reasonable person," etc.

7 Here I subscribe to the "narrow" definition of interpretation, according to which we interpret legal provisions only when they are unclear (Wróblewski 1992). Otherwise we merely "apply" them to facts.

In the event of thick[8] visuals being used as evidence to determine the concrete facts, arguers and audiences have more room to rely on elements from outside the immediate legal framework, such as their personal values that they can read into the premises. This is more difficult when it comes to thin visuals in clear cases, where their perception and thus also evaluation are semantically narrowed down to a greater extent than in unclear cases. In such cases, there are several possible interpretations of a thick visual, and this means that arguers have more potential to be effective in suggesting their version of a reasonable interpretation to their audience.

The situation where thick visuals are used as evidence and invite several possible meanings for judges to consider is semantically quite similar to the problem of unclear texts, where the values of judges can also be discerned in their rulings. Thus, there would be no single answer but several possible directions, a factor that is often manifested in divided courts with the opinions of different judges on the table.

In this respect, semantically thick (legal) words, being part of the logical mode of the upper premise, present similar problems as thick visuals (as part of visual argumentation preceding the establishment of the lower premise). They both invite alternate modes of arguing (i.e., emotional and kisceral being intuitive arguments such as personal values), as not strictly legal materials in a legal case, to fill out "blank" (logical) legal arguments (see also Novak 2020a, 2020b). Arguers such as judges are embedded in their social and psychological environments that they share with their audiences, and the legal logical mode through their arguments is only able to generalize clear legal situations. Since "a picture is worth a thousand words," it seems that (thick) pictures create greater semantical gaps than (thick) words, and when the two of them are combined the semantic problem is even exacerbated.

Thus, when visuals are part of legal argumentation, the visual and verbal modes interact. There are a number of different situations that can make the case clear or unclear. Already at the level of visual argumentation, there could be thin or thick visuals, which can also be accompanied with a thin or thick verbal text. Generally, a thin verbal text would anchor a thick visual, which could not be the case with a thick verbal text in combination with an either thin or thick visual. This becomes even more complex when visual argumentation enters legal argumentation, with the upper (legal) premise being represented by thin or thick words. Imagine "translation" and interpretation problems when thick visuals meet thick texts of legal norms.

Next I present an unclear case with a thick visual where the evidence provided an opportunity for judges to use different (multi-modal) argumentative-rhetorical moves to justify their decision on the case at hand.

8 If "clear" can be associated with "thin," "unclear" is not necessarily "thick," because thick would imply several meanings, whereas unclear might entail none.

3.3 A Case Analysis: *Grims v. Mladina*

3.3.1 Facts and Legal Procedures

In March 2011, *Mladina*, a Slovene left-wing weekly, published two photos next to each other titled "Not Every Dr G. is Already Dr Goebbels"[9] in its satire feuilleton (Mladinamit): What was on the black-and-white photo placed to the left side was the Nazi Goebbels with his wife and three children, all of them smiling to the camera. On the right side, there was a color photo of the right-wing Slovene politician Grims with his wife and three children sitting in a relaxed atmosphere in front-row chairs at an Easter mass.

Underneath the headline, the two photos were accompanied by the following text:

> Our former associate, Sena Driskić, compared Dr Grims with Dr Goebbels on his Facebook profile. The editors of Mladinamit join his protest. It might seem that Dr Grims follows his role model, but he still lags behind him. He needs more training in manipulation. *Sieg*!

In the editorial introduction of the same magazine, and in three texts of the following edition, *Mladina*'s editors commented as to why they had made the comparison between Mr. Grims, a prominent right-wing Slovene politician, and his family with the family of Dr. Goebbels, the Nazi minister of propaganda. They wanted to criticize Mr. Grims's activities of political propaganda that largely focused on manipulating the general public, of which his latest reports about an alleged imminent threat from migrants to Slovenia were particularly bad examples.

Grims then sued *Mladina* before the District Court, which dismissed the lawsuit in July 2013, by reasoning that *Mladina* criticized Grims's political activities to a justifiable extent in the manner of political satire. The court stressed that Grims took advantage of the media for his political promotion in the same manner as Goebbels. There was allegedly no direct comparison between the two families and both the pictures must have been understood in a broader context, together with the accompanying text.

Grims appealed and the appellate court reversed the first court judgment in February 2014 (No. I Cp 3057/2013), ordering *Mladina* to publish the judgment, apologize to Grims, and award him damages. The court reasoned that "The publication of photographs can encroach on people's integrity more severely than words." They even mentioned the idiom "A picture is worth a thousand words." They continued:

> Although the freedom of expression includes publishing photographs, when courts balance various interests or the freedom of expression

9 Capital letters in the Slovene original.

> against personality rights, they may need to separate the text from the published photographs, and make a separate balancing of the opposite interests in connection with the photographs.

To support their reasoning, they cited ECtHR's *Rothe v. Austria*.[10] They added that photographs and pictures cause multilayered effects and highlighted the openness of non-verbal communication. Thus, in their opinion, journalists must be more careful when dealing with pictures and photographs. Moreover, despite the fact that Grims was a crafty politician, he was also the father of a family, and the journalists' criticism went way beyond the limits of a reasonable critique by comparing him with a mass murderer, who also agreed to poison all of his six children at his wife's behest.

In the judgment rendered on September 10, 2015 (No. II Ips 93/2015), the Supreme Court affirmed the appellate court's judgment. They reasoned that the photographs in that case, as a separate totality, went beyond the limits of the comparison of the methods of propaganda used by Grims and Goebbels. What was crucial was the comparison between the ideal family life demonstrated in both the photographs and the fact that Goebbels had killed all of his children. In the judges' opinion, any criticism should not be more vulgar, insulting, intimidating, or less dignified than the political activities criticized.

Mladina subsequently appealed to the Constitutional Court, which upheld (by Decision No. Up-407/14 dated December 14, 2016) the Court of Appeals' and the Supreme Court's decisions. They emphasized the general power of pictures (also emotional) and agreed to the separation between the photographs and the text when balancing the freedom of expression against the personality rights by the lower courts. They reiterated that the image of the father of a family during an Assumption-Day mass at Brezje, Slovenia's most famous pilgrimage site, should be protected from a comparison made with a mass murderer in another photo. The case was decided by seven votes in favor and two against. The dissenters pointed to the fact that the political satire in that case should have been protected under the constitutional freedom of expression and that the majority erred when protecting the right of a father to safeguard the collective reputation of his family, which was allegedly not even argued in the case.

3.3.2 A Multi-Modal Reconstruction

To what extent is the previous case multi-modally relevant? Was it not decided upon solely on the basis of the (legal) logical and verbal mode? Where can we discern the traces of multi-modal argumentation in this case?

10 There are certainly other cases in which the ECtHR did not evaluate pictures separately but in the entire context of the case. See, e.g., *Wirtschafts-Trend Zeitschriften-Verlagsgesellschaft m.b.H v. Austria*, which the Slovene Court did not consider relevant in this case.

In the process of justification, judges would usually be reluctant to admit that they are also – as other people normally are – trapped in a hermeneutic circle, as in their reasoning they would only say that they apply "objective" criteria. Therefore, judges' separate opinions would promise more materials for discerning their subjective views than majority ones whose style is generally more official. It is thus the task for legal academics in particular to reconstruct their decisions in a multi-modal way, along with the standard argumentative reconstruction of legal decisions as suggested by mainstream legal argumentation theory, which is usually concerned with what kind of legal arguments were used in legal decisions and whether they could be used in a better, that is, more rational/reasonable, manner. This additional kind of "multi-modal reconstruction" as suggested here will extend the mainstream argumentative reconstruction of the reasoning of legal decisions further. In contrast with mainstream reconstruction, the multi-modal reconstruction of legal, mostly judicial, decisions would follow a different aim than the mainstream reconstruction. It could be used as an additional tool to study the potential for multi-modal arguments and rhetorical devices to be used and would be secondary to typical legal arguments. It would provide us with additional information that would allow us to obtain insights into the argumentative and rhetorical colorfulness of the environment in which the legal logical mode is used.

3.3.2.1 Logical and Visceral Argumentation

Lawyers used to the (legal) "robust" logical[11] (and verbal) mode will take such a case for granted. They would reason that there were simply two different legal positions in that case and one of them prevailed. However, a careful eye that is able to perceive the subtleties of multi-modal details will perhaps see such a case in a different light, finding both the premises indeterminate (the major vague, and the minor ambiguous due to the thick visual based on which that premise was established differently, at different court levels and by different judges).

First, the relevant legal norms (in the universal premise – *Mp*) in the case, as the logical mode's substance in this case, were on one hand from the Code of Obligations (at the level of ordinary courts' procedures) and Art. 35 of the Constitution (the right to the protection of integrity and reputation, at the level of constitutional review). They provide the grounds for legal redress if one is "defamed by another person." On the other hand, Art. 39 of the Slovene Constitution, which was also potentially relevant, ensures "freedom of expression," which at the level of constitutional review failed to overrule

11 What is typical for the legal logical mode are the (i) form of logical argument (most frequently deductive syllogism) and (ii) substance inclusive of legal norms (rules and principles) being the core of any legal system.

the right not to be defamed as a personal right. Both *Mp*s in this case are quite vague: on one hand, we have freedom of expression protecting political satire while, on the other, we have the father of a family who took them to a mass and for that reason is compared with the family of one of the worst Nazis. In the whole procedure, it was unclear which position would ultimately succeed: on one side, there were the positions of the District Court and the Constitutional Court's dissenting minority, on the other the court of appeals, the Supreme Court, and the Constitutional Court's majority. This was certainly not visual vagueness or "thickness" but normative-legal. Constitutional norms, such as the freedom of expression and personality rights as applying in this case, are generally thick, and their balancing even contributes another dimension to their thickness.[12]

Second, in terms of the factual (particular) premise that was presented at the level of the constitutional review as challenging the court decision, the photographs were presented in the magazine in the visual (or visceral) mode, with scant verbal explanation about the comparison. The text that initially accompanied the photographs tried to anchor them, obviously unsuccessfully as determined by the senior courts. Frankly, the initial verbal text published above the photographs was quite ambiguous (thick), whereas the editors' additional comments made the anchorage firmer by pointing to the reason why the politician was criticized in the mentioned manner. The final anchor had been accepted by the first-instance court, however not by the higher courts that retrieved it in order to make the photographs' comparison thick (again) in order to open the gate for them to introduce the argument/value of the reputation of a family father, as a personality right to be protected against the journalists' freedom of expression. Thus, the thick image "translated" in the said manner was then placed in the thick framework of balancing the two constitutional norms. The visual comparison of the two photographs was striking to the extent that the verbal anchor used could not achieve its purpose. However, the Constitutional Court's dissenting judges would share the same opinion.

In order for the photographs to be classified as concrete facts subsumed under the relevant legal norm, despite some small verbal text, they needed to be "translated" to the verbal mode as a legal position pointing to the existence of (no) defamation. Notwithstanding the aid of such a "translation," the photographs compared were "thicker" (Kjeldsen 2015) than the words that tried to anchor them. Indeed, the judges made them such (i.e., thick) when they retrieved the verbal anchor used and found the personality right of the family father to be protected. Due to the vague legal provisions and the judges' divergent reasons with respect to the evaluation of the comparison of the two photos, the decision cannot simply be taken for granted as a kind of "neutral" application of the law. Thus, the case could have been understood

12 Some theorists do not list the argument of weight or balancing among interpretative legal arguments but among constructive legal arguments (e.g., Guastini 2014, 407).

in two different manners, by seeing either a crafty politician who deserved to be criticized (the lowest court and the dissenting minority) or an exemplary father who was worthy of protection (all the other judges). The case was not only normatively thick (vague) but also factually thick due to the thick visuals as evidence to determine the factual premise in this case.

Apart from the visceral mode, the kisceral mode as well as the emotional mode must have been relevant in this case. To see Mr. Grims also as a father and not only an annoying politician necessarily entails that one should resort to family values and the father as a family protector. The judges expressed this openly when they stressed the importance of a comparison of the photographs in isolation from the accompanying text, which they said was an example of an admissible political critique. Also, the Nazi horrors that they despised and the family relations that they cherished, as emotional arguments – as used, certainly, in the "safe harbor" of legal logical syllogism, were also expressed by the judges.[13]

Therefore, in this case, the visceral argument (C – The Grimses and Goebbelses being two similar families; R – Their photos being published together) opened up room for other alternate arguments to step in, in the absence of a more precise argumentative framework concerning the comparison and given the vague legal provisions that applied. Thick visual evidence (actually made thick by the courts) from the lower premise have met thick words of the upper premise. But that is a typical situation in hard legal cases – in clear or easy cases, their premises tend to be clear. Consequently, the positions of the two judges were possible in that case: (i) if the comparison is considered in the context of the whole story, and Mr. Grims were looked upon more as a prominent politician, then the political satire account would be supported, whereas (ii) if the photos are taken separately from the text, his role as a father figure would be protected.

3.3.2.2 The Kisceral Argumentation of Values

In a hermeneutical situation, one that is all the more so when unclear legal cases are resolved, what is important are also judges' inner (personal[14]) values that include both their intuitions and emotions. It is well-known that neuroscience and cognitive psychology connect cognition with emotions when values are psychologically experienced. According to Thagard, "values are mental (neural) processes that are both cognitive and emotional. They combine cognitive representations, such as concepts, goals, and beliefs, with

13 About the role of intuition and values, and their connection with emotions, see more next.

14 Here I use the adjective "personal" (meaning subjective) because values in law can also be objective: as part of legal provisions such as equality before the law and legal certainty that are in fact constitutional provisions.

emotional attitudes that have positive or negative valence" (Thagard 2013). In the view of Oyserman, "values can be thought of as priorities, internal compasses or springboards for action." They are "implicit or explicit guides for action, general scripts framing what is sought after and what is to be avoided" and "ultimate rationales for people's action." They are at play on both the individual and group levels. Even at the individual level, they are internalized social representations or moral beliefs that people appeal to and are internalizations of sociocultural goals. "Values are not simply individual traits: they are social agreements about what is right, good, to be cherished." They contain cognitive and affective elements and have a selective or directional quality being internalized (Oyserman 2001).

Values most often give judges indications as to how to further construe legal premises. As already mentioned, as a rule, they are not directly and openly expressed in the written materials of judges' deliberations or their reasoning. Yet this is not to say that they were not present, and sometimes in a very influential manner. It seems that the less legal premises are determined, the more room there is for them to step in.

It should be stressed that for Jung, but also contemporary psychologists interested in cognitive science and neuroscience who base their findings on numerous experiments with human brain activities, there are two types of thinking – "fast" or automatic and "slow" or analytical, also termed System 1 and System 2 (Kahneman 2011), which are very much related. Fast thinking relies on emotions and intuitions, to which I would also add physicalities, for which the right hemisphere of the brain is "responsible." In human evolution, this is the older part of the brain while slow thinking, which is more rational or what some call critical thinking, is more logical, analytical, technical, and developed later in evolutionary terms. When it comes to multi-modes of argumentation, I would ascribe the (legal) logical mode to System 2, and other alternate modes to System 1.

Accordingly, in connection with the aforementioned two systems of thinking, the problem with unclear cases is the following. In clear cases, as their counter examples, the premises of legal syllogism are very much developed, and in a modern legal system they are expected to be analytically, coherently, logically interrelated, and connected so that the principle of legal certainty is upheld. We could say that this is an expectation for System 2 to operate. However, when there are gaps, ambiguities, and vagueness in the premises in the legal context of judicial proceedings, there is more room for System 1 to step in and direct the manner in which System 2 develops. This is an opportunity for values to step in for the initially unclear legal premises and do the job for them. A typical example of such is a constitutional review in which the clashes of values are commonplace because there are different judges with different worldviews.

Moreover, Mercier and Sperber claim that most reasons are "after-the-fact rationalization." Their main role is to "explain and justify" our intuitions but not in the process of intuitive inference itself. They are social constructs and are meant for social interaction, having "a central role in guiding cooperative or antagonistic interaction, in influencing reputations, and in stabilizing social norms." They continue that "the way we infer our reasons is biased in our favor. We want reasons to justify us in the eyes of others." And "they represent our inferences as rational in a different, socially relevant sense of the term where being rational means being based on personal reasons that can be articulated and assessed. To be socially shared they need to be verbally expressed" (Mercier, Sperber 2018, 110–144).

It was Kelsen who said that "the interpretation of a statute, need not necessarily lead to a single decision as the only correct one, but possibly to several, which are all of equal value, though only one of them in the action of the law-applying organ (especially the court) becomes positive law." Kelsen asserted that when legal practitioners interpret laws by means of their cognition (logical and rational),[15] they could only establish what the frame of that law is and within it there are "several applications possible." He contrasted his view with traditional jurisprudence, which claimed that it had found legal methods of how to correctly fill in the ascertained frame. He continued that "[t]raditional theory will have us believe that the statute, applied to the concrete case, can always supply only one correct decision and that the positive-legal 'correctness' of this decision is based on the statute itself." Further, it would seem

> as if the law-applying organ had to use only his reason but not his will, and as if by a purely intellectual activity, among the various existing possibilities only one correct choice could be made in accordance with positive law. . . . All possible methods of interpretation developed so far lead only to a possible, not necessary, result, never to one which is alone correct.

Thus, "it is futile to justify 'legally' one at the exclusion of other." In such

> it is not cognition of positive law, but of other norms that may flow here into the process of law-creation – such as norms of morals, of justice, constituting social values which are usually designated by catch words such as "the good of the people," "interest of the state," "progress," and the like.
>
> (Kelsen 1989, 351–354).

Kelsen understood the problem that I indicate here perfectly. His criticism of apparently "legal" argumentation seems to refer mostly to the so-called unclear cases. In clear cases, his critique is, I must say, exaggerated. His

15 Compare this with Jung's interpretation of cognition, which includes the irrational functions of perception, sensation, and intuition.

conception of the legal "mode" is, however, close to what I understand here by the "legal logical mode": mostly legal norms of positive law composed in a body of laws that we call the legal system.

Thus, if legal premises are vague and ambiguous, which is true as a rule in unclear cases, there is room for values or arguments of values to have their say. They are not part of the traditional legal logical mode, and thus when basing their decisions and reasons on values, judges in unclear cases would argue that what they apply is strictly law, and that their reasons and arguments necessarily only follow from the legal text. This should certainly be criticized, as it makes decision-making and reasoning less transparent by leaving out something that is tremendously important. In such cases, judges should admit that what they do is also legal policing and moral legislating, since the values behind their "legalistic" activity can be of moral, social, and political importance for their community.

Also, if factual premises are vague and ambiguous due to thick (visual) evidence to determine such, there is room for judges' values to step in. Thus, having both premises unclear complicates the case's argumentation even more. In the case at issue, provided the unclear upper premise(s), the judges retrieved the journalists' verbal anchor from the photographs compared, just to resort to the value behind the mentioned personality right of the family father that they disclosed and then protected.

Based on the previous theoretical discussion of the importance of judges' values, can we discern them in the text of the reasoning of the decision? The perception of values as internal mental representations is to a great extent connected with intuition. This is the reason why the kisceral mode of argumentation is discussed, and this mode of argumentation is relevant for legal argumentation when legal arguers base their legal arguments on the values that they subscribe to. Certainly, these values need to be recognized by the legal order; however, it would be difficult to find a major value that has not been embedded in the constitution as the supreme legal act of a certain society. These values are directly referred to, or at least implicitly incorporated, in specific constitutional legal norms.

Well, it certainly follows from the majority reasoning of the decision that it explicitly emphasized the value of a father-protector image, which the majority recognized from the photograph of Grims and his family. Jung would explain that, apparently, the father archetype was well integrated into the majority judges' personalities. His family role, or the role of a "family father" who wanted to protect the reputation of his family by suing the magazine, seems to be more important to them than the value of free speech, in which criticizing a prominent politician for his political activities is an important liberal value in limiting government and individual freedom. Moreover, the fact that Grims was the father of a religious family at a religious ceremony contributed further to protecting conservative values in society.

In the mentioned case, the kisceral argument read as follows: C – the value of a family (and family father) was violated; R – the photographs (in which an ideal Grims family was compared with the Nazi family). That kisceral argument was read into the following constitutional argument: C – the personality rights were unconstitutionally violated; R – when balanced against the freedom of expression, the personality rights were too much interfered with. However, the case was not decided kiscerally only but in an important connection between the kisceral and legal logical premises.

3.3.2.3 Emotional Argumentation

In this case, in their "sober" logical reasoning, the judges used a number of emotionally loaded words to support their rejection of the photos' comparison, which is proof that they resorted to certain emotionally loaded rhetorical devices in order to be more persuasive in relation to their audience. They used the following emotional words: the "horrible" contradiction between ideal family life and "cruel" historical evidence; a "shocking" comparison; a general symbol of "evil"; the metaphorical dimension of "bestiality."

Despite the fact that emotions are very important in people's lives and also in the (professional) activity of legal arguers and audiences, in this kind of research, where I examine lawyers' and judges' reasoning in the written text, one cannot expect them to enjoy a greater role. In justifying their decisions, lawyers rely on legal provisions and their reasonable interpretation. Emotions are rarely found, mostly only in the judges' separate opinion when they get more personal and sometimes make use of emotional rhetorical devices. I do not deny that another study, perhaps a psychological one that tries to get into the mind of judges, or a study focusing on the psychological dynamism in a courtroom where also a jury is involved, would prove that they have a greater role.

Emotional argumentation in that case would read as follows: C – the judges' emotions hurt; R – the photographs compared: the "horrible" contradiction between an ideal family life and "cruel" historical evidence; a "shocking" comparison; a general symbol of "evil"; and the metaphorical dimension of "bestiality." This is not how one would suspect the judges felt when seeing the comparison of the two photographs, but that is what they wrote in the text of the Constitutional Court decision and can be found there as their rhetorical devices used, which may also have an argumentative value (Perelman, Olbrechts-Tyteca 1969). As already mentioned, neuroscientists admit that perception of values is intuitive-emotional, thus when confronted with the photographs' comparison, they used the kisceral and emotional arguments to read them into the legal arguments.

Accordingly, was the use of the said emotional figures rhetorical or argumentative? I guess both aspects are possible. Rhetorical argumentation theorists claim that rhetorical figures (such as emotional figures used in this case) may be argumentative if they bring about a change of perspective and the adherence of the hearer (senior judges or other audience members); if that is not the case, they will be considered as an embellishment or a figure of style (Perelman, Olbrechts-Tyteca 1969, 169).

3.4 Conclusion

The presentation of problems associated with the legal interpretation of visuals as evidence used to determine the factual premise, and how that interacts with the legal premise, seems to be innovative and important for legal argumentation scholarship. These relevant nuances seem to have been neglected so far.

When legal reasoning is taken descriptively, Beck claims that, apart from its scientific model in which judges follow legal *topoi* (such as legal provisions, established arguments, and methods of interpretation and argumentation), we also need to consider its heuristic (non-formalist) model with extra-legal steadying factors (of a moral, economic, or political character) (Beck 2012, 24–27). These extra-legal steadying factors include a judge's need to attract public confidence in their judgments; the fact that they can(not) be always absolutely politically constrained and judicially self-restrained; their inclination to be politically fashionable and correct; adherence to their professional and institutional ethos that have particular characteristics; and an inability to always neutralize their personal elements (such as their personal beliefs, values, and interests) when making and justifying their judgments (Beck 2012, 35–50).

The combination of the scientific and heuristic model to some extent converges with my multi-modal approach to legal argumentation. Firstly, there is a more formal framework for the logical mode. Secondly, there is also a multi-modal argumentative dimension of legal reasoning. It is this rhetorical aspect of argumentation (Tindale 2004) that brings legal arguments closer to the real life of arguers and their audiences. When legal argumentation is taken as rhetorical argumentation, we not only recognize logical arguments (*logos*) but also kisceral (*ethos*), emotional (*pathos*), and visceral (*physis*) that arguers use in order to persuade their audiences (Novak 2020a).

The mentioned approach is not a theoretical speculation but is built on analyzing the justifications of legal/court decisions. Beck's, as well as multi-modal "alternate" modes, should not be used to constitute independent premises because that would entail non-legal reasoning. To qualify as legally relevant, they must always be used in connection with legal norms, by giving them a certain meaning, especially when they are indeterminate.

Thus, although the legal context is a formalized framework, in judicial proceedings there is also room for multi-modal argumentation. In this respect, so-called unclear legal cases, those with vague and ambiguous premises are particularly interesting. In these, it is possible to discern *loci* or "traces" of the mentioned multi-modal argumentation. They communicate the message that, for a realistic account of legal argumentation at least, one needs to take into account modes beyond the traditionally accepted logical mode.

Stemming from a descriptive point of view, it is important to realize the presence of the alternate modes in legal argumentation since the legal logical mode is reductionist. From a normative aspect it is, however, difficult to say how much of such heuristics is allowed for decisions to be still considered legal. It seems that only a general principle can be given that they must be relevantly linked to legal norms, and potential deviations from that are evaluated by competent legal authorities on a case-by-case basis. This is, however, the material for another topic to be discussed, of fallacies of multi-modal arguments in legal argumentation.

References

Barthes, Roland. 1967. *Elements of Semiology.* London: Jonathan Cape.

Bateman, John A. 2014. *Text and Image. A Critical Introduction to the Visual/Verbal Divide.* London: Routledge.

Beck, Gunnar. 2012. *The Legal Reasoning of the Court of Justice of the EU.* Oxford, Portland, Oregon: Hart Publishing.

Blair, Anthony J. 2015. "Probative Norms for Multimodal Visual Arguments." *Argumentation*, 29: 217–233.

Forceville, Charles. 2020. *Visual and Multimodal Communication: Applying the Relevance Principle.* Oxford: Oxford University Press.

Gilbert, Michael A. 1997. *Coalescent Argumentation.* Mahwah, New Jersey: Lawrence Erlbaum Associates, Publishers.

Groarke, Leo. 2017. "Multimodality and the Law." In Manzin, Maurizio, Puppo, Federico, Tomasi, Serena (Eds.). *Multimodality and Reasonableness in Judicial Rhetoric.* Studies on Argumentation & Legal Philosophy/2. Trento: Università degli studi di Trento, Quaderni della Facoltà di giurisprudenza.

Groarke, Leo, Tindale, Christopher W. 2004. *Good Reasoning Matters! A Constructive Approach to Critical Thinking.* Don Mills, Ontario: Oxford University Press.

Guastini, Riccardo. 2014. *La sintassi dei diritto.* Torino: G. Giappichelli editore.

Jewitt, Carey (Ed.). 2014. *The Routledge Handbook of Multimodal Analysis* (2nd ed.). London: Routledge.

Jung, Carl G. 1971. *Psychological Types.* London: Routledge.

Kahneman, Daniel. 2011. *Thinking, Fast and Slow.* London: Penguin Books.

Kelsen, Hans. 1989. *Pure Theory of Law.* Gloucester, Massachusetts: Peter Smith.

King, Rodney, Spagnola, Lawrence J. 2012. *The Riot Within: My Journey from Rebellion to Redemption.* New York: HarperOne.

Kjeldsen, Jens E. 2015. "The Study of Visual and Multimodal Argumentation." *Argumentation*, 29: 115–132.

Kjeldsen, Jens E. 2016. "Symbolic Condensation and Thick Representation in Visual and Multimodal Communication." *Argumentation and Advocacy*, 52: 265–280.

Kjeldsen Jens E. 2017. "The Rhetorical and Argumentative Potentials of Press Photography." In Tseronis, Assimakis, Forceville, Charles (Eds.). *Multimodal Argumentation and Rhetoric in Media Genres.* Amsterdam: John Benjamins Publishing Company.

Koon, Stacey C., Deitz, Robert. 1992. *Presumed Guilty: The Tragedy of the Rodney King Affair.* Washington, DC: Regnery Gateway.

Kress, Günther. 2010. *Multimodality: A Social Semiotic Approach to Contemporary Communication.* London: Routledge.

Kress, Günther, Van Leeuwen, Theo. 2001. *Multimodal Discourse: The Modes and Media of Contemporary Communication.* London: Arnold.

Mercier, Hugo, Sperber, Dan. 2018. *The Enigma of Reason, A New Theory of Human Understanding.* London: Penguin Books.

Novak, Marko. 2020a. "Multi-Modal Argumentation and Rhetoric in Judicial Proceedings." *Argumentation and Advocacy*, 56 (1): 41–60.
Novak, Marko. 2020b. "Rooting Gilbert's Multi-Modal Argumentation in Jung, and Its Extension to Law." *Informal Logic*, 40 (3): 383–421.
Oyserman, Daphna. 2001. "Values: Psychological Perspectives." In *International Encyclopedia of the Social and Behavioral Sciences.* Amsterdam: Elsevier Science Ltd.
Perelman, Chaïm, Olbrechts-Tyteca, Lucie. 1969. *The New Rhetoric: A Treatise on Argumentation.* Notre Dame: University of Notre Dame Press.
Smith v. United States. 1993. 508 U.S. 223.
Thagard, Paul. 2013. *The Brain and the Meaning of Life.* Princeton: Princeton University Press.
Tindale, Christopher W. 2004. *Rhetorical Argumentation, Principles of Theory and Practice.* Thousand Oaks, California: SAGE Publications.
Tseronis, Assimakis, Forceville, Charles (Eds.). 2017. *Multimodal Argumentation and Rhetoric in Media Genres.* Amsterdam: John Benjamins Publishing Company.
von Engisch, Karl. 1943. *Logische Studien zur Gesetzensanwendung.* Heidelberg: Carl Winter, Universitätsverlag.
Wróblewski, Jerzy. 1992. *The Judicial Application of Law.* Dordrecht: Springer Netherlands.

4 Kisceral Argumentation in Law

Between Past and Present

4.1 Introduction

According to Gilbert, "kisceral" (from the Japanese *ki* meaning energy) is one of the four modes of argumentation and refers to various kinds of intuition (1997, 2011). In addition, an argument is kisceral when it is drawn from that mode with respect to its reasons (Gilbert 1994, 166). Recognizing kisceral argumentation as a specific mode of argumentation entails a broadening of the concept of rationality, with an alternative to logical rationality in its narrow conception (Tindale 2021).

In psychological terms, the question of what is kisceral or "intuitive rationality" follows, importantly, from Jung, who also termed it passive thinking or intellectual intuition,[1] where thinking is decisively influenced by intuition (1971). With respect to legal intuitive thinking, in the extraverted type it is directed to the object (i.e., legal sources and facts of the case), where a lawyer finds a quick diagnosis for the case based on a superfast syllogism in which the facts are subsumed under hundreds of possible major premises of legal norms and their hunch stops at a particular one (or several of them), being those that they "recognized" using their "sense of the law" (German: *Rechtsgefüehl*) as the right ones. This might analytically be a wrong guess, so what is also needed is a full analysis to follow, something Kahneman would designate as slow thinking (2011). It could also be called "instrumental intuition" (Novak 2016). There is, however, another version of intuition that is important in legal evaluation, namely "creative intuition" (Novak 2016). It is its introvertive variant, where a thinker is led by their (internal) ideas, archetypes, and values (Jung 1971) especially where, in the case of a legal thinker, premises for their evaluation are vague, ambiguous, and gappy so that they read their values into abstract and general premises (Novak 2016). The reason why such an intuition can be termed creative is that it is on this basis that lawyers, most often judges, create or construe

1 See also Kahneman's "fast thinking" variant (2011).

DOI: 10.4324/9781003433767-5

additional norms by reading their kisceral reasons into the pre-existing ones that are, as a rule, uncertain.[2]

A closer look at legal argumentation also even finds kisceral arguments in modern Western law that claim to be logical, as well as some historical examples from Oriental law and the Middle Ages, and Sharia law both past and present. The easiest way for critics of kisceral argumentation to argue against it would be to assert that it is simply "irrational." The much more difficult way would be to admit that we all, even overtly "rational" Westerners, sometimes rely on these types of arguments.

4.2 The "Golden Age" of the Kisceral in Western Law

Kisceral legal argumentation as argumentation in which the evidence/reasons for a legal claim are intuitive, and such intuition, mainly as a "sense of justice," is even decisive for a final judgment, initially flourished in a model of law that Weber designated as "formally irrational."[3] This is the case "when one applies when in lawmaking or lawfinding means which cannot be controlled by the intellect, for instance when recourse is had to oracles or substitutes thereof" (Weber 1978, 656). Following Weber, these kinds of reasons, or grounds with regard to evidence obtained from divine intervention, involved ordeals, drawing lots, combat, or oracular pronouncements. These kinds of revelation in law, otherwise determined by some supernatural entity, were as a rule interpreted by magicians, sages, prophets, or priests (760–761). Such argumentation – and it could be termed argumentative as it is possible to imagine potential differences in opinion or disagreements – was typical for Oriental law as well as for Western law in the Early Middle Ages, when mostly Germanic tribes settled in new territories and established their barbaric or pre-feudal states.

It is interesting that such kinds of argumentation had been suppressed to a considerable extent in ancient Greece and Rome; however, not to the same extent as it is today. What would be typical for Ancient Greece was the birth of logic (and rational thought), which to an important extent also applied in Rome. But the presence of a kisceral mode of arguing reemerged with Germanic tribal law and was kept in existence up until the Renaissance. A decisive step in its suppression seemed to be the establishment of the first universities, where scholars began to study Roman law in a rational-logical manner (through analysis, comparison, generalization, systematization, and

2 It is particularly in the area of constitutional review, where judges in especially hard and novel cases resort to their values when they discover new norms from an implied text, concretize constitutional principles, balance constitutional principles, and create value hierarchies between norms. See also Guastini (2014, 407).

3 According to Weber, formalism applies to "utterances of certain words, the execution of a signature, or the performance of a certain symbolic act with a fixed meaning" (657).

interpretation). Moreover, the Church modernized its procedures by introducing inquisitorial procedures developed from the old Roman procedure of *cognitio*. Furthermore, in the 13th century, Aquinas rationalized metaphysics by linking it with the rational thought of Aristotle (Kelly 1992). Moreover, at the Lateran Council in 1215, the Holy See forbade its priests from participating in trials by ordeal. This move had a lasting impact on the development of procedural law in Continental Europe. Unlike ordeals and compurgation, inquisitorial procedure emphasized the importance of empirical evidence, such as documents, witnesses, and confession. The previously mentioned metaphysical means of evidence were gradually superseded by witnesses (who were to testify from their own experience) and confessions with the aid of torture (Robinson, Fergus, Gordon 2000). Furthermore, ordeals were also forbidden in England in 1219, and in some Habsburg lands in 1277.

A prominent example of unlimited kisceral argumentation was trial by ordeal, in which it was held that God would not allow the innocent to suffer and would therefore reveal the truth through their reaction to the ordeal (Robinson, Fergus, Gordon 2000, 28). Perhaps the most famous example of such would be from Oriental law where, according to Art. 2 of the Code of Hammurabi, if a person accused another person of magic but could not prove this fact, the accused needed to immerse themselves in a river. If the river "took him," their accuser would be entitled to keep his house for himself. However, if the river showed that the accused was innocent by leaving him alive, the accuser would be executed, and the released person would get their house (Roth 1997, 76–81). Trial by ordeal was also common in various Germanic tribes. For example, the Salian Franks, in their customary law (*Lex Salica*), instead of an ordeal presided over by river gods, practiced trial by boiling water (Robinson, Fergus, Gordon 2000). Furthermore, other types of ordeals were practiced, such as duels and the use of a red-hot iron that needed to be brought by a suspect from the entrance of a church to its altar in order to prove their (absence of) guilt.

Another example was compurgation, the practice by which a person's innocence or the truth of their claim was maintained, not on the basis of any objective (i.e., empirical) evidence, but by summoning sufficient oath-helpers who could swear to his or her good character, credibility and general fairness simply from their conscience and conviction. This kind of evidence was very much practiced in the framework of Germanic customary law (Robinson, Fergus, Gordon 2000, 28). It was important that such oath-helpers were sworn in before God, typically in religious premises and while touching a sacred object. It was a religious act in the then very religious community as a guarantee such person would not lie, otherwise they would face divine condemnation of their soul. Both judgments by ordeal and compurgation were used as evidence in cases in which there were no firm evidence about the defendant's guilt.

In the manner of kisceral argumentation of that time, in a religious aspect, the judge (typically a priest) would make a claim (judgment) based on his intuitive interpretation of a certain circumstance that occurred in such a trial, being evidence or "reasons" for that claim. They strongly believed that God was able to intervene in physical events and thus the fact that one combatant won a duel against another was a result of divine intervention. Likewise, oath-helpers would not take an oath to support the plaintiff if that person was not trustworthy, since otherwise they might run the risk of divine "revenge." This kind of knowledge was not based on (logical) cause-effect spatial and temporal relations but on a notion that there is a divine "knowledge" of things possessed by a supernatural being that controls the universe. For the same reason, the River God in a trial by ordeal carried out in Babylon would not allow an innocent person to drown but would only take the guilty.

What was typical of the predominant cultural psychological typology of these cultures, according to Carl Jung, was the subordination of their cognitive function of underdeveloped thinking, which was thus auxiliary to the dominant function of intuition. Such an intuition is driven by inner ideas or archetypes, in the case of these societies represented initially by pagan gods and later by the Christian God. This was a cultural typological pattern that normally applied to law as well as being a socially predominant structure. The kisceral mode simply prevailed over some kind of "logical mode." Nowadays we would be struck by such ordeals and would surely call them irrational, to say the least. But our thinking is much more developed after hundreds of years of evolution, beginning in Ancient Greece with the birth of logic or analytic thinking, which in the case of law was even upgraded with Roman law. Today, at least with respect to law, we could say that the predominant cultural pattern is the predominance of the cognitive function of thinking. Intuition, as far as it exists, is subordinate to it as an auxiliary function. Yet, with the decay of the ancient world, the aforementioned "irrationalism" in law reoccurred.

When judging kisceral societies with our modern eyes, we risk committing at least two fallacies: the first would be the "point of view" (Tindale 2021, 4–5), when we develop our view of those societies from our own position whose predominant cultural psychological-typological pattern is very different. The second problem is how we define reasonable (Tindale 2021, 4–5), which is very different from their conception of reasonableness. For those cultures, evidence or reasons to support judgments were simply different.

What was typical for such metaphysical societies was an uncritical following of means of revelation without serious rational evaluation, where rationality is associated with logic and critical thinking (i.e., the logical mode). However, with the advent of Ancient Greek civilization, with the turn from *mythos* to *logos* (Marcic 1969, 152), this changed and developed further in Roman law. Rational thought and argumentation changed the status of kisceral argumentation in making it "interstitial," in the shadow of *logos*, logical thinking and reasoning. The logical mode came to prominence.

4.3 The Kisceral in Law in the Modern Age

4.3.1 The Rise of the Legal Logical Mode

By the Late Middle Ages, important social changes had begun to occur in European societies, which caused their gradual rationalization. The birth of universities provided a fertile arena for the study of Roman law in a systemic and analytical manner. The legal institutions of Roman law were much more suitable than those of feudal law for newly emerging capitalistic economic relations. It seems that it was the reception of Roman law in particular that boosted the development of a modern logical mode of legal argumentation in the broader sense. That was even strengthened in subsequent centuries, culminating in the codification movement at the end of the 18th century and throughout the 19th century, which brought tremendous civil codifications, such as Code Civil (1804), the Austrian ABGB (1811), and the German Civil Code (BGB) in 1900. Intellectually, the "spirit of the time" regarding law in the 19th century was one of legal formalism and legal positivism (Kelly 1992). The ideal and *forma mentis* as such was reflected in the German school of mechanical jurisprudence, according to which the role of the judge was to be merely a subsumption (automatic) machine that would perform their judicial work in a perfectly logical manner: subsuming facts under legal norms and coming to conclusions. It seems that the Industrial Revolution of that time also found its expression in law, by praising a very technical and mechanistic (logical) mode in law. At least formally, kisceral arguments were ousted from the official picture of law.

A renowned embodiment of that *Zeitgeist* was surely the German sociologist and lawyer Max Weber, who wrote (yet never finished) his magnum opus, *Economy and Society*, in the 1920s. He designated ideal modern law as "formally rational," which was "found where the legally relevant characteristics of the facts are disclosed through the logical analysis of meaning and where, accordingly, definitely fixed legal concepts in the form of highly abstract rules are formulated and applied" (Weber 1978, 657). For example, Weber was very critical of the common-law institution of the jury, since it makes an independent verdict on the guilt of a defendant without producing reasoning in which reasons as the basis for their decision-making could be checked. Thus, at least theoretically, such a verdict could be purely intuitive, or kisceral. Weber thought that the institution of the jury was a remnant of pre-modern law, "qadi justice" (Weber 1978, 892–895).

What is typical of such logical rationality, is systematization, formalism, generality, abstractness, etc., and these were thus essential features of the great Continental civil codes mentioned earlier. They were typical products of bourgeois law, which by their general and abstract legal rules brought important values of legal equality and certainty to the fore. These values were constitutive of the demands of bourgeois revolutions: equally applying rules of business in territorial terms, stable (precisely determined) legal relations, free workers and consumers.

In that model of law, there was no place whatsoever for the kisceral, as intuition was viewed as purely subjective, unscientific, and a remnant of historical past. The most important legal source was the statute, an act of the legislature. Thus, statutory positivism was especially important, as it particularly favored (abstract and general) legal rules, leaving no room for legal principles[4] to have a major role in legal decision-making. Furthermore, legal formalism and (statutory) positivism also echoed in the common-law world, particularly through Bentham and the British positivist movement. Bentham was a great proponent of statute as a legal source, which in his view better ensured legal certainty than precedents without a stricter doctrine of *stare decisis* in force at that time. He accused common-law judges of too freely considering past precedents when relying on them. He pointed out that reasoning from the spirit of a case of what was relevant and binding in a previous case was too intuitive and arbitrary, thus the doctrine of *rationes decidendi* was born (Kötz, Zweigert 1998).

A clear proponent of formality in the logical mode on the Continent was Hans Kelsen, who in his *Pure Theory of Law* (Kelsen 1989) wanted to cleanse law of all the external elements that he felt were foreign to the concept of law. What was to remain in his concept of law was (logical) cognition, rational and formal. Thus, there was no place for intuition and the kisceral in his definition of law.

This extreme logical and formalistic model of law resulted in the "eclipse of reason" (Horkheimer 1974), with the effect that law was justified as valid as long as it met the formal (logical) criteria of validity, regardless of its content. That resulted in, e.g., the Nazi Nuremberg laws of the 1930s, which deprived Jewish people of their basic human rights. Those laws were adopted through legally and logically correct procedures, as consistent and systematically and hierarchically well-arranged, but still led to such horrible results to constitute extreme human rights violations. Therefore, after World War II, it became clear that a vision of law that does not respect basic human values, morality, and ethics, or denies them in extreme cases (such as with Nazi, fascist, and communist "laws") does not deserve to be called law (Radbruch 2003). After that, even legal positivists such as Hart included the minimum content of natural law (linked with morality) in their concept of law (Hart 1994), and it was Dworkin who stressed the importance of moral principles in giving us solutions even in hard cases (1997b).

Consequently, the door was again opened for moral intuitions, a version of kisceral arguments, to play a certain role in reasons to support certain legal decisions. The door, however, was not wide enough for the kisceral as it had been in the pre-modern law described at the beginning of this contribution.

4 As abstract and general legal norms, they are able to accommodate judges' moral (i.e., kisceral) intuitions to a much greater extent than legal rules.

The role of kisceral arguments, while recognized, was limited to merely an "interstitial" relevance.

4.3.2 The Postmodern Return of the Kisceral to Legal Decision-Making and Argumentation

The development of law after World War II witnessed a major increase in the importance of human rights and legal principles. National constitutional courts (as "moral legislatures") were established, international human rights conventions adopted, and tribunals to protect them introduced. Particularly emphasizing the importance for law of human rights provisions and moral legal principles, which are typical repositories of human values, (moral) intuitions of judges, through which they have access to their inner values,[5] are no longer seen as arbitrariness necessarily detrimental to law and legal decision-making, but also as a virtue that help judges to make their logical decisions in certain situations more just.

However, the kisceral mode in law was no longer supreme as it had been in pre-modern times. Its role in law today is "interstitial": predominantly in hard cases, when legal rules to precisely regulate factual situations run out, we can find it "alive" when judges ground their decisions on moral legal principles and constitutional rights, thus relying on their own conscience and personal values in such abstract legal provisions (see also Cahill-O'Callaghan 2020).

Accordingly, in unclear legal cases, what is important are also judges' inner (personal)[6] values perceived to an important extent through their intuition. In the absence of an explicit text, these values give judges a basis to further construe legal premises. As it transpires, this is not a mere speculation because we can find traces of that even in their written reasoning.[7] It seems that the less legal premises are determined, the more room there is for their values to step in. In interpreting unclear legal norms, judges are bound to follow objective legal values, i.e. the values of the legal system, such as legal certainty, equality, social security, human rights, which are specifically provided for by being determined in the legal systems. However, it is their discretion to make such a selection or emphasize a particular point.[8]

5 At least in civil law systems, judges need to promise before a high state official that they will adjudicate according to the constitution, statutes, impartially, and according to their own "conscience" before they are sworn in.

6 Here I use the adjective "personal" (meaning subjective) because values in law can also be objective (or social): as part of legal provisions enacted, such as equality before the law (the value of universalism behind) and legal certainty (based on the value of security), that are in fact constitutional provisions (Cahill-O'Callaghan 2020).

7 Cahill-O'Callaghan used a coding scheme to detect this in the judgments of the UK Supreme Court (33–34).

8 When they resort to the so-called constructive arguments that surpass mere interpretation: e.g., balancing conflicting principles, creating value hierarchies between legal norms, resolving antinomies, and filling gaps in the law (Guastini 2014, 407).

As an example, let me again refer to Kahneman's two systems of thinking. System 1 is "fast" thinking based primarily on intuition and emotion. System 2 is "slow thinking grounded in logical evaluation and analysis (Kahneman 2011). In connection with the aforementioned two systems of thinking, the problem with unclear cases is the following. In clear cases, as their counter examples, the premises of legal syllogisms are very much developed, and in a modern legal system they are expected to be analytically, coherently, logically interrelated, and connected so that the principle of legal certainty is upheld. However, when there are gaps, ambiguities, and vagueness in the premises in the legal context of judicial proceedings, there is more room for System 1 to step in and direct the manner in which System 2 develops. This is an opportunity for values to step in for the initially unclear legal premises and do the job for them. A typical example of such is a constitutional review in which the clashes of values are commonplace because there are different judges with different worldviews.

Thus, if legal premises are vague and ambiguous, which is true as a rule in unclear cases, there is room for values or arguments of values to have their say. They are not part of the traditional legal logical mode, and thus, when basing their decisions and reasons on values, judges in unclear cases would argue that what they apply is strictly law and that their reasons and arguments necessarily only follow from the legal text. This should certainly be criticized, as it makes decision-making and reasoning less transparent by leaving out something that is tremendously important. In such cases, judges should admit that what they do is also legal policing and moral legislating, since the values behind their "legalistic" activity can be of moral, social, and political importance for their community.

Accordingly, although of crucial importance for law, legal deciding, and legal justification, the logical mode of arguing is unable to satisfactorily justify the resolution of various problems that judges face when they (un)consciously rely on their personal values. Therefore, it needs to be supplemented in the most demanding cases by the kisceral mode, at least in the dimension indicated next.

4.4 The Rhetorical Model of Legal Argumentation and the Kisceral

4.4.1 Shortcomings of the Dialectical Model of Argument

It was already stressed that the logical mode, in its dialectical version, is central for legal argumentation. At least in theory, the dialectical model of legal argumentation is a normative (ideal) requirement if we want to call a decision legal. In the area of law as a special social discipline, facts are to be evaluated on the basis of legal norms in order to establish their legal status or compliance with law. That is at least the demand of the rule-of-law principle as the meta-principle in the legal domain, in which one can find the sub-principles of legal certainty and trust in the law, encompassing some of the most important social values such as order, justice, stability. Furthermore, the dialectical model of legal argumentation is not only to serve as a departure point for a legal reasoning to be considered valid, but also as the final product's structure of a judgment's reasoning, to explain that certain facts were subsumed under specific legal norms and a legal decision followed.

However, the dialectical model of legal argumentation alone "works" well only for the easiest or clearest legal cases. The rhetorical method of legal argument, where we rely on additional interpretative arguments to explain the upper premise, and evidence to additionally explain the lower premise, is not needed in this situation because both premises are clear enough. Furthermore, the rhetorical model where legal arguments are subject to different audiences does not seem to work here either. Because of their clarity, legal arguments in such a situation have a strong inter-subjective value "speaking for themselves" and do not seem to be audience-dependent. At this point, I do not agree that any legal argument is subject to an audience to the extent that, even if the premises are clear, it is never independent from the audience, as Perelman would claim (2008, 19).

However, such a case might become complicated and change its character, from being a clear case to an unclear one. In such situations, we need an additional criterion to justify the use of the dialectical model of legal argumentation. It is the rhetorical model of legal argumentation that further justifies either an unclear major premise (legal norms) or minor premise (facts). In such a manner, unclear legal norms are first additionally justified by different canons of interpretation that have been established in legal theory. Second, if the facts are unclear or contested, they are further proved by evidence.

Why would that fall within the rhetorical model of legal argumentation?

4.4.2 The Need for a Rhetorical Model of Legal Argumentation (the Kisceral and Ethos)

In the framework of the dialectical model of legal argumentation, which is based on logical criteria, there is seemingly no important role for kisceral arguments. However, it is a rhetorical model of argumentation that seems to be more promising to explain the role of the kisceral in legal argumentation, at least in certain types of cases. The rhetorical model of argumentation goes beyond mere logical means of persuasion and justification, which simply run out in the most demanding legal cases.

Although rhetoric is popularly (and primarily) associated with effectiveness, with reasonableness only being its outer framework of legitimacy (consider van Eemeren's (2010) concept of "strategic maneuvering"), here it is considered to be more than that. To separate effectiveness from reasonableness implies that these are two separate things. It presupposes that an arguer is aware in advance of more than one reasonable (and "just" in the case of law) way of resolving a dispute and decides for one as long as it benefits them in winning the argument. In such a view, there seems to be something eristic about effectiveness. However, when an arguer purports to pursue a "just" solution that seems the only reasonable one to them, a goal in itself, no matter how effective it is at that point, it seems that it ceases to be appropriate to distinguish effectiveness from reasonableness. In such unclear cases when arguers try to "justify their claims under conditions of uncertainty as an attempt to convince a relevant audience of a claim about what we collectively should do or how we should act" (Zarefsky 2014, 3), it appears that there is something heuristic in their undertaking. In *Phaedrus*, Plato highlighted that all discourse is rhetorical, even when the speaker is simply trying to communicate the truth – indeed, true rhetoric is the art of communicating the truth (notice the broad sweep of the discussion of discourse at 277e5–278b4). Rhetoric is present wherever and whenever people speak (261d10–e4 and context) (Plato 1993). Even when one is not sure what the truth is, and even when one is thinking through something by oneself – carrying on an inner dialogue, as it were – discourse and persuasion are present (Griswold 2020).

In such unclear situations, both arguers and audiences do not know exact ("just") answers in advance. They do not have previously established clear upper premises at their disposal to subsume lower premises to them, and decide on past cases, like in the case with forensic rhetoric according to Aristotle (2004). Although they are deemed to decide on past cases, they in fact need to construe the upper premise further so they act, at least partially, like legislators in the manner of deliberative rhetoric deciding on future cases.

This seems to relate to the most difficult cases in law, where dialectical legal arguments run out because the premises are enthymematic (i.e., unclear, gappy, ambiguous, or vague), such that those who are to resolve such a case necessarily navigate their thoughts in the dim light of such unclear premises. Such cases could even be termed "very hard" ones and would include the hardest topics in constitutional law, such as cloning, euthanasia, abortion, gay marriage, etc. In these kinds of cases we actually have upper premises, such as constitutional norms (principles and human rights norms), but they are particularly abstract and general. Furthermore, we usually do not have previous similar decisions to follow as precedents.

Supreme or constitutional court judges, being the last judicial resort in a country, also have an audience that surpasses the immediate parties to a case before them, as does the European Court of Human Rights in human rights cases. Their general audience are people populating the jurisdiction on the top of which these judges sit. When appointed by representatives of parliament, these judges are entrusted with specific powers, not only as lawyers with an excellent knowledge of law but also as "moral legislators" (Dworkin 1997a) that embody certain values that they share with those who appointed them. Thus, they are entrusted with the power to be "reserved" legislators especially in controversial cases. Certainly, even in such cases, they need to rely on legal norms but the legal norms in such situations are often very abstract provisions. In such cases, the judges find the meaning of these partially enthymematic premises through reading in their personal values. This brings an ethotic rhetorical element to legal argumentation. The audience generally follows them, but in case they do not want to, they propose a constitutional amendment to overcome their decision.

These kinds of judgments are particularly judgments of value. The impact of judges' personal values on their decision-making can be found in their opinions where they rely on different values to justify their decisions. The rhetoric of values, and thus kisceral arguments, because we generally have access to our inner values through the cognitive function of intuition, come into play where there are no firm dialectical proofs to rely on. Given such partially enthymematic premises, judges' opinions are therefore very much divided. Thus, it seems that a dialectical model is unable to justify the normative reason/choice for selecting one of the dialectical arguments. Thus, they need to be justified further by the value choices of judges.

Let me point once again to O'Callaghan's demonstrating the role of the personal values of UK Supreme Court judges in their decisions. Especially when complicated cases are controversial and include several dissents, the judges use a discretion that is influenced by their personal traits, most importantly personal values, "which act at a subconscious level in decision making." They do not even deny this fact (Cahill-O'Callaghan 2020, 596–598; Posner 2010).

A similar analysis could be made with respect to the judgments of highest courts in the legal family of civil law, either constitutional or supreme courts.[9] For example, in the previously mentioned case of whether a referendum to be held on gay marriage is constitutional, the majority relied on the values of conservation, such as tradition and conformity, while the minority who wanted to ban the referendum (since it is not allowed against human rights), resorted to the values of openness to change, including self-direction and stimulation, as well as universalism and as much equality as possible (Schwartz et al. 2012).

In such cases, it is not difficult to point to their legal-political character. As already established, in such situations they not only follow forensic oratory when they are to adjudicate on past actions. In such a manner, very hard cases invite judges to set precedents in novel cases and engage in semi-political, i.e., deliberative, oratory to set new standards in landmark decisions, and act like legislators in carrying out distributive and not only commutative justice.

4.4.3 Kisceral Argumentation in Islamic Law[10]

As already indicated, the role of kisceral arguments in contemporary Western law is predominantly "interstitial," which points to their limited significance

9 Since the majority decisions of these courts are more official in style, and not so much analytic and discursive as those from their common-law counterparts, dissents are a better terrain to find judges' expressions of their personal values justifying their decisions.

10 My presentation of the role of kisceral arguments in Sharia law is merely descriptive.

– mostly in very hard cases. There seems to be, however, greater promise for them in Sharia law,[11] even though that type of law has also gone through a modern transformation in the last two centuries (Hallaq 2009). Even so, the Sharia system of adjudication is less formalized than adjudication in Western legal systems. There is a greater insistence on religious and community moral values and social customs in addition to legal texts. What is embedded in the heart of Sharia is that "the content of rational thinking must be predetermined, transcendental and above and beyond what we can infer through our mental faculties of reason. . .. It marries reason and revelation, where rational thought is insufficient" (Hallaq 2009, 12–15). It traditionally recognized the supremacy of the unwritten codes of morality and morally grounded social relations (Hallaq 2009, 62), where communal values of honor, shame, integrity, and socio-religious virtue entered and intermeshed with legal practice and the prescriptive provisions of the law (Hallaq 2009, 164).

The basic judicial institution in Sharia is the qadi, the magistrate or judge of a Sharia court, who also exercises extrajudicial functions, such as mediation, guardianship over orphans and minors, and the supervision and auditing of public works. Not infrequently, the qadi's ambition is not only to apply black-letter law to a dispute but also to reinstate social harmony in a community in which the dispute arose, concerning which perhaps mediation could be a better option than adjudication. Thus, they are considered to advocate a moral logic of distributive justice rather than the logic of winner-takes-all (Hallaq 2009, 175–176).

In the past, no body of Islamic positive law had come into existence, and the first qadis therefore decided cases on the basis of the only guidelines available to them: Arab customary law, the laws of the conquered territories, the general precepts of the Quran, and their own sense of equity, where they relied on their personal values being in consistency with religious and moral values of Islam. In the case of a qadi, legal norms and social morality were inseparable, one feeding on and simultaneously sustaining the other, where the Muslim court was the product of the very community it served. Once this law had formed, however, the role of the qadi underwent a profound change. No longer free to follow the guidelines mentioned earlier, a qadi was now expected to adhere solely to the new Islamic law, and this adherence has characterized the office ever since (Hallaq 2009, 64).

Traditionally, the power of the qadi to interpose his own judgment was legitimized by the belief that adjudication in conformity with divine law is one of those duties that some individual must perform on behalf of all in the society for it to remain a proper community of believers in the eyes of Allah (Juynboll 1961; Schacht 1964, 206). Although the traditional role of the qadi has been greatly altered by the introduction of Western codes and the

11 Islamic religious law has the validity of positive law in certain areas of legal regulation in Muslim countries.

development of bureaucratic structures, the quest in many Muslim countries for an authentically Islamic way of life has given renewed emphasis to the classic precepts of Islamic jurisprudence (Rosen 1980–81, 218).

Less formalized adjudication in Sharia law also stems from how the appeal against qadi justice is organized. The *mazalim*[12] is a court (presided over by the supreme ruler or his governor) that hears complaints addressed to it by virtually any offended party. Since Islamic law did not provide for any appellate jurisdiction but regarded the decision of the qadi as final and irrevocable, the *mazalim* court functions as a kind of court of appeals in cases where parties complained of unfair decisions from qadis. The *mazalim* judge is not bound to the rules of Islamic law (*fiqh*), nor for that matter is he bound to any body of positive law, but is free to make decisions entirely on the basis of considerations of equity. The *mazalim* court thus provided a remedy for the inability of qadis to freely take equity into account. It also made up for certain shortcomings of Islamic law, for example, the lack of a highly developed law of torts, which was largely due to the preoccupation of the law with breaches of contracts. In addition, it hears complaints against state officials (Ahmed 2018).

Weber juxtaposed the rational interpretation of law on the basis of strictly formal concepts to a kind of adjudication that is primarily bound to hallowed traditions. According to this notion, individual cases cannot be unambiguously decided by tradition on the basis of concrete revelation (oracle, prophetic dicta, or ordeal – in Oriental law) or informal judgments rendered in terms of concrete ethical or other practical valuations. He continued that "*Qadi* justice" knows no rational rules of decision. But he was in a similar manner even critical of the common-law jury, calling it empirical justice. The problem with juries was, in his opinion, the fact that after rendering a verdict, the members of a jury do not give reasons for their decision (Weber 1978, 976). Weber was critical of a system in which judges have recourse to a general set of ethical precepts unevenly employed on a case-by-case basis rather than to a series of rules abstractly formulated and uniformly applied (Turner 1974, 107–121). However, even Weber's *Kadijustiz* principle does not say that a qadi would administer justice according to "his own arbitrary whim or momentary fancy," but their discretion is to be carried out in accordance with popular conviction (the sound feeling of the people) following the religious or ethical value system prevailing at that time and place (Rheinstein 1967, xlvii).

In order to follow a relatively large extent of discretionary deciding and justifying decisions that (still) allow qadis and their appellate bodies to make kisceral arguments embedded in Muslim religion and local customs, let us examine a few legal cases. From 1967 to 1978, Rosen made several field trips to Morocco, to the city of Sefrou, where he observed the work of a qadi court.

In *Hussaini v. Alahami*, which was decided in 1965, the plaintiff requested the return of his wife, the defendant, who left him several months ago.

12 See, for example, *divan al-mazalim* (or Grievance Board) from Saudi Arabia.

Represented by her father, the defendant claimed that the plaintiff had indeed divorced her, producing a document claiming that 50 people had testified to the fact before a notary. The plaintiff denied this, arguing that those 50 people brought by the defendant should not be trusted, as they were her close relatives. The qadi found for the plaintiff and ordered the defendant to return to her husband because she failed to produce a special document about divorce that needs to be attested by a notary (the so-called *stisfar*). The defendant then appealed, relying on a special provision of the Code of Personal Status, which provides that if there are witnesses to a divorce that is said to have occurred in the absence of notaries then this testimony must itself be notarized. The defendant thus produced a document in which 12 witnesses stated that they knew the couple had been married for a little over one year, after which the husband repudiated his wife. The plaintiff presented the notarized testimony of 12 witnesses who stated that the couple had been married for four years, and that all of them were present at the wedding, and that the plaintiff had never divorced his wife (Rosen 1980–81, 224–225).

The appellate court affirmed the qadi's decision. Confronted with two sets of witnesses, it chose to assume that those living in the same settlement as the couple were more likely than those living at some distance to know the actual state of their relationship. Additionally, they argued that the husband was eager to live with his wife or he would exercise his legally recognized right to divorce her unilaterally. Because no charges of mistreatment from his side were made, it could be suspected that the wife's family had played an important role in creating the dispute. Thus, this is an example of cultural assumptions and legal presumptions that shape the qadi's discretionary powers (Rosen 1980–81, 226). Thus, an example of kisceral reasons in his argument was his "gut feeling" that the locals would know better about their marriage than those distant people.

In case there is no evidence on either side to support the parties' assertions, the court has the power to require litigants to support their claims with a holy oath, which is commonly taken in the presence of two notaries at a mosque, a saintly shrine, or in the lodge of a religious brotherhood. Such an oath apportions the burden of swearing and the legal presumptions that accompany its use (Rosen 1980–81, 226). It usually takes the following form: for example, the court demands that the defendant take an oath swearing that he did not take any of his wife's belongings with him upon their divorce. If the defendant takes the oath, he will be presumed innocent. If, however, the defendant refuses to swear, the plaintiff must take the oath, and if the latter does so, the case will be awarded to him or her. But the sequence of oathtaking could be reversed depending on the situation. What is important is the power that such oaths are believed to contain, since there is a real fear that a false oath will result in harsh supernatural punishments. It is also not very uncommon that, when asked to take an oath, a person refuses to do so and thus surrenders the case. Accordingly, the presumptions and the order of oathtaking may be deciding factors in a case (Rosen 1980–81, 227). Again, this is (merely) kisceral evidence that a defendant was innocent because they would not lie in front of God.

A qadi's equitable discretion even allows them to decide differently when the law on a matter is quite clear and when they nevertheless feel that justice may be violated by the strict application of the law. A case in point is *al-Haji v. Hedraz*, from 1961, where the plaintiff stated that her husband, the defendant, has been sent to jail for two years. But for three years and two months prior to that he did not support her and their young daughter. She wanted the qadi to divorce her because she could not wait for the husband to come back from prison. In fact, she had sued him before several times, and the court always ordered him to support her, but he refused every single time to do so. Although technically following the "letter of the law" in that situation the qadi could only grant her a revocable divorce, meaning that the husband would be able to take the wife back after a certain period of time, he decided that the situation was so outrageous that it would be unfair to do so, and he decided for an irrevocable divorce. In his opinion, the qadi not only pointed to the husband's bad record but also to the fact that the plaintiff had constantly displayed the characteristics of a respectable woman since her neighbors regarded her as circumspect, well-behaved, and long suffering. From that it seems that by using his powers of consultation and utilitarian reasoning, even the present-day qadi may be able, from a formal point of view, to make a lawless (*contra legem*) decision. However, this is substantively justified in terms of the countervailing equities (Rosen 1980–81, 235–240).

Another example of discretion in Islamic law is *tazir*, which refers to punishment for offenses at the discretion of the judge (*qadi*) or ruler of the state. It is one of three major types of punishments under Sharia law: *hadd*, *qisas*, and *tazir* (Cammack 2012, 1–7). The punishment for the *hadd* are determined by the *Quran* or *Hadith*, *qisas* allow equal retaliation in events of intentional bodily harm, whereas *tazir* refers to punishments for less serious offenses that are not specified in the Islamic sacred texts (El-Awa 1993), such as thefts among relatives, attempted but unsuccessful robbery, fornication that does not include penetration, and homosexual contact such as kissing that does not result in fornication (Bassiouni 1992). The punishments include prison terms, flogging, fines, banishment, and seizure of property (Baldwin 2012, 117–152). In this respect, the judge enjoys considerable leeway to use an appropriate form of punishment, neither the punishment needs to be consistent with respect to other defendants or over time, and the qadi has also the discretion to forgive *tazir* offenses (El-Awa 1993).

From the previous examples we can see that the level of judges' discretion is (still) much higher in Sharia law than in modern Western law. This is a definite cultural difference; still, it is far from claiming that Western judges are akin to "logomachs." Why would this feature of adjudication be connected with rhetorical argumentation rather than with dialectical (or logical) argumentation? A crucial point is that in uncertain legal situations their discretion is quite extensive, much more so in Islamic law than in Western. It is the Islamic audience that trusts their *qadis* to a great extent, and they adhere to their audience to find a suitable solution in clear but also problematic cases. The audience trusts their (moral) authority to the extent that they find the best legal solution relying on their (expert) intuition, which is not absolute and unlimited but embedded in Islam. This is then justified by means of kisceral arguments.

Both in the form of either value judgments from Western law or discretion in the framework of Sharia law, it seems that kisceral arguments based on arguers' intuitions are still present in contemporary law in a more or less restricted manner. In this way, judges' own sense of justice supplements positive law due to various reasons (indeterminacy, obsolescence, injustice, etc.). When judges are sworn in, they generally promise not only to uphold the constitution and statutes, and adjudicate impartially, but also to follow their conscience (i.e., morality), regardless of which version of morality they will be bound to follow.

4.5 Conclusion

Kisceral (i.e., intuitive) arguments, as those in which their reasons are found in one's intuition, are (unlike their historical predecessors) very limited in their recognition and application in (Western) modern legal systems. One of the chief reasons for that is the modern conception of the rule of law, according to which laws are democratically (collectively) enacted in parliaments whose legal texts also need to be followed by courts. In addition, serving the same principle of the rule of law, courts are bound by their previous decisions. To rely on kisceral arguments to the contrary of the aforementioned may imply arbitrary decision-making and justifications.

Still, from present reports and experiences too numerous to cite, it follows that in at least quite unclear cases laws cannot prevent legal decision-makers (most typically, judges) from relying on their kisceral arguments when they need to act in a discretionary manner. After all, the genius of creativity very much depends on intuition, with the same being true for judicial creativity as well. However, then again, such creativity can be once welcome and another time self-willed and arbitrary. By all means, it needs to provide reasons that the audience accepts every time, or not.

References

Ahmed, Rumee. 2018. *The Oxford Handbook of Islamic Law*. Oxford: Oxford University Press.

Aristotle. 2004. *Rhetoric*. Mineola, New York: Dover Publications, Inc.

Baldwin, James E. 2012. "Prostitution, Islamic Law and Ottoman Societies." *Journal of Economic and Social History of the Orient*, 55: 117–152.

Bassiouni, Cherif M. 1992. *The Islamic Criminal Justice System*. London, New York: Oceana Publications.

Cahill-O'Callaghan, Rachel. 2020. *Values in the Supreme Court.* Oxford: Hart Publishing.
Cammack, Mark. 2012. "Islamic Law and Crime in Contemporary Courts." *Berkeley Journal of Middle Eastern & Islamic Law*, 4 (1): 1–7.
Dworkin, Ronald. 1997a. *Freedom's Law: The Moral Reading of the American Constitution.* Cambridge: Harvard University Press.
Dworkin, Ronald. 1997b. *Taking Rights Seriously.* Cambridge: Harvard University Press.
El-Awa, Muhammad S. 1993. "Punishment in Islamic Law." *American Trust Publications*, 1–68.
Gilbert, Michael A. 1994. "Multi-Modal Argumentation." *Philosophy of the Social Sciences*, 24 (2): 159–177.
Gilbert, Michael A. 1997. *Coalescent Argumentation.* Mahwah, NJ: Lawrence Erlbaum Associates, Publishers.
Gilbert, Michael A. 2011. "The Kisceral: Reason and Intuition in Argumentation." *Argumentation*, 25: 163–170.
Griswold, Charles H. 2020. "Plato on Rhetoric and Poetry." *Stanford Encyclopedia of Philosophy.* https://plato.stanford.edu/entries/plato-rhetoric/ (15.4.2021).
Guastini, Riccardo. 2014. *La sintassi del diritto.* Torino: G. Giappichelli editore.
Hallaq, Wael B. 2009. *An Introduction to Islamic Law.* Cambridge: Cambridge University Press.
Hart, Herbert L. A. 1994. *The Concept of Law.* Oxford: Clarendon Press.
Horkheimer, Max. 1974. *The Eclipse of Reason.* London: Continuum.
Jung, Carl G. 1971. *Psychological Types.* London: Routledge.
Juynboll, Theodor W. 1961. "Adhab." In Gibb, Hamilton A. R., Kramers, Johannes H. (Eds.). *Short Encyclopedia of Islam.* Leiden: E. J. Brill.
Kahneman, Daniel. 2011. *Thinking, Fast and Slow.* London: Penguin Books.
Kelly, John M. 1992. *A Short History of Western Legal Theory.* Oxford: Oxford University Press.
Kelsen, Hans. 1989. *Pure Theory of Law.* Gloucester, Massachusetts: Peter Smith.
Marcic, René. 1969. *Rechtsphilosophie. Eine Einführung.* Freiburg: Verlag Rombach.
Novak, Marko. 2016. *A Type Theory of Law: An Essay in Psychoanalytic Jurisprudence.* Dordrecht: Springer.
Perelman, Chaïm, Olberchts-Tyteca, Lucie. 2008. *The New Rhetoric.* Notre Dame: University of Notre Dame Press.
Plato. 1993. *Symposium and Phaedrus.* New York: Dover Publications, Inc.
Posner, Richard. 2010. *How Judges Think.* Cambridge: Harvard University Press.
Radbruch, Gustav. 2003. *Rechtsphilosophie.* Heidelberg: C. F. Müller.
Rheinstein, Max. 1967. *Introduction to Max Weber, on Law in Economy and Society.* New York: Simon and Schuster.
Robinson, Olivia F., Fergus, David T., Gordon, William M. 2000. *European Legal History.* London: Butterworths.
Rosen, Lawrence. 1980–81. "Equity and Discretion in a Modern Islamic Legal System." *Law & Society Review*, 15 (2): 217–246.
Roth, Martha T. 1997. *Law Collections from Mesopotamia and Asia Minor.* Atlanta: Scholars Press, Society of Biblical Literature.
Schacht, Joseph. 1964. *An Introduction to Islamic Law.* Oxford: Clarendon Press.
Schwartz, Shalom H. et al. 2012. "Refining the Theory of Basic Individual Values." *Journal of Personality and Social Psychology*, 103: 663.

Tindale, Christopher W. 2021. *The Anthropology of Argument*. London: Routledge.
Turner, Bryan S. 1974. *Weber and Islam: A Critical Study*. London: Routledge, Kegan Paul.
van Eemeren, Frans H. 2010. *Strategic Maneuvering in Argumentative Discourse*. Amsterdam: John Benjamins Publishing Company.
Weber, Max. 1978. *Economy and Society*. Berkeley: University of California Press.
Zarefsky, David. 2014. *Rhetorical Perspectives on Argumentation: Selected Essays by David Zarefsky*. Dordrecht: Springer.
Zweigert, Konrad, Kötz, Hein. 1998. *An Introduction to Comparative Law*. Oxford: Oxford University Press.

5 Emotional Argumentation, Law, and ADR

5.1 Introduction

Law has traditionally been suspicious about the role of emotions, in particular with respect to judicial decision-making. An ideal judge has been portrayed as a "sober" logomachy who is capable of an (absolutely) objective and rational judgment by withstanding all the attempts of his or her emotions to influence the judgment. However, the development of neuroscience has brought problems to this ideal picture, by establishing important connections, even a kind of interdependence, between emotions and the capacity for logical thinking in human brains. Accordingly, a new approach to emotions in legal argumentation theory must necessarily be more tolerant toward emotions connected with legal arguments. Accordingly, today we will not discard them all together but would consider their relevance to an extent that could be accommodated with the requirements of the justification of judicial decisions. Nevertheless, specific problems with their presence in such justification still remains.

In this chapter, I first outline the modern development of emotional argumentation theory in general argumentation. Then, I try to see how emotional arguments could work in the legal context, either as grounds in legal arguments, specific premises in law creation procedures, or premises in the framework of ADR. Finally, I discuss the role of the emotional expression of legal (dialectical) arguments.

5.2 Modern Development of Emotional Argumentation Theory

In modern argumentation scholarship, unlike traditionally, it is quite normal to claim that there exists something that could be called emotional argumentation (Carozza 2007, 179). Indeed, almost 20 years ago already, Walton argued that emotional arguments, such as *ad misericordiam* and *ad baculum*, can in some cases be reasonable and not fallacious (1992). Furthermore, in his seminal article on the multi-modal theory of argumentation, Gilbert found that emotions can be used to express arguments (1994). He discussed emotions in relation to arguments mainly in two ways: (i) as reasons or grounds for a certain claim and (ii) as means of expressing a certain argument.

DOI: 10.4324/9781003433767-6

His distinction of the two types of emotional arguments to some extent resembles O'Keefe's legendary distinction between argument 1 and argument 2 (1977). While argument 1 refers to a result (product) of an individual's making an argument, argument 2 denotes a process in which two arguers are engaged when having an argument. According to Wenzel (1979), the first concept designates a logical, in particular "structural" or static approach to argument, whereas the second dialectical and rhetorical, a dynamic perspective on how arguments are made in real life.

Gilbert also demonstrated that emotional arguments can also be dealt with normatively and thus evaluated by the informal-logic standards of relevance, acceptability and sufficiency (Gilbert 2004). He wanted to demonstrate that they are at least reasonable, if not rational, and their structure "logical." However, the most important caveat with respect to such claims refers to an area and extent to which such arguments are permitted. For example, in certain areas, it is completely reasonable to make emotional arguments: friends A and B, or spouses C and D argue over their friendship or love, where emotional arguments are frequently used especially when they are about to settle a dispute within such a relationship.

There have been others who continued to deal with emotional argumentation. Ben-Ze'ev asserted that emotions do constitute a particular kind of argumentation, are rational, and constitute efficient argumentation. For Ben-Ze'ev an emotional argument is specifically one that has emotion(s) used as reason(s) for a claim or action (Carozza 2007, 200; Ben-Ze'ev 1995).[1] Moreover, Plantin (1998) claimed that the emotional dimensions of argument can be investigated by recognizing "emotional sentences," those sentences that tell us that someone is experiencing an emotion, and by locating the "experiencer," the subject experiencing the emotion, plus the "emotion terms," which are the societal labels that get attached to emotions.[2] His work focused on emotions as claims (Plantin 1998, 5–7). His theory relies on emotions that are declared in the context of argumentation, (Carozza 2007, 200). Carozza developed a tool for dispute resolution practitioners, the social style model (Furlong 2010), which can help argumentation practitioners better understand and navigate emotional arguments (Carozza 2020). Finally, Wohlrapp claims that there are three ways emotions can be related to an argument such that (i) emotion appears instead of an argument, (ii) emotion is an argument, or (iii) emotion appears in an argument (2006).

But is that relevant also for the domain of legal argumentation knowing that valid arguments more or less depend on the field in which they are used? Law as a special social field of communication and argumentation has its own rules. From the aforementioned about the emotional argumentation theory,

1 Similar to Gilbert's emotional argument 1.
2 This resembles Gilbert's emotional argument 2.

it seems that two types of emotional arguments are typical: E-argument[3] 1 (as dialectical) and E-argument 2 (as rhetorical). Accordingly, in the continuation, I will test their applicability in the field of legal argumentation.

5.3 Two Types of Emotional Arguments in Law

In real life there are ample examples of emotional argumentation. However, legal disputes in courts are (normatively) not to be resolved in the emotional mode of argumentation. Nevertheless, they most often involve emotional communication and argumentation between the parties to such a dispute, prior to and during the trial. That is a realistic picture of people's disputes that are often heated by emotions. In the traditional (formal) picture of judicial decision-making and justification of judicial decisions, where the figure of a judge appears to be a third person, objective and impartial, to resolve such a dispute the emotional mode should not be present. However, if it appears, and realistically can appear, because not only the parties but also the judge is a human being with all the emotions, it should be subordinated to the logical mode of argumentation. Thus, a failure to abide by this normative requirement frequently results in legal errors typically established by appellate courts.

Although recently many studies exist that demonstrate how difficult it is or impossible, from a psychological point of view, to separate logical decision-making from emotional, this is not a concern for argumentation scholars. Behind the formal veil of logical argumentation, a set of emotional arguments may exist in the process of self-argumentation in the heads of judges as decision-makers. That is, however, the task for psychologists and neuroscientists to deal with (Feteris 1999). Argumentation scholars are interested in what kinds of emotional arguments are institutionally possible in a legal game, mostly in the sense of the possibility of existence of emotional arguments in the justification of judicial decisions.

Due to the institutional normative constraints in using legal logical arguments, in which the facts of a case are subsumed under legal norms and legal decisions are inferred accordingly, emotions should not be used as reasons or grounds for making separate arguments, in the aforementioned Gilbert's (and Ben-Ze'ev's) sense of emotional argument 1 converging with the idea of O'Keefe's argument 1. Moreover, in Wohlrapp's language, emotions cannot be separate legal arguments in the legal context; however, in the dynamic process of a legal game in which arguers such as parties, judges, and attorneys have arguments (O'Keefe's argument 2), they do appear in an argument. Therefore, they can be used in a narrow rhetorical sense as means of expressing legal logical arguments, which is the second type of their possible usage according to Gilbert.

3 E- in the argument stands for "emotional."

Thus, what is institutionally prohibited in law is to make E-argument 1, which is about separate emotional premises in a legal argument. This applies because the premises constituting the typical structure of a legal deductive syllogistic argument are to be about legal norms – the upper include the legal facts in the legal norm(s), whereas the lower include those concrete facts taken from the brute facts of a certain case to meet the legal facts of the upper premise. Institutionally, there is no proper place for emotions in the said premises. Emotions can be abstracted in the legal facts or appear in brute or concrete facts, but in no manner as specific grounds/premises in the legal argument. Next I refer to E-argument 1 as the (dialectical) possibility of emotions being part of the premises/grounds in a legal argument.

Emotions can be present in the upper premise of deductive syllogism but only as corollaries or "remnants" of emotions transcribed into the abstract language of the logical mode of legal provisions. For example, the criminal offense of insult has incorporated the possibility of severe emotional distress caused to an injured party that would constitute that criminal offense. But such emotion was lifted to the level of the logical mode by finding its place in a general and abstract legal rule of the penal code. By that it ceased to exist as a separate way of emotional argumentation.

However, the aforementioned applies to administrative or judicial argumentation as the process of law application, in which individual legal acts (decisions and judgments) are made. Emotions can be separate premises, and as such constitute arguments in the framework of legislative procedures or ADR procedures. It is common that members of parliament rely not only on their rational interests and motives but also emotions when enacting a certain law. For example, they might be afraid of intensified terrorism, and such a fear may be an additional justifiable reason/premise in order to strengthen the existing anti-terrorist measures in a law. Likewise, within mediation two spouses divorcing may consider their love for their own child as a special premise in order to reach a good compromise for her well-being, since such a compromise does not need to depend only on legal rules. Still, a legislative procedure does not need to be considered as a legal procedure but a political one, and mediation, when strictly speaking, is not part of a narrow concept of law.

If there is a problem with using emotions as separate grounds/premises in law (as E-argument 1), it is much easier to use them as E-argument 2 – as expressions of arguments, when emotions are not arguments (or part thereof at least) but appear in an argument. There are legal institutional limitations with regard to how far lawyers (judges) can go in this respect, but they may use them to such extent.

5.3.1 Emotions as Grounds in Legal Arguments

As already mentioned, next I present two exceptions to the notion that emotions should not appear in legal arguments as separate grounds/premises. The first refers to the legislative procedure, and the second to the ADR procedure dealing with mediation.

5.3.1.1 Law Creation (Legislation, Constitution-Framing)

The application of law could also be understood, in a narrow sense, as a legal process in which courts and other legal bodies apply pre-existing law to factual situations. In such, they generally follow the deductive pattern of subsuming facts under legal norms (both of them being premises, as grounds, reasons, or evidence, in the deductive syllogistic argument), and making a conclusion on the basis of them. Institutionally, i.e., formally, and normatively speaking, in such a typical process of law application, there seems to be a strong agreement among legal theorists that no room for emotions as independent premises exists in such a deductive legal argument.

However, the situation is a little bit different when it comes to the process of law creation in the framework of which the legislative procedure is typical. In such a procedure, it seems that the inductive argument is at the forefront. When a new statute or amendments to an existing statute are enacted, the legislature makes inferences from several individual or specific premises to a general claim/standpoint being represented by the final statutory texts. These premises may be of a different character: pre-existing laws, social or individual interests of a political or economic character, values, but also people's emotions or sentiments. Imagine MPs deciding on an anti-terrorist statute, who perhaps witnessed the horrific consequences of a terrorist attack the other day, and along with their (rational) deciding cannot avoid the fear that something like that could repeat. In such a context, in terms of political induction, following which a legal text is created, their separate emotional premises seem to be legitimate ones.

In the same manner, Sajó claims that sentiments (i.e., emotions) have an important role in setting up constitutional designs and arrangements. He points to fear being present in the making of many constitutions, in order to achieve assurances against constitutional oppression, mob rule, and factional passions (in the case of the US Constitution). Moreover, compassion and indignation are emotions behind the regulation of many human rights. In a similar vein, disgust, indignation, and empathy were behind the abolition of slavery, and the prohibition of cruel and unusual punishment clause (2011). Thus, emotions are also one of the motivational impetuses behind what we design not only into our constitutional law but also other areas of law. For example, it is not difficult to imagine that, when the postwar German federal constitution was being adopted, one of the premises on which it was built, especially with respect to human dignity being the most important human right therein, and the prohibition of amending the Constitution in that part, was the collective emotion of disgust with all the horrors caused by the Nazi regime.

However, through a legislative and constitution-framing procedure, emotions become legal (or institutional) facts and, as such, part of legal arguments in a dialectical sense.

5.3.1.2 ADR

Even if courts are in general successful in resolving people's disputes, their decision could sometimes be harmful for continuing the parties' relations. Imagine two business firms, one suing another for a large amount of money allegedly owed to firm A but vigorously defined by firm B. Concerning that alleged debt, they could have a completely different view of what is lawful and just in such a case. If the court agrees with the existence of the debt not being returned and decides entirely in favor of firm A by ordering firm B to pay, e.g., EUR 1 million, it is quite likely to assume that the defendant in that case would refrain from continuing the business relationship with firm B in the future. The reaction would also be emotional, of course, but that is what occurs in real life. However, if the parties tried to resolve their dispute "peacefully," based on a compromise or settlement, their business relationship has a much better chance of being preserved, as they would not be as frustrated. Thus, apart from being more expensive and time-consuming, the courts' logical manner of dispute resolution could also be harmful for parties' entire relationships that not only consist of logical and legal dimensions but also emotional dimensions.

In ancient China, according to the *Li* principle, people were reluctant to bring their disputes to courts because they believed the disputes should be resolved within the community in order that universal harmony, of which social order is a part, is preserved. They believed individuals are tied in a community not only formally but also with a myriad of different emotional, intuitive, and physical elements. So a dispute should be resolved by paying attention to all these elements not just formal aspects (Zweigert, Köetz 1998). Legal anthropologists find similar patterns of resolving disputes between individuals in old African tribal communities (David, Grasmann 1988). Thus, techniques of alternative dispute resolution (hereinafter ADR) were rediscovered in the Western world in the 1960s, 1970s (Roach Anleu 2000), most prominently mediation, to be complementary to traditional legal or judicial proceedings that are predominantly formal and logical. In that kind of proceeding, open and direct emotional communication and argumentation play a more important role than in traditional legal proceedings.

One could say that is true, but ADR is not part of law, narrowly speaking. Frankly, this argument could be accepted in a narrow sense, which is why we use the adjective "alternative" (to judicial proceedings). However, in a broader sense, law as a concept is wider than law-court. ADR has not only been frequently used in commercial and family legal disputes, but has also been extended to other areas of law, such as administrative law and consumer disputes. Moreover, in many civil codes it is procedurally required to try mediation before trial, otherwise the lawsuit might be dismissed. We also deal with court-annexed mediation, meaning that judges in their free time, certainly not in their own cases, work as mediators for the parties who initiated court proceedings. This is the reason why today ADR is so pervasive in connection with legal proceedings, thus it seems reasonable for it to be included in a broader definition of law (Novak 2016).

Concerning ADR and mediation as an alternative to traditional formal and logical judicial procedures, it seems that Gilbert's theory of coalescent argumentation (1997) is very useful to describe the situation in which logical (legal) argumentation interacts with emotional argumentation in order that a dispute is resolved in a holistic and lasting manner.

Gilbert built his theory of coalescent argumentation as a normative continuation of his more descriptive theory of multi-modal argumentation. The idea is to "join together of two disparate claims through recognition and exploration of opposing positions." He stated two main reasons to develop such a theory: (i) to focus on a real-life or "human-based nature of argument" as opposed to a more idealized and limited logical argument; and to (ii) emphasize "agreement" or the "likelihood of agreement arising from between dispute parties" (Gilbert 1997, 102). For that reason, he differentiated between claim and position, the first being merely the "icon" for the position that is much richer and deeper, which is a "matrix of beliefs, attitudes, emotions, insights, and values connected to a claim" (Gilbert 1997, 105). To understand position, one must be aware of all the modes of argumentation, i.e., the logical, emotional, visceral, and kisceral (Gilbert 1997, 109). Thus, any claim might at the same time be supported by various premises of "reasons," and they could be multimodal: logical relating to our thoughts; logical inferences and connections; emotional, stemming from our emotions; visceral, related to our physicalities (basically our senses but according to Gilbert also power and environmental relations); and kisceral, referring to our intuitions.

According to Gilbert, disagreements that should be turned into agreements might be related to a specific mode, where we explore (i) vertically, how deep such disagreement is with respect to a specific mode; (ii) horizontally, to find out whether the disagreement in one mode is also a disagreement in another mode; or even (iii) diagonally, when we compare different modes and see where they (dis)agree (Gilbert 1997, 114–115).

Furthermore, Gilbert developed a five-rule procedure in order that two positions coalesce. The first step is "prior to encounter," in which the proponent is to reflect on his or her face and strategic goal prior to stating his or her (dis)agreement. The second step is "discovering the opposer's position" as to the same goals. The third step is to "identify commonality" as to common elements between the parties. The fourth step is dedicated to "examining modes" to realize whether the parties operate in the same mode, which is the mode of disagreement, and "might utilization of other modes be helpful." The last step "examines depth of goals" and potential motives, values, etc., if goals are in conflict (Gilbert 1997, 123).

Bearing in mind the connection between Gilbert's multi-modal argumentation and Jung's psychological types (Novak 2020), it would perhaps be interesting to emphasize that a similar protocol as Gilbert's five-rule procedure concerning the coalescence of arguments is followed in Jungian psychotherapy.

For example, when a couple has problems in their relationship and the therapist decides to resort to psychological-type therapy, he or she would first explore what is the psychological-type structure of both partners (which is their dominant, inferior, and tertiary function). Then he or she would try to disclose through a conversation with both of them which is the function that causes them problems and will perhaps try to find the function that is most likely a common ground for their common interests and eventual agreement or compromise. If the cognitive functions are replaced with modes, we get a similar picture, which would be typical of ADR, and no wonder why some put ADR on the list of therapeutic justice techniques (Abadinsky 2003, 356). A dispute is tried to be resolved out-of-court not only logically, but holistically, in which emotions and emotional argumentation play an important role.

In fact, Gilbert wrote:

> Resistance on the emotional level, for example, might be dealt with by an analysis on the logical level. This is the approach taken in rational-emotive therapy where strong feelings and fears are explored through logical analysis until their attitudinal nature must be directly confronted. (Gilbert 1997, 114)

In a specific case of family mediation, after the settlement reached before the court concerning the custody, contacts, and support for children following their divorce, the ex-spouses came to a mediator because they could not divide their joint property. Through several separate and joint meetings with the parties, the mediator realized that the problem was not legal but emotional. What turned out to be the most important for him was that the mediation proceedings were not open, as he was afraid that in court proceedings the public would learn that he spent money for his "hobbies," including visiting casinos and brothels. What was the most important for her was that her ex-husband, although he was the breadwinner in the family, recognized her contribution to the upbringing of their children and her diligent work in the household (Jäger 2019). When their emotional arguments, i.e., his fear of publicity to ruin his reputation and her feeling of inferiority, were properly addressed, they were finally willing to compromise so the legal problem of the division of the joint property was resolved.

Accordingly, although in mediation the critical-logical mode is also used to help parties reach an agreement, "it seems possible that well 'reasoned' arguments, strong standpoints, can [often] be peripheral to solving disagreements," and "there is no good reason to prioritize reason (which was obviously present) over empathy, or intuition, or connection, or symbiosis" (Carozza 2020, 8–9).

5.3.2 The Emotional Expression of Legal Logical Arguments

Accordingly, the judicial institutional framework, formally speaking, does not allow the possibility of E-argument 1, meaning that emotional reasons would constitute separate premises in a legal argument. The so-called emotional grounds or reasons will not be considered valid in the legal domain. Legal procedural rules require dealing with legal logical arguments; emotional arguments need to be subordinated to those, if they are allowed to be made at all within court proceedings.

What about E-argument 2, where emotions are used to express logical (dialectical) arguments?

In courtrooms, lawyers daily resort to *pathos* when addressing judges and juries in their oral advocacy. Furthermore, legal counsels write briefs in which they try not to be overly emotional due to their attempt at a convincing or persuasive analysis of legal provisions and facts of the case, and their adherence to the audience of judges, who are also to operate syllogistically in their reasoning of the decision. However, there is usually some room for them to utilize rhetorical *pathos* in their briefs mainly using various rhetorical devices (figures and tropes). In a similar manner, but not to the same extent, the rhetorical style (*elocutio*) is sometimes used, in the form of *pathos.* Moreover, emotions to express legal arguments are often used when judges write their separate (i.e., concurring or dissenting) opinions, in which they criticize majority decisions that as a collective product are, as a rule, written in a dry logical style.

Frost reminds us that

> Quintilian also warned against boring the judge with all the available arguments, against dry repetition of facts which may suggest the advocate's lack of confidence in the judge's memory, and against over-elaboration of arguments, a practice which makes judges suspect that the advocate is not confident about the argument.
>
> (2005, 63)

Moreover, the classical rhetorical analysis of how judges responded to emotional appeals was closely linked to the five-part structure for legal arguments (i.e., opening sentence, statement of the case, argument summary, argument, and closing argument) (Frost 2005, 63–65). Greco-Roman legal rhetoricians were aware that emotions were very important; however, differently concerning different parts of the trial. Different emotions would apply to different parts (and different audiences), in which the opening statement is different from the closing argument. According to them, they played an important part in a persuasive discourse (Frost 2005, 67).

What kind of emotions are used by the parties and attorneys in a case depends on the audience to which they are addressed. If they are intended for lower court judges, so lower court judges would also use them for their audience, senior court judges. And highest court judges would use them to address a general (legal) audience. Still, because in the legal context, especially modern, the logical mode of argumentation predominates, they would be used rhetorically not dialectically, that is, interstitially.

In such a manner, Frost analyzed Justice's Scalia dissent in the case of *United States v. Virginia*, also from the view of *pathos* used in his dissent. He discussed its use in terms of the introduction (*exordium*), the main part (*partitio*), and the conclusion (*peroratio*), with the introduction and conclusion being the most important part concerning the use of emotions. He also pointed to Scalia's parallel structure, metaphors and similes, antithesis, rhetorical questions, and his forensic style (Frost 2005, 126–132) in order to invoke an emotional response in his audience.

5.4 Conclusion

Today's legal argumentation theory's position toward emotional arguments is more favorable than was the traditional approach. Still, there are some serious limits to the recognition of their validity in the legal context. In the formal judicial context that is very much influenced by the logical-type evaluation of arguments, not much space will be left for evaluating emotional arguments as grounds since logical tools are simply not equipped to do that – emotional arguments will not work properly in logical spaces (Carozza 2022, 570).

There is no doubt that many emotions have been institutionalized in the process of law creation and, as legal facts, constitute upper premises in logical legal arguments. However, in legislative procedures and ADR procedures (including restorative justice and care pedagogy approaches (Carozza 2022, 578–579)), emotional arguments may appear as separate arguments.

It is also undisputed, in the framework of legal argumentation, that emotions may be present, to some extent, as manifestations or expressions of dialectical legal arguments, in the form of rhetorical devices of pathos in expressing the mentioned dialectical arguments. To the extent they are allowed, they appear as devices having an argumentative value.

References

Abadinsky, Howard. 2003. *Law and Justice.* Upper Saddle River, New Jersey: Prentice Hall.

Ben-Ze'ev, Aaron. 1995. "Emotions and Argumentation." *Informal Logic*, 17 (2): 189–200.

Carozza, Linda. 2007. "Dissent in the Midst of Emotional Territory." *Informal Logic*, 27 (2): 197–210.

Carozza, Linda. 2020. "Diversity, Conflict Resolution, and (Dis)agreement." *12th OSSA*, Windsor: University of Windsor.

Carozza, Linda. 2022. "Amenable Argumentation Approach: Accommodating Emotional Arguments." *Informal Logic*, 42 (3): 563–582.

David, Rene, Grasmann, Günther. 1988. *Enführung in die grossen Rechtssysteme der Gegenwart.* München: C. H. Beck'sche Verlagsbuchhandlung.

Feteris, Eveline T. 1999. *Fundamentals of Legal Argumentation.* Dordrecht: Kluwer International.

Frost, Michael H. 2005. *Introduction to Classical Legal Rhetoric: A Lost Heritage.* Aldershot: Ashgate.

Furlong, Gary T. 2010. *The Conflict Resolution Toolbox: Models and Maps for Analyzing, Diagnosing, and Resolving Conflict.* Mississauga, Ontario, Canada: John Wiley & Sons.

Gilbert, Michael A. 1994. "Multi-Modal Argumentation." *Philosophy of the Social Sciences*, 24 (2): 159–177.

Gilbert, Michael A. 1997. *Coalescent Argumentation.* Mahwah, NJ: Lawrence Erlbaum Associates, Publishers.

Gilbert, Michael A. 2004. "Emotion, Argumentation and Informal Logic." *Informal Logic*, 24 (3): 245–264.

Jäger, Nina A. 2019. *Pravna kultura v slovenskih osnovnih šolah s poudarkom na mirnem reševanju sporov z uporabo mediacije.* Nova Gorica: Evropska pravna fakulteta Nove univerze.

Novak, Marko. 2016. *The Type Theory of Law: An Essay in Psychoanalytical Jurisprudence.* Cham: Springer.

Novak, Marko. 2020. "Rooting Gilbert's Multi-Modal Argumentation in Jung, and Its Extension to Law." *Informal Logic*, 40 (3): 383–421.

O'Keefe, Daniel J. 1977. "Two Concepts of Argument." *Journal of the American Forensic Association*, 13: 121–128.

Plantin, Christian. 1998. "Arguing Emotions." In van Eemeren, Frans H., Grootendorst, Ron, Blair, Anthony J., Willard, Charles A. (Eds.). *Proceedings of the Fourth Conference of the International Society for the Study of Argumentation.* Amsterdam: Sic Sat.

Roach Anleu, Sharon L. 2000. *Law and Social Change.* London: SAGE Publications.

Sajo, Andras. 2011. *Constitutional Sentiments.* New Haven, London: Yale University Press.

Walton, Douglas. 1992. *The Place of Emotion in Argument.* University Park: Pennsylvania University Press.

Wenzel, Joseph W. 1979. "Jürgen Habermas and the Dialectical Perspective on Argumentation." *Argumentation and Advocacy*, 16 (2): 83–94.

Wohlrapp, Harald. 2006. "Who is Afraid of Emotion in Argument?" *ISSA Proceedings 2006.* Amsterdam: Sic Sat.

Zweigert, Konrad, Köetz, Hein. 1998. *An Introduction to Comparative Law.* Oxford: Oxford University Press.

6 The Legal Appraisal of Multi-Modal Arguments

6.1 Introduction: Arguments' Appraisal

In addition to the rules of a general (philosophical) framework of argumentation, there are also specific rules for argumentation in special fields. These special rules also refer to arguments' appraisal, on the basis of which we can find sound and less sound arguments but also those that do not pass the minimum test of validity in a specific discourse such that they could be called mistakes, fallacies, derailments, errors, or simply violations of that discourse. The appraisal or evaluation of arguments is a normative approach to argumentation, where certain criteria are developed on the basis of which we evaluate their soundness or validity in a certain argumentative context. Different contexts develop different criteria to appraise arguments according to the contexts' special requirements. Sometimes these criteria overlap, but what is important is to evaluate arguments pursuant to the "genuine" criteria of a field for which these arguments are meant. Hence, we not only deal with different fields but also different systems (or orders) of argumentation and their specific requirements. For example, if we appraise arguments in an informal-logical context, we need to respect the theory of fallacies. Furthermore, a rhetorical context has its own rules of evaluation, which also applies to multi-modal argumentation, as well as, finally, the legal field.

Multi-modal arguments could also be appraised according to specific criteria of a particular mode. The logical mode does not differentiate much from the informal-logic context, while the alternate modes present a different issue. Therefore, the emotional mode has emotional criteria to evaluate its soundness. The same applies to the visceral mode, where physical criteria can be developed to evaluate whether arguments in that mode adhere to what is sound in the visceral mode. Likewise, kisceral arguments will be evaluated according to what are specific criteria of validity in the kisceral mode. For example, to remain within their natural mode, their own criteria of evaluation should not follow the ones from informal logic (as it applies, e.g., to emotional arguments (Carroza 2022)). Let us call the violations of multi-modal argumentation simply (multi-modal) "mistakes," to point to the criteria specific for the multi-modal system of argumentation of what is sound argumentation.

DOI: 10.4324/9781003433767-7

Fallacies are, generally speaking, errors in reasoning, which refer to how seemingly sound arguments are built and inferences made. They are dealt with by informal logic (and pragma-dialectics), and are examples of arguers' failing to carry out their dialectical commitments with respect to the "structure of the argument developed" (Tseronis, Forceville 2017, 6). Furthermore, one can speak of derailments, where arguers fail as to their rhetorical commitments with respect to "constructing or addressing a specific audience in a certain rhetorical situation" (van Eemeren 2010; Tseronis, Forceville 2017, 6).

Finally, the criteria to appraise arguments in the system of legal argumentation, if they are to remain within the field of law, need to follow the so-called legal errors determined by positive (procedural) law. As a special type of discourse, law has its own rules to appraise legal arguments and establish legal errors or legal violations on the basis of which, typically, in court proceedings on appeal a judgment of a lower court is found to have committed errors referring to either (i) facts or (ii) substantive or (iii) procedural law.

In this chapter, I discuss (i) how evaluation requirements from the different argumentation systems overlap or not with legal errors and (ii) how multimodal arguments are able to pass the muster of the requirements of legal errors, to qualify them to become sound legal arguments.

6.2 Mistakes of Multi-Modal Arguments

Violations of specific modes within multi-modal argumentation can simply be called "mistakes." It is a situation in which a wrong mode is used to express an argument in the context of another mode. For example, by using logical arguments in an emotionally sensitive situation, we make a mistake. This would occur when a creditor claims his money back from the debtor's heirs on the exact day of the first-year anniversary of the debtor's death. It is logically justified that a debtor, or his heirs if they inherited from him some property, need to return the debt to the creditor. But it is emotionally improper that the creditor requests from the deceased's heirs to do that at an event dedicated to remembering the deceased by his still grieving relatives.

As already mentioned, emotional arguments, like other alternate arguments, should have their own criteria, pertaining to their own mode, of what is a sound (multi-modal) argument (Carroza 2022). Likewise, Tindale argues that each of the alternate modes should define such criteria for itself. What is acceptable, plausible, has sufficient support, or is able to withstand refutation is to be measured in the framework of the respective mode (Tindale 2022).

A multi-modal mistake diametrically occurs when in a certain situation people should argue logically but they decide to argue emotionally. In order to resolve a technical problem people should argue logically, not emotionally. For example, in the frame of argumentation among building experts whether a bridge is supported by sufficient supporting construction, an (emotional) argument that one is afraid of its collapsing misses the appropriate mode if it is not grounded on a previous technical argument. Furthermore, kisceral arguments are not appropriate when one should argue in a logical mode. If you want to prove someone's guilt, you should not argue based on a hunch – with applying a proper legal norm and evidence. However, if you like to make an argument based on internal values it is not enough to only rely on logical arguments. If you want to rely on a gut "feeling," you do not seek empirical evidence.

We could continue trying to find all possible combinations among all four modes, but what we will realize eventually is that to make appropriate arguments in a specific mode we need to argue in that mode. Moreover, to make arguments sound in a specific mode, sometimes it is not enough to only argue in that mode but also to argue well in that mode. To appraise whether multimodal arguments in a specific mode are good enough, the test from informal logic (Gilbert 2004)[1] can be used: (i) we evaluate whether argument in that mode is acceptable (claiming money back from the relatives at the anniversary event is surely unacceptable); (ii) whether it is relevant for the conclusion (in order to resolve a technical dispute you should not argue that you are afraid); as well as (iii) the criterion of sufficiency requiring that a certain claim is sufficiently supported by the premises in a specific mode. For example, in the deceased-debtor case, the creditor should express his argument sufficiently in the emotional mode by first expressing condolences to the relatives of the deceased and then either indicating softly enough that there is something to talk about or at least waiting for some time before coming up with his logical argument.

What is important to stress is that even if the test of arguments' soundness was taken from informal logic, it was evaluated according to the requirements of alternate modes. This is so because the form or structure of argument is always logical, but it is the material part that is taken from the alternate modes. However, with respect to the logical mode we have a double logical "situation" – both the formal and material components of the argument are in the logical form.

It turns out that the evaluation requirements of specifically alternate modes, would often contradict those of valid legal arguments, which means that alternate arguments would result in legal errors. In dealing with multi-modal legal argumentation, I am more interested to see which multi-modal arguments, of them those pertaining to the alternate modes, would survive the test of legal errors, and work in this manner as valid legal arguments.

6.3 Fallacies and Legal Errors

In informal logic, fallacies denote a bad reasoning. There are many fallacies established to show the pitfalls of practical reasoning. There also exists a

1 He wanted to show that even emotional argumentation can be rational, not that the test can be used to establish appropriate emotional argumentation.

grouping of such fallacies into different categories, of which formal and informal fallacies are among the most known (Hansen 2015). While formal fallacies with deficient argument forms are always invalid arguments, informal fallacies are not always such.

To establish what kind of reasoning is fallacious or to test/evaluate if certain arguments are good enough, special models have been invented: e.g., the Relevance-Sufficiency-Acceptability model (Johnson, Blair 1993) or the Acceptability-Relevance-Sufficiency Test (Groarke, Tindale 2003). According to the latter, with regard to acceptability, premises or reasons are acceptable if they are either true or meet the standards that are accepted by the members of a particular field (more appropriate in practical-reasoning situations). Relevance refers to the requirement of premises being relevant for the claim, and, finally, sufficiency (or adequacy) requires that the premises should be strong enough to support the conclusion (Groarke, Tindale 2003).

What about the fallacies and finding out what kind of reasoning is fallacious in the context of law? Although the general tenets and requirements of practical reasoning, which would also include the idea of fallacies, would more or less also apply to law, it has developed its own institutional criteria of argument appraisal in the framework of legal procedures. These are standards that have been accepted by members of the legal field, and usually encoded by the legislature, in the form of general procedural legal norms. Despite the fact that there are overlappings between the informal logic's model of fallacies and the criteria used in legal procedures, to establish what is legally valid we need to follow the law's criteria. Failings to meet such criteria are called "errors" of law and fact, respectively. The law has developed its own criteria in different procedural codes (most specifically criminal, civil, and administrative) that are better attuned to problems of the legal field.

In order to establish what is an error of law/fact, one needs to consult procedural codes. Such errors are found in all kinds of legal proceedings at various levels of decision-making within a legal system. When it comes to court proceedings, they are generally sanctioned as invalid legal arguments by appellate courts when these review the reasoning of judgments of first instance courts with regard to potential errors. Such errors are of three categories, two of them of a legal character and the third one is factual. First, they can be substantive-law errors, meaning that in a specific case the court of first instance did not or did erroneously apply the substantive law it should have applied properly. Second, they can be procedural-law errors, in the sense that certain rules of procedure were not at all or were improperly followed. Third, errors of fact signify that the factual situation necessary for the application of a legal norm was deficiently or mistakenly established. In typical legal deductive syllogism, the errors of law (substantive and procedural) concern mistakes in the major premise, whereas the errors of fact deal with mistakes in the minor premise.

Certainly, there are important overlappings between the aforementioned fallacies and the legal errors. The strongest one is with regard to formal fallacies as errors in logic that can be seen in problems with respect to the argument's form so that such arguments can also be called *non sequiturs.* A similar situation can be found in law, e.g., in court proceedings where the reasons of a judgment contradict its operative provisions or are (usually partially) missing in the judgment. Such errors of (procedural) law violating the procedural rules that require that inference based on deductive syllogism leading to a decision is properly described in the reasoning of the judgment, are considered as substantial violations of procedure and are monitored by appellate courts *ex officio.*[2] Accordingly, formal fallacies are also always invalid in the legal context, thus it is more interesting to focus on informal fallacies and establish when they constitute, or not, legal errors.

When it comes to informal fallacies and their counterparts, i.e., legal errors, in law, although there are many resemblances, certain differences exist as well.

An example of overlapping between fallacies and legal errors is the example of the informal fallacy of *ad hominem,* which means attacking the arguer instead of the argument. In legal proceedings, a similar "error" could be committed when, instead of what the defendant did (the act), who the defendant is (the person) is taken into consideration by the judge. In such a situation, the judge might have some positive affection concerning such a person and might even be closely related to them, so they consider that person's wrongful act less severely than if there were no affection for the person. Thus, in such a situation, if the judge is not recused from deciding the case, their adjudication would not be impartial and thus would be invalid, violating the rules of legal procedure.

There is, however, also a difference between the criteria of valid reasoning in informal logic from what is still valid reasoning in the legal domain. Saunders claims that concerning the fallacies, considerations that are contrary and even misleading to purely rational discourse in philosophy may be relevant and valid in law. He actually maintains that requirements of what arguments are still valid, and not fallacious, in law are lower than in philosophy, where normative or ideal types of reasoning are sought for. This is due to a mixture of rational and logical debate, factual issues, and demands of justice, which signifies that law tolerates a wider variety of arguments. This basically refers to informal fallacies that unlike in other fields can be acceptable as valid legal arguments (Saunders 1993, 245, 381–382).

2 For example, according to Art. 371 of the Slovene Criminal Procedure Act, there is a substantial violation of the Act, e.g., "where the operative provisions of the judgment are incomprehensible or contradictory in themselves or in contradiction with the reasons of the judgment; where the judgment lacks reasons altogether or reasons relating to crucial facts are not adduced or are completely vague or considerably inconsistent in themselves; or where there is considerable discrepancy between the statement of reasons relating to the content of documents or the records of statements given in the course of proceedings on the one hand and these documents or records themselves on the other." This is not a peculiarity of Slovene legislation, because other Continental criminal procedure codes have similar provisions.

6.4 Rhetorical Failures and Legal Errors

Rhetorical failures or "derailments" (van Eemeren 2010) are arguers' unreasonable moves failing to persuade their audience. They entail failed rhetoric concerning its several components. Orators should master, first, different tasks, which in the event of written rhetoric include ***inventio*** (invention; discovery), ***dispositio*** (disposition; organization), and ***elecutio*** (style). Second, in the framework of rhetoric, orators use three means of persuasion: *logos*, *ethos*, *pathos*, and *physis* as a multi-modal addition (Novak 2020, 11). All the mentioned crucial rhetorical elements may result in good or bad rhetoric depending on how reasonably they are used in a certain text.

For example, with respect to rhetorical *logos*, there could be failures as to a certain topic selected, the structure and organization of arguments, or the text's style (rhetorical figures, such as ***parallelism or antithesis***). Within the pragma-dialectical theory of argumentation, van Eemeren deals with derailments as failures concerning "strategic maneuvering." This is a rhetorical move that arguers resort to when trying to be effective to steer the discussion in a certain direction, by the elements of topical selection, adaptation to audience, and presentational devices (van Eemeren 2010). According to van Eemeren, "if arguers' reasonable exchange is overruled by their eagerness for achieving effectiveness, their strategic maneuvering has got derailed." Furthermore, "all derailments of strategic maneuvering are fallacies in the sense that they violate one or more of the rules for critical discussion" (van Eemeren 2010, 198).

Moreover, in line with classical rhetoric, one needs to mention also *ethos* and *pathos*, as well as *physis* being a multi-modal addition, as non-logical means of persuasion. Rhetorical failures, or derailments if we may borrow van Eemeren's term and extend it beyond rhetorical logos, occur here as well since all of the non-logical means of persuasion can end up being used in an unreasonable manner. They can all be fallacious in the legal context, and as such can also be errors of law and facts, respectively. For example, *pathos* can be used by a judge in their first-instance judgment in a manner so much favorable to one party that the appellate court would question their impartiality to the effect of being an unreasonable move. Concerning *ethos*, a judge would rely in their judgment on the value of justice, being a supreme moral value, in a lengthy discussion to support their decision. However, the problem could be that such a move is unreasonable because it has no palpable connection with existing legal provisions on which their judgment should be based. Finally, in a copyright case to decide on a possible infringement, the judge would rely on comparing the taste of two varieties of cheese, but the problem would be that it changes through time, so their move could be seen as unreasonable.

Having established that the criteria of evaluating arguments from other argumentation systems (e.g., informal logic and rhetoric) can also match legal errors, let us now see more precisely how multi-modal arguments would pass, or not, the muster of legal errors. In such a manner, we are able to distinguish legally valid multi-modal arguments from those that are invalid.

6.5 The Four Modes and Their Legal Errors

We have seen that the multi-modal theory of argumentation can to some extent also be extended to law and legal argumentation. Thus, it seems necessary to establish certain criteria to evaluate which multi-modal arguments are acceptable and which are not in the area of law (Groarke 2017). This is a normative issue dealing with argument evaluation that separates admissible arguments from those that are inadmissible. In the area of law, violations of admissible argumentation are called legal errors, as already mentioned.

Next, all four modes of multi-modal argumentation are analyzed to establish the limits of specific modes in the legal context. In informal logic, it is important to make a list of fallacies in order to make a distinction between valid and invalid reasoning. A similar system applies in law where legal systems provide extensive lists of errors applying to a specific legal area, which are encoded in procedural rules of that specific area such that valid legal reasoning is separated from invalid.

6.5.1 *The Logical Mode*

As already emphasized, the logical mode of argumentation has traditionally been the central mode of legal argumentation. Legal errors from the logical mode typically refer to legal provisions (either procedural or substantive legal errors) and facts that we find in the premises of deductive legal syllogism.

Procedural legal errors violate procedural rules. For example, formal "violations" deal with mistakes concerning logical inferences, rational links, and connections with a legal argument. One such legal error that is, in civilian legal systems, usually classified as an essential violation of legal procedure is when the operative provision of a judgment contradicts itself or reasons of the judgment. Such a formal mistake concerning formal inconsistencies within legal logical reasoning that should be very rare in legal procedures corresponds to the formal fallacy of *non sequitur*, meaning an invalid argument whose conclusion is not supported by its premises.

Furthermore, another kind of legal error is of a substantive character, when a lower court violates a substantive statute in the sense of applying an incorrect legal provision, which is perhaps not relevant for the case at issue. Finally, with respect to the factual premise, there can be a violation due to erroneous or incomplete finding of state of facts.

All these types of legal errors have been well established in law and legal argumentation theory, so there is no need here to go further into that.

6.5.2 *The Visceral Mode*

In the context of law, the "visceral" mode is relevant when our five senses are concerned with respect to how people (differently) perceive (i) legal evidence (of "visceral nature") and the (ii) (visceral) elements of certain intellectual property rights (i.e., copyrights, trademarks, and industrial designs), and argue on the basis of such. Concerning such, "multi-modal" evidence and (the constitutive elements of) such rights would be visual, auditory, or similar that are not fully captured by their verbal expression since their message is to an important extent non-verbal (such as photo, picture, painting, soundtrack, video). These kinds of arguments can be valid or invalid legally when they are used in legal proceedings and appraised by relevant courts.

With respect to (i) visceral evidence, for example, the painting by Margaret Mead in the Honolulu court was used as evidence to prove that she was the right creator of the Big-Eyed Children paintings. However, the video clip of Stanley "Tookie" Williams as evidence containing the prosodic information to show that the gang leader became a better person did not persuade the governor of California to pardon him. In civil-law judicial proceedings, courts (most often judges) decide whether (such) evidence are strong enough to pass a certain standard of proof. If that is not the case, they, typically on appeal, establish errors of facts, meaning that the establishing of facts was deficient or improper. In common-law systems,

> a claim that the trier of fact improperly found a fact may be reversed by the trial court on the ground that the verdict was against the weight of the evidence, or by an appellate court on the more limited ground that the jury could not have reasonably found the facts it did.
>
> (Gifis 1991, 164)

That mostly concerns the factual or lower premise of legal logical deductive syllogism.

Concerning (ii) visceral arguments dealing with intellectual property rights, first the copyright, the same case of painter Margaret Mead can be used in order to evaluate a copyright violation. An original painting is not only a piece of evidence (in its "material property" dimension) but also incorporates a concrete legal norm (copyright)[3] (its "intellectual property" dimension).

A similar situation with regard to the separate value of visceral arguments would also refer, e.g., to trademarks and industrial designs. All these types of intellectual-property cases could involve problems with evidence, especially due to their predominately non-verbal character (as described earlier), but could also constitute errors of substantive law, when an administrative body (Intellectual Property Office) or a lower court, for example, erroneously concludes that all the conditions for registering a trademark were fulfilled, thereby violating the Industrial Property Act.

3 Its abstract legal norm dimension is situated in the proper statutory provision of the Copyright Act determining that copyrighted works are legally protected.

6.5.3 The Emotional Mode

In the field of legal argumentation, the premises are to be composed of legal norms and facts, not (independent) emotions, in the form of emotional arguments. If legal arguments are instead based on emotions with no relation to legal norms, they are legally invalid for structural reasons since such an argument would be based on a wrong premise when emotions as (legal) grounds are used instead of legal norms. In the legal deductive syllogism, we only have one legal and one factual premise, with no room for additional emotional premises. Otherwise, the requirement of the rule of law calling for the objectivity and impartiality of legal decision-making, cannot be met. This would be a case, for example, where a judge convicts someone because he does not like that person, without any reliance on the legal norm and the facts, and this would be an essential error of (substantive) law. Such extreme situations almost never occur in modern law, I believe.

More frequent are examples where emotional arguments are less clearly used. A legal norm could be used in a specific direction because of a judge's (emotional) bias. The judge is perhaps related to some extent to one of the parties, and there is a danger that, in addition to the legal and factual premise, another, emotional premise sneaks into the decision-making of that judge. This could also be an error of law, however of a procedural character since the procedure is to ensure impartial adjudication. To prevent such situations, there is the institution of recusal. When a judge is too emotionally attached to a party, they need to request their recusal (or a juror's dismissal though the *voir-dire* examination). The so-called objective reasons of recusal exist when there are some close family ties, while the so-called subjective reasons for recusal when the judge feels that he or she is simply too emotionally affected by a certain party that he or she cannot adjudicate impartially.

Moreover, a third possibility exists when emotional arguments are used, in a rhetorical manner, as expressions of legal arguments. This could also constitute an error of (procedural) law, which prohibits contempt of court, when in defending their rights in court a party would insult the other party or the judge. A similar situation occurred when an appellate judge, who was angry and disappointed at the first-instance judge in a case decided on appeal, not only dismissed the latter's arguments as erroneous and remanded the case for new decision-making (logos), but also made several comments, in a pathetic manner, about how that judge was ignorant, illiterate, and overall incompetent such that he did not deserve to perform the office of judge. This could constitute an error of law, but of a "softer character" by violating the Code of Judicial Ethics, which requires judges to be respectful with respect to their colleagues and take care for the reputation of courts and judges in public. In an extreme case, it could lead to disciplinary proceedings.

6.5.4 The Kisceral Mode

Kisceral arguments applicable in the legal context are chiefly about arguing on the basis of values. Intuition, being a common cognitive function on the basis of which kisceral arguments are made, is certainly a very broad concept and a psychological function that covers many phenomena. On first glance, like emotions, values based on intuitions seem extraneous to the legal framework, in which the objectivity/rationality of decision-making and justification is imperative; however, a closer look would disclose that, realistically, there is much more to that.

A kisceral argument directly used in the legal context would constitute a legal error, for example, when a jury would find an Afghan migrant guilty of robbing an elderly Canadian woman without clear evidence. Instead of relying on the evidence in that case, the jurors would base their intuition on a value of security shared among many people who are afraid of migrants because some of them are criminals. In that case, two types of errors could be committed: (i) the error of fact could point to that there was no evidence for the charge made, while (ii) the error of law would emphasize that what the migrant did to that woman, if he did something at all, was not a criminal offense. Perhaps there was no force exerted from the migrant or the woman gave him some property voluntarily because she felt sorry for him but later changed her mind.

However, if a kisceral argument, such as a judge's moral conscience, was used to interpret an unclear legal norm or fill in a gap in the law, it would be another matter, not erroneous. There have been many examples of that discussed in the preceding pages.

6.6 Conclusion

The area of law like other argumentation systems (such as informal logic and rhetoric) has developed its own system of argument appraisal that, like other systems, distinguishes between valid and invalid arguments. The invalid legal arguments commit thusly errors of fact or errors or law (substantive or procedural).

However, not all multi-modal arguments are invalid in the area of law, and it is from those valid arguments that legal argumentation theory and practice should learn in developing their horizons. In such a manner, the logic of legal argumentation must also be examined in its multi-modal perspectives, which brings both law and legal argumentation closer to the reality of our life.

References

Carroza, Linda. 2022. "Amenable Argumentation Approach: Accommodating Emotional Arguments." *Informal Logic,* 42 (3): 563–582.

Gifis, Steven H. 1991. *Law Dictionary.* New York: Barron's Educational Series, Inc.

Gilbert, Michael A. 1997. *Coalescent Argumentation.* Mahwah, New Jersey: Lawrence Erlbaum Associates, Publishers.

Gilbert, Michael A. 2004. "Emotion, Argumentation and Informal Logic." *Informal Logic*, 24 (3): 245–264.

Groarke, Leo. 2017. "Multimodality and the Law." In Manzin, Maurizio, Puppo, Federico, Tomasi, Serena (Eds.). *Multimodality and Reasonableness in Judicial Rhetoric*. Studies on Argumentation & Legal Philosophy/2. Trento: Universita degli studi di Trento, Quaderni della Facolta di giurisprudenza.

Groarke, Leo, Tindale, Christopher W. 2003. *Good Reasoning Matters! A Constructive Approach to Critical Thinking*. Toronto, New York, Oxford: Oxford University Press.

Hansen, Hans. 2015. "Fallacies." *Stanford Encyclopedia of Philosophy*. https:/plato.standford.edu/entries/fallacies (6. 11. 2023).

Novak, Marko. 2020. "Multi-Modal Argumentation and Rhetoric in Judicial Proceedings." *Argumentation and Advocacy*, 56 (1): 41–60.

Saunders, Kevin W. 1993. "Informal Fallacies in Legal Argumentation." *South Carolina Law Review*, 44: 343–382.

Tindale, Chris. 2022. "On the Kisceral Mode of Argumentation." *Informal Logic*, 42 (4): 603–621.

Tseronis, Assimakis, Forceville, Charles (Eds.). 2017. *Multimodal Argumentation and Rhetoric in Media Genres*. Amsterdam: John Benjamins Publishing Company.

van Eemeren, Frans H. 2010. *Strategic Maneuvering in Argumentative Discourse: Extending the Pragma-Dialectical Theory of Argumentation*. Amsterdam, Philadelphia: John Benjamins Publishing Company.

7 Multimodal Legal Argumentation in EU Trademark Disputes

7.1 Introduction

I have already emphasized that apart from Gilbert's theory of multi-modal argumentation, there also exists the multimodal theory of argumentation, one of its founders being Groarke. Although there are differences between the two theories, there are also overlaps. Of all four of Gilbert's modes, the visceral mode is a crucial point where the theories meet (Groarke 2022). When their strengths and weaknesses are generally compared, Gilbert's version of multimodality seems to be broader by providing feasible alternatives to making premises in a logical manner. However, concerning the comprehensiveness of an analysis dealing with the dichotomy between verbal and non-verbal semiotic resources, on the basis of which people argue, multimodal argumentation has gone further. After all, the verbal–non-verbal distinction is not even an essential feature of Gilbert's approach. I have already referred to certain findings from the multimodal theory of argumentation in this book, particularly when discussing the visceral mode (see, for example, visual argumentation). It seems to be a necessary addition to the multi-modal theory of argumentation at least in certain areas of discussion, one of which being trademark law.

In this chapter, I firstly present some basic issues concerning EU trademark law and disputes about that, especially for those readers who are not particularly familiar with the topic to follow the discussion in this chapter more easily. Then, I outline some fundamental points from the multimodal argumentation theory as necessary tools to analyze various problems associated with trademark disputes. After that I discuss different levels of multimodality with respect to arguments, including trademarks and the trademarks themselves, as well as the problem of trademarks' presentation. Then, we look into the matter of EU trademark disputes, where the multimodal Sabel test developed by the Court of Justice of the EU (hereinafter the ECJ) is mainly discussed, to be followed by the Guidelines of the European Union Intellectual Property Office (hereinafter the EUIPO) that were created to apply the Sabena test to examination practices by the Office and other national offices. Finally, further challenges in the area of trademark examination and argumentation that the new or non-traditional trademarks brought are discussed from a multimodal perspective.

DOI: 10.4324/9781003433767-8

7.2 EU Trademark Law and Disputes in a Nutshell

Trademarks as rights to exclusively use a sign on products to identify their origin have been used from ancient times (Dutfield, Suthersanen 2008). In the modern era, with international legal documents adopted at the end of the 19th century, their regulation was unified globally to a large extent.[1] Still, national systems of trademark law provide some differences. In this contribution, I focus on the unified system of trademark law within the EU, which had existed since the early nineties of the previous century and was importantly amended by a new EU regulation in 2017. The last amendment took into consideration the global development of information technology by introducing the protection of so-called non-traditional (or non-conventional, sometimes even simply referred to as "new") trademarks.

Within that system, the "traditional" trademarks have included: (i) word trademarks consisting of any words irrespective of the fact that they have a particular meaning (e.g., Adidas). It could be one word or a combination of several words. (ii) Figurative trademarks include visuals of any sort, which could also be combined with verbal elements (e.g., a panther accompanied with the word Puma). Generally, the word and figurative trademarks are still the most used trademarks, although other traditional trademarks include (iii) shape trademarks (three-dimensional – e.g., the Coca-Cola bottle); (iv) position trademarks (e.g., the three stripes on Adidas sports shoes); (v) pattern trademarks (e.g., a certain pattern drawn on the surface of a product); and (vi) color trademarks (one color or a combination of colors).[2]

In order to register a trademark at the European Union Intellectual Property Office (hereinafter EUIPO), according to the (previous) 1993 EC Regulation, it was required that signs must have been graphically presentable in the EUIPO Register. To some extent that prevented technological progress because it was possible to register only those signs that could be verbally or (at least) visually depicted on paper. That impediment was eventually removed in the 2017 EU Regulation, in which the electronic format was recognized equal to the paper as a means of representing trademarks. This amendment opened the gate for the following non-traditional trademarks: (i) sound trademarks; (ii) motion trademarks; (iii) hologram trademarks; and (iv) multimedia[3] trademarks (including visual, sound, and motion elements).[4]

1 The Paris Convention for the Protection of Industrial Property was adopted in 1883.
2 See EUIPO – Home (europa.eu) (June 5, 2023).
3 From the discussion in this book, it seems that in this context perhaps "multimodal" would be a better term than "multimedia," with medium having the meaning of "intermediate" for the purpose of communication, while a mode is the way of presenting a sign being somewhat closer to its creation.
4 Certain non-EU jurisdictions recognize also other types of trademarks, such as taste, scent, texture or feel, and gesture trademarks.

However, some of the just mentioned non-traditional marks could even before be represented graphically in the trademark register. For example, a sound mark containing music was represented by musical notation; a motion mark by a sequence of certain visuals, which could also be the case for a hologram mark. This was of course a limited possibility since not all sound marks could have been presented in such a manner, and there was absolutely no possibility of graphically representing a multimedia mark. This problem was solved by the 2017 EU Trademark Regulation, which abandoned the requirement of the graphical representation in the register. The new relevant provision of Article 4 reads as follows:

> An EU trade mark may consist of any signs, in particular words, including personal names, or designs, letters, numerals, colours, the shape of goods or of the packaging of goods, or sounds, provided that such signs are capable of:
>
> (a) distinguishing the goods or services of one undertaking from those of other undertakings; and
> (b) being represented on the Register of European Union trade marks ('the Register'), in a manner which enables the competent authorities and the public to determine the clear and precise subject matter of the protection afforded to its proprietor.

In 2018 the Commission Implementing Regulation was adopted, which detailed certain requirements for registration, in particular concerning the new marks. Art. 3 of the implementing regulation reads as follows:

> The trade mark shall be represented in any appropriate form using generally available technology, as long as it can be reproduced on the Register in a clear, precise, self-contained, easily accessible, intelligible, durable and objective manner so as to enable the competent authorities and the public to determine with clarity and precision the subject matter of the protection afforded to its proprietor.

What are meant by "available technology" are electronic media carrying visuals, sounds, and their combinations, such as JPEG, MP3, and MP4. Art. 3 of the Implementing Regulation classifies ten types of marks (i.e., word, figurative, shape, position, pattern, color, sound, motion, multimedia, and hologram); however, there is also the possibility of a mark that does not fit into any of the mentioned categories. Word, figurative, shape, sound, hologram, and multimedia marks can be presented in a (classical) graphical or electronic manner, but no (verbal) description to accompany such representation is allowed since that could confuse consumers. However, descriptions are allowed with respect to position, motion, pattern, and color marks, as well as any mark that cannot be categorized, in order to additionally explain the sign to be registered. According to Art. 3 of the Implementing Regulation, where the representation is accompanied by a description, such description should accord with the representation and should not extend its scope.

The procedure to register an EU trademark begins by an application submitted to the EUIPO.[5] At first it examines whether the formal requirements have been met in the application, and then it checks if any absolute grounds to refuse a trademark exist.[6] Should a sign to be registered as a mark passes the test of the absolute grounds for refusal, it is published in the EUIPO official bulletin. Once it is published, interested parties have a three-month period to oppose the mark pending on the basis of a previous trademark. This is the so-called opposition procedure in which the parties invoke the so-called relative grounds for refusal, which are usually also called "private grounds."[7] This kind of objection by the owner of a previous trademark, pointing in particular to the pending mark being identical or too similar to the previous mark such that consumers could be confused, is decided upon by the EUIPO. If the opposition is unsuccessful the EUIPO registers the trademark.

Appeal from the EUIPO, as a first-instance authority, is possible to be lodged with the Board of Appeal, who is independent from the EUIPO, although it has been established within its structure. Furthermore, aggrieved parties may seek judicial review against the Board of Appeal by filing an action with the EU General Court. Finally, the Court of Justice of the EU is empowered to grant leave to appeal from the EU General Court's judgment.

Although legal disputes with respect to (EU) trademarks may be manifold, and at different tribunals, in order to present findings from multimodal argumentation theory to benefit legal argumentation with respect to trademarks dispute, I focus in this chapter primarily on cases in the opposition procedure (i.e., the issue of identity or similarity with a previous mark likely to cause confusion).

5 The electronic form of application has increasingly been encouraged, although a classical paper application with electronic attachments when necessary is still recognized.

6 These include the so-called public reasons for refusal, such as violating Art. 4 of the 2017 Regulation concerning "signs of which an EU trademark may consist, being devoid of distinctive character, signs having become customary in the trade, being contrary to public policy and morality, etc.

7 Art. 8 of the 2017 Regulation determines the following:

"Upon opposition by the proprietor of an earlier trade mark, the trade mark applied for shall not be registered:

(a) if it is identical with the earlier trade mark and the goods or services for which registration is applied for are identical with the goods or services for which the earlier trade mark is protected;

(b) if, because of its identity with, or similarity to, the earlier trade mark and the identity or similarity of the goods or services covered by the trade marks there exists a likelihood of confusion on the part of the public in the territory in which the earlier trade mark is protected; the likelihood of confusion includes the likelihood of association with the earlier trade mark."

7.3 Multimodal Argumentation Theory for Trademark Disputes

The most important lesson from multimodal argumentation theory seems to be the knowledge that it is very difficult, if not impossible, for words to entirely capture non-verbal signs by interpretation, translation, or transliteration. According to Kjeldsen (2016), in translation, conversation, and eventual presentation of the reconstruction of multimodal arguments, it is particularly difficult for the analyst to be certain about the intended meaning, since the verbal means do not actually suffice to capture the rich information communicated by non-verbal resources to an audience. Blair (2015, 220) claimed that, in such a situation, the verbal is to be understood as a "placeholder" for the visual (or any other non-verbal mode), not a "translation" of it. According to him, "verbal reconstruction rarely captures all that was expressed in the visual argument, but is a placeholder for it, and provides us with a reference for use in evaluating the cogency of the visual argument."

This seems to be relevant for any area, even law, where non-verbal utterances appear together with words. One such typical area of law is trademark law. In the legal argumentation of intellectual property cases in general (copyright and industrial property, particularly trademarks), insights from multimodal argumentation theory can be very useful to understand the "physical" character of such cases (Novak 2020). The "physical character" refers to a number of non-verbal signs that are used today in trademark law, independently or in combination with words, to designate the origin of products and services. Such physicalities include visuals, sounds, smells, tastes, gestures, etc. It is important to be aware that we are able to argue by such non-verbal signs solely, without any presence of verbal utterances. These types of non-verbal phenomena are generally used within argumentation as reasons (evidence) to back our claims, which can be verbal.[8]

Groarke, who developed the multimodal theory of argumentation, focused in particular on visual at first and then, to some extent, also on acoustic argumentation[9] and claimed a logical structure of multimodal arguments. If we want to have multimodal argumentation, at least one of the essential elements of an argument, most often one of the premises, must be in a non-verbal form. Today it is widely accepted within the multimodal argumentation community that non-verbal discourse is able to create and express propositions, and that what was primarily done in the visual mode can be extended to other modes (Tseronis, Forceville 2017, 6). If all the premises and the conclusion are in one mode only, we would deal with monomodality.

8 One of the meanings of old Greek *logos* was also "word," meaning verbal. Thus, in terms of the semiotic resources of a specific mode, one of the typical characteristics of the logical mode could also be that it is almost exclusively verbal.

9 See also Eckstein (2017) and Kišiček (2018).

Moreover, Tseronis argued against a strong divide between visual and verbal arguments and called for studying their interaction (2018). This position is important because we could extend it to other visceral arguments, not only visual ones. In the interaction between non-verbal modes and the verbal mode, there are at least three possibilities: (i) the non-verbal mode has an important and direct impact on constituting the essential elements of the argument (the premises and the conclusion); that impact can be (ii) indirect or less important, or, finally, just (iii) peripheral (Tseronis 2018).

What also seems necessary to consider from the multimodal argumentation theory for the discussion of trademarks is the distinction between thick and thin (Kjeldsen 2015). It is certainly something different and poses many more problems to deal with signs that have multiple meanings (thick ones) than the ones with narrow meanings (thin ones). The thicker a sign the greater the scope of discretion when it is interpreted. That basically applies to all semiotic resources, including words.

Tseronis and Forceville (2017, 5) suggest as the most obvious the following semiotic modes: written language, spoken language, static images, moving images, music, non-verbal sound, gestures, gaze, and posture. However, they emphasize this is not a definite list. Furthermore, Groarke (2022) adds olfaction, taste, and touch. A vast majority of these can potentially be important for a burgeoning area of non-traditional trademarks, which further depart from the traditional use of verbal language.

Moreover, what is also important to consider is the role and function of the various semiotic modes, and the differences between them. Each semiotic system has its own affordances, which can be shown to be more suitable for one function than for another. For example, we consider and evaluate static images following their texture, composition, use of color, etc., while in the event of moving images we consider their sequencing in time (Tseronis, Forceville 2017, 9).

7.4 Multimodal Argumentation and EU Trademark Law

7.4.1 Two Levels of Multimodality

With respect to the issue of multimodal argumentation when trademarks are dealt with, we need to consider that there are actually two aspects or levels of multimodality. There is the multimodality of trademarks themselves and also the multimodality of argumentation about trademarks. The combination of the two levels can contribute to complex situations that one needs to deal with. What is important in this context is an awareness, which was stressed several times in this book, that different modes bring different aspects of a story and that full translation from one mode to another is extremely difficult, if not impossible.

The first multimodality deals with their trademarks' required representation that with respects to certain marks needs to be multimodal. Like in the case of motion or multimedia marks. However, we also have monomodal marks, such as word, visual, or sound marks. Thus, we have different modes in which specific trademarks need to be represented, in order to be eligible for registration. Thereby the verbal mode is combined with other non-verbal modes. The application to the EUIPO is filled out in the verbal form, and the multimodal signs to be registered as marks are submitted in the electronic format or otherwise presented (mostly in the visual mode). Moreover, the non-verbal modes are often accompanied by descriptions, being in the verbal mode. I discuss the problem of different modes appearing at this level (the representation level) next. From that follows that the framers of the Regulation and the Implementing Regulation have already understood to a certain extent the problem of different modes interacting with one another, which is one of the core topics of the multimodal argumentation theory. They paid attention to making a distinction between situations in which non-verbal elements can be accompanied with description and those that would be too confusing for consumers.

The second level, for which the representation level is important, is the argumentation level of multimodality, which is my major concern in this article. Different modes are used when intellectual property offices or courts decide and argue in trademark disputes. The two levels are certainly interconnected not only that the argumentation level necessarily follows the representation level but also that without understanding the multimodal dimension of the representation level it is impossible to argue multimodality well in the framework of the argumentation level. Moreover, in the continuation, it will follow that that the multimodal approach developed by the ECJ, from within the argumentation level, was then used by the EUIPO in developing guidelines for prospective parties to register their trademarks at the representation level to avoid unnecessary disputes in the future.

7.4.2 The Problem of Trademarks' Representation

The new marks, i.e., sound, motion, hologram, and multimedia marks, are strictly speaking not completely new. Except for the multimedia mark, the others could have been registered already under the previous Regulation's system of graphical representation. In addition to the possibility of their representation today, which is mostly in the electronic manner, they can still be represented graphically. That used to be the only option before. Their graphical representation, as the secondary option, is still explicitly determined in the Implementing Regulation. This second option of their representation is generally considered to be equivalent to their electronic version, but from a more nuanced (multimodal) view it is questionable whether that is really the case. What is problematic is the view that the same sign is able to be equivalently represented in different modes without losing some (important) content. Is the musical notation for some melody entirely equivalent to its melody played? If not in any other manner, there is the difference of an instrument by which the melody is played. Moreover, is a sequence of moves really equivalent to the motion recorded? I guess there is still a gap, which is greater in some than in other approximations concerning the traditional and electronic representation of certain marks.

Let us take the sound mark first. According to the Implementing Regulation, it can be "represented by submitting an audio file reproducing the sound or by an accurate representation of the sound in musical notation." The crucial word from the previous citation is "accurate," since there is a question of whether all music notations are accurate representations of the sounds recorded. Even the same musical notations will sound different when played by different instruments, or even by the same instruments that are differently tuned. However, this will work when musical notation is registered as a sound mark and will keep being represented by musical notation. Moreover, only music sounds can be represented by musical notation, not other sounds that may be registered. In sum, what is expected to predominate is the electronic version of a sound's reproduction as a primary means of representation, with the graphical reproduction as the secondary option becoming superfluous.

A similar problem might be in relation to the motion mark. Pursuant to the Implementing Regulation, this kind of mark is to be "represented by submitting a video file or by a series of sequential still images showing the movement or change of position. Where still images are used, they may be numbered." Again, it is far from obvious that such a series of sequential still images could be equivalent to the video file as we deal with two different modes. The same problem appears to be with the hologram mark, which should be represented by submitting a video file or a graphic or photographic reproduction containing the views that are necessary to sufficiently identify the holographic effort in its entirety.

Only the multimedia mark, which has not existed before in any manner, can only be "represented by submitting an audiovisual file containing the combination of the image and the sound." In such a case, there has never been an attempt of trying to represent it in a graphical version. That would definitely be doomed to fail. As a matter of fact, such a view seems to be in a complete accord with the findings of multimodal argumentation theory.

Aside from the problem of "translating" between the modes, is the problem of (verbal) description as an additional means of explanation when the mark is submitted for registration. Unlike the previous regulation, the existing one leaves out such description with respect to word, figure, shape, sound, and hologram marks since that could confuse customers. However, when the matter concerns position, pattern, color, and motion marks the primary and secondary means of representation may be accompanied by description detailing the mentioned representation.[10] In connection with such, there is a general provision in Art. 3.2 of the Implementing Regulation, stipulating that when

10 This also applies to the so-called sui generis mark, which is not covered by any of the mentioned taxonomies.

the representation is (allowed to be) accompanied by description such should accord with the representation and should not extend its scope. I do not want to say that such possibilities never exist, but once we admit that words can only be placeholders for non-verbal signs, the argument that "description is generally able to accord with the representation and generally does not extend its scope" is untenable.

7.5 EU Trademarks' Disputes and Argumentation

7.5.1 Introduction

Argumentation comes in view when there are disagreements, and it is particularly law that is intended to be the last resort for resolving them. When EU trademarks are concerned, potential disputes can initially be dealt with at the EUIPO, at the two levels of administrative procedure. If the parties are unsatisfied with the resolution of the dispute at the EUIPO, they can submit their case for a judicial resolution to either national or EU courts. My intention here is not to discuss the details of their jurisdiction or all the possible grounds to file a lawsuit seeking the judicial protection of one's EU trademark in the case of its infringement. Generally, the procedure of registering trademarks is quite harmonized around the globe, including the EU system: once an applicant files their application to register a trademark, the competent office will check whether the so-called absolute (or "public") requirements for registration are fulfilled. For example, a trademark that can be registered must be distinctive enough from the products it designates (it must not be generic in the sense of representing the products by the very means of its appearance – e.g., a 3D trademark in the form of a bottle to designate bottled beverages), it must not be in conflict with public morality, if it is in the form of a national symbol there must be an appropriate approval by the relevant state body, etc. If all these absolute requirements are met, the trademark is published in the office's official bulletin and the deadline of usually three months begins to run, in which persons interested might object to it before it is finally registered (the so-called relative or "private" grounds for objection). The most common reason for such would be that it is too similar to a pre-existing trademark such that consumers will be confused in the sense of not being able to distinguish between the previous and the new trademark's owners with respect to the specific products such a trademark is to designate.

In the case of the mentioned relative objections in favor of a previous trademark, the objector is to claim that the signs used in the two trademarks are too similar so it would be difficult for consumers to make a distinction between the two. As already mentioned, traditionally the most frequent trademarks have been word and figurative trademarks. With respect to the reasoning concerning a word trademark, the traditional monomodal, that is, exclusively verbal argumentation applies in the form of words, and the verbal format normally suffices.

However, concerning figurative trademarks, also one of the most common types of trademarks so far, they could either appear in the form of visual signs (as an image, picture, logo, etc.) solely or in combination with words. That difference is important because words added to a visual can either extend or narrow down the semantic scope of the visual. At least in recent years, authorities that have dealt with disputes concerning trademarks, in the case of the EU trademark either the Board of Appeals of the EUIPO, national courts, or the EU General Court, when resolving such disputes began to include visuals along with the text describing the situation, interpreting the visuals and explaining the decision on the dispute in the reasoning of the decision. A prior practice was that these authorities only discussed the problems even with the visuals only verbally, i.e., monomodally, in the reasoning of the decision. Obviously they became aware that when it comes to figurative trademarks the argumentation in the reasoning of the decision must be multimodal because words do not suffice to deal with all the possible nuances of the visuals when evaluating two figurative trademarks that are in conflict. Perhaps their intention was at the beginning to only be more transparent or clear to also show, not only describe, the visuals themselves that were at issue. However, as we will see next, that created an important precedent beyond just what applied to visual argumentation in the case of EU figurative trademark disputes. In any case, visual argumentation in figurative trademark disputes has paved an important way for cases of disputes to be dealt with in other cases, especially dealing with nontraditional trademarks but also with those that the EU trademark system does not (yet) accept (i.e., trademarks in the form of olfaction, taste, and touch).

7.5.2 The "Bible" of an EU Trademark Case Analysis: The Sabel Test

Back in 1997, the ECJ to some extent already recognized the multimodal dimension of trademark disputes, without explicitly using the word "multimodal."[11] Before the case went all the way to the ECJ, it had originated at German intellectual property offices and courts. In the case of *Sabel v. Puma* (C-251/95 of November 11, 1997), the Dutch company SABEL BV submitted a sign to be registered as a trademark in Germany in classes 18 and 25 of the Nicean classification. That black-and-white sign consisted of the picture of a cheetah running in the right direction, along a line stretching on the left side of the animal. Below the animal was the word sabèl in small letters. The logo with the animal and the word was put in brackets.

However, the German company Puma AG, Rudolf Drassler Sport, lodged opposition to the registration of that mark on the ground that Puma was the proprietor of the pictorial mark of the silhouette of a black puma running in the right direction.

11 We should bear in mind that its "sister" theory, the multi-modal theory of argumentation, was hardly born at that time.

For a better perception of the two logos contested, I strongly suggest the reader to check the mentioned ECJ judgment on the Court's official website.

The German Patent Office considered there to be no resemblance for the purposes of trademark law, thus Puma appealed to the Federal Patent Office, which found a resemblance between the two marks with respect to SABEL's goods in classes 18 and 25 (the "double identity" rule). Therefore, SABEL appealed to the German Federal Court of Justice, which, provisionally, held that there was no likelihood of confusion as regards the two marks in question following German law. However, since the matter concerned the implementation of an EU directive, it decided to send to the ECJ the question for a preliminary ruling about the meaning of the phrase "includes the likelihood of association with the earlier trademark" from the Directive.

In its reply to the aforementioned question for a preliminary ruling, the Court introduced the so-called global approach to considering aural, visual, and conceptual elements when establishing a similarity between a trademark and a sign to become a trademark. The ECJ referred to the arguments by the Belgian, Luxembourg, and Dutch governments, which also contributed their written observations in the case. They explained that the term "likelihood of association" was included in those provisions of the Directive at their request, in order that they should be construed in the same manner as the relevant provision of the regional Uniform Benelux Law on Trade Marks that had adopted the concept of resemblance between marks, rather than that of the likelihood of association/confusion, in defining the scope of the exclusive right conferred by a trademark.

Those governments referred to a judgment of the Benelux Court, which had held that there was resemblance between a mark and a sign when, taking account of the particular circumstances of the case, in particular the distinctiveness of the mark, the mark and the sign, considered separately and together, present aurally, visually, or conceptually a similarity such as to establish an association between the sign and the mark (judgment of May 20, 1983, in Case A 82/5 *Jullien v. Verschuere*, Jur. 1983, vol. 4, p. 36, (para. 15).

According to the Court, that global appreciation of the (i) visual, (ii) aural, or[12] (iii) conceptual similarity of the marks in question must be based on the overall impression given by the marks, bearing in mind, in particular, their (iv) distinctive and (v) dominant components. It continued that the wording of Article 4(1)(b) of the Directive – "there exists a likelihood of confusion on the part of the public" – showed that the perception of marks in the mind of the average consumer of the type of goods or services in question played a decisive role in the global appreciation of the likelihood of confusion. The average consumer normally perceives a mark as a whole and did not proceed to analyze its various details (para. 23). It concluded that "the mere association which the public might make between two trademarks as a result of their

12 This is not to be considered as a disjunction but a conjunction.

analogous semantic content" (this would entail conceptual similarity) was not in itself a sufficient ground for concluding that there was a likelihood of confusion within the meaning of that provision (para. 26).

Although the ECJ did not decide finally on the dispute between Sabel and Puma, which obviously was not its task in the framework of the preliminary ruling procedure, where only (uniform) interpretation of an unclear EU law provision is made, it seems to suggest the following, taking into account both the actual wording of its opinion and the material facts of the case. First, a likelihood of confusion presupposes the likelihood of association or similarity between two marks. Second, in such a situation, an insignificant similarity is not important because anyone could find an element in one sign that might be similar to another sign compared. Third, what matters is conceptual similarity where two marks use images with analogous semantic content. These kinds of images would constitute dominant or distinctive elements in the mark. Fourth, even though there is eventually a conceptual similarity that is not enough because one should not take that in isolation, but what counts is the overall impression given by the marks. Fifth, the global appreciation of the marks in question is made by considering the visual, aural, or conceptual similarity. Sixth and finally, what is relevant is the perception of marks in the mind of the average consumer of the type of goods or services.

The multimodality of the global test is found in its several modes referred to: (i) the verbal mode not only with the conceptual part dealing with logical thinking when concepts are concerned, but also with verbal discussion and argumentation in general. Moreover, there are also the (ii) visual and the (iii) aural modes.

Following the global test made in this case, we find a similarity between the two cases in that in both marks there is a bounding feline, being a symbol of velocity, vitality, and strength (sports when translated into human condition). Furthermore, the importance of this dominant and distinctive image[13] is in its conceptual similarity. However, if we take on an overall comparison of the marks, we need to consider also the visual elements, where only the silhouette of the animals is to some extent similar. If we are more careful visually, we can see actually another kind of animal in the second mark, not a puma but a cheetah: not only their color (black v. black with white dots) is different but also other shapes of the body, such as their heads. Moreover, there are other visual differences: sabel also has two half circles on both sides of the animal, and a line in the middle. There is also the word sabel, which is not only a visual and verbal difference with Puma but could also be an aural one when you pronounce the word.

The introduction of the aforementioned (multimodal) global test was a more than welcome addition to trademark law in order to better understand

13 The important distinctiveness of a puma, on the first mark, follows particularly from its renown market status.

and analyze signs that appear in trademarks. It is already important for traditional trademarks, not to mention the new, non-traditional, ones. What is, however, missing is the development of more structured and nuanced categories of the already-mentioned similarities. For example, when we compare various visual elements, we need to know, at least to some extent, some basics of visual grammar[14] (from multimodal social semiotics) (Leborg 2006; Kress, van Leeuwen 2006) that tells us more about relations between the elements. Thus, comparison within the three similarities should be elaborated in more detail, which seems to be a task for courts to do in their daily practice. Without such additional categories, it seems quite easy for different stakeholders to find similarities or differences as they want, meaning that their approach can be quite arbitrary.

7.6 The EUIPO Guidelines

7.6.1 In General

Based on the mentioned global test to apply to the examination of objections arguing the identity or similarity of signs to be registered as trademarks with previous marks, the EUIPO adopted the following methodology of examining marks or comparing signs that it included in the Examination Guidelines for EU trademarks.[15] It is not a regulation but a list of best practices in trademark examination. In such a way, the EUIPO makes three steps: (i) the two signs are presented in a table, whereby a description is also possible if still allowed according to the newest approach; (ii) relevant distinctive as well as dominant[16] parts of both the signs compared are established, whereby insignificant parts do not need to be considered; and (iii) the visual, aural, and conceptual aspects of the signs compared are taken into account. To find a similarity either great (more than average) or small (less than average), it is enough that the signs meet in one of the previously mentioned three aspects. If a similarity between the signs is found, it is then examined whether (iv) that could lead to the probability of consumer confusion. What are thereby considered are the relevant territory and public where such confusion could occur relating to the origin of goods or services.

In view of the criterion of distinctiveness[17] between signs, there exist (i) powerful marks, in which the more distinctive the sign or mark the greater

14 Other (non-verbal) modes have also their distinct grammars, e.g., notes for music.

15 At https://guidelines.euipo.europa.eu/1935303/1950066/trade-mark-guidelines (28.12.2022). What is important in comparing two trademarks is the so-called double identity between the sign and the goods or service protected by such a sign.

16 According to the EUIPO, this is usually the element that is visually outstanding concerning the position, size, or use of color in the sign. Also, the sign must have at least two identifiable elements, whereby word marks do not have dominant parts.

17 According to the Court's reasoning in C-342/97, this entails a greater or smaller ability of a certain mark to designate the belonging of certain goods or services to a specific company and distinguish them from the goods or services of another company.

consumer confusion is caused by the similarity with another mark, which also entails that such a mark is difficult to copy. (ii) Weak marks' signs are not especially distinctive with respect to other marks, are not particularly known, and have little imaginative content. In such a case, even if the marks are similar it is not expected that the consumers will be confused. Such marks are easy to be copied, and stronger criteria need to be applied to examine their similarity.[18]

7.6.2 Visual Comparison

Concerning visual comparison between two signs, the EUIPO is aware that public perceives word elements differently than other elements. These can be read and understood as a sequence of letters, while others are cognized through their graphic or figurative characteristics. For this purpose, it created special rules for visual comparison that differ among themselves due to the type of marks compared. Thus, special rules have been elaborated to mutually compare word marks, word marks with figurative ones including word elements, only figurative marks, between figurative marks with figurative marks with word elements, black-and-white and color marks, and marks with only one letter. Special attention was also dedicated to motion and multimedia marks.

What are particularly interesting are practices regarding new trademarks, both motion and multimedia marks. The practices with motion marks imply special distinction between verbal, figurative, and motile or transformative elements. With respect to the transformative elements, the EUIPO emphasized:

> A certain movement that is explicit and distinctive is enough to find out that the mark is to a certain extent visually similar although it concerns a case where distinctive elements are verbal. In addition to motile elements, a motion mark can include other transformative elements, such as a changing of colors or the transformation of one element into another. These changes need to be considered when the visual similarity of marks is evaluated. However, a sudden change of position or the change of colors in itself will not have a major effect on the result of the comparison of marks and generally will not lead to finding visual similarity.

The Guidelines are results of best practices originating from the specific cases of the examination of objections by the EUIPO, which are constantly adjusted. Their real value depends on the type and number of cases decided either by the EU General Court (abbreviated as T) or the EUIPO Board of Appeal (abbreviated as R). Since there has generally not been a lot of cases of the new trademarks before the EU General Court, and there have only been a few at the EUIPO, the Guidelines use hypothetical cases from the EU

18 Sabel, ibid.

Intellectual Property Network's "Common Communication on New Types of Marks: Examination of Formal Requirements and Grounds for Refusal (CP11)." Concerning visual comparison only the motion and multimedia marks have been dealt with. In the event of the comparison of multimedia marks the Office has so far only developed comparison between the graphical presentation of verbal elements with figurative elements, even though that type of mark is one of the most complex.

In creating the rules for the comparison of both multimedia as well as motion marks, the Office has consistently used e-links to the original trademarks, which seems to be fully in conformity with the multimodal argumentation theory's approach arguing that verbal descriptions can never entirely capture non-verbal elements. Such a practice needs to be suggested for the EU General Court, as well as the ECJ, when disputes concerning such marks appear before them.

7.6.3 Aural Comparison

Aural comparison between EU trademarks' signs initially deals with whether both signs are able to be pronounced (like a word mark) or concern a specific sound. These elements will not be found in a figurative or similar mark (such as three-dimensional, color, and position marks). All EU official languages need to be taken into account in pronouncing an EU mark. Thereby the number and sequence of syllables, joint rhythm, and the intonation (i.e., the pitch) need to be paid attention to. What is compared is joint syllables and their similar combinations.[19]

Sound trademarks consist of: (i) sounds, including musical elements; (ii) natural sounds from nature (e.g., dogs barking); (iii) verbal elements sung or spoken; as well as (iv) other sounds. Sound marks can be sonically compared with other sound marks and multimedia marks, as well as with other marks if they comprise a verbal element. The EUIPO Guidelines, or the Offices' Joint Standpoints where no practice of such has occurred at the EUIPO/Board of the General Court, compare the signs in the following manner.

Only those motion marks having verbal elements can be sonically compared. These will include word marks or figurative marks with verbal elements. Multimedia marks can always be compared sonically with other multimedia marks as well as with marks containing verbal elements.[20]

New marks must be e-linked (see Table 7.1) especially when the sign cannot be presented graphically. This more or less applies to all new marks, i.e., sound, motion, hologram, and multimedia marks, since their graphical approximations (e.g., notes for a sound (musical) mark or a sequence of moves for a motion mark) never fully capture their dimension.

19 The EUIPO Guidelines.
20 Ibid.

Table 7.1 An Example of Sound Trademark Comparison from the EUIPO Guidelines

Previous mark (sound trademark)	*Sign to be registered (sound trademark)*	*Case No.*
♫ Link	♫ Link	Primer T/R Hypothetical case

7.6.4 Conceptual Comparison

This is the third level of comparison stemming from the Sabel test. It deals with finding whether compared signs form certain concepts in the background. What is thereby meant is a specific semantic meaning that is created by a certain sign or a combination of signs. In this sense, the EUIPO Guidelines present with examples a different combination of signs that in the following situations signify conceptual similarity between marks compared: both marks contain a word or expression; two words refer to the same semantic expression or its variants; two exclusively figurative marks represent the same or similar concept; figurative or color marks with a word represent a concept that is formed in the background of the word; two marks have figurative elements with the same or analogous concept, whereby one or both contain word elements; two signs consist of a joint meaningful word that is distinctive, whereby one of them contains an additional word or a figurative element without any meaning; a personal name that is common to two signs.[21] There are also examples of conceptual comparisons between sound, motion, and multimedia marks[22] and between letters themselves.[23]

From the multimodal perspective, this kind of comparison implies logical argumentation that is explicitly verbal, as conceptual logic has been part of logic since Ancient Greece. What would be a special challenge from the view of multimodal argumentation is creating and comparing concepts made from non-verbal signs.

7.7 Non-Traditional Trademarks' Visceral Argumentation Going Further

The task of the verbal description and evaluation of the two visuals compared, such as in this case, is a challenging one. Still, in (figurative) trademark cases various authorities are required to do so since that falls within their jurisdiction. To get a full idea of what has been at issue in the event of such comparison, it seems better to publish visuals along with a text than publish the text

21 Ibid.
22 Ibid.
23 Ibid.

alone. There is a necessary "semiotic" gap between visuals and their verbal equivalents, which also follows from the analysis of the involved authorities' reasoning concerning the comparison between the visual signs.

It is not my intention to make evaluation of whose position was more correct, but to point to a gap that existed between the images and their verbal description, and what an authority making such evaluation misses if it does not publish disputed images along with their verbal description. In order to prove that there is a gap between the word description and a visual, we could make a test of trying to draw an image from its previous verbal description without seeing the image first, and we will realize how far our drawing differs from the actual image.

The tribunals, most prominently courts, dealing with cases of traditional trademarks, in particular those including visual representations, have successfully bridged the gap between the traditional monomodal verbal argumentation and the need for including visual argumentation. They did that by simply publishing visuals along with the text in the reasoning of their decisions. Not in all cases, but at least generally, it seems that they have understood that there was a gap they filled by multimodal argumentation. However, that pattern of argumentation has not been followed in the first cases concerning the non-traditional trademarks at least at the EU level.

There have been a number of non-traditional trademarks already registered at the EUIPO, and some cases already reached the Board of Appeals. They both issue their decisions electronically following the pattern of deciding disputes concerning visual trademarks (multimodal: mixed verbal-visual argumentation). That means that they make links to the text, thereby including the non-traditional signs (mostly sounds and videos).

Hence there has been almost no cases at the EU General Court yet to deal with disputes concerning non-traditional trademarks. There was only one case concerning a sound trademark. In that case it was claimed that the sound trademark for a soda drink was not distinctive enough to pass the test of fulfilling the absolute grounds for registration. The EU General Court upheld the argument against its registration, but it failed to follow the requirement of multimodal argumentation, which in that case included acoustic argumentation. It only verbally described the sound sign by the following words: "after opening the can there is approximately one second of silence and then approximately nine seconds of rustling."[24] Does that really fully describe that sound?

7.8 Conclusion

Traditional legal argumentation has been verbal and will probably predominantly remain that way for the foreseeable future. Words are very powerful semiotic resources and very well fulfill their important role in people's

24 T-668/19 (*Ardagh Metal Beverage Holdings v. EUIPO*).

communication and argumentation. Even when we have other semiotic resources, such as visuals, sounds, etc., in case of disagreements about them a resort to words would very much help to resolve such disagreements. In such cases, we use words for description, evaluation, and justification. They can make (legal) arguments clearer, firmer, and stronger.

But words as signs are far from being omnipotent, especially when we have cases in which other semiotic resources determine the propositions (premises) to an important extent. And it seems that many trademark cases are of such a character. It seems that, in the reasoning of their decisions on trademark disputes, the courts have understood that issue to some extent, at least in the cases of visual argumentation (with respect to visual trademarks – most prominently figurative ones). Both national, as well as EU, courts have realized that non-verbal signs (so far visuals) must be presented along with their verbal description in the reasoning.

However, the Sabel test applied in such cases seems to be vague enough to allow different perspectives too easily. This is why, taking some lessons from different modes' grammar as developed in social semiotics, would definitely improve the reasoning of decisions that adjudicators make in such cases.

Moreover, the approach described in this chapter will have to be applied also to non-traditional trademark cases, a path that the EUIPO Board of Appeals has already taken. However, in my opinion, this kind of coherence and consistency will have revolutionary implications as, at least in non-traditional trademark cases, it would oust the traditional paper-format publication of judgments from its use in legal communication. They would need to stick to an electronic format only in order to ensure the full transparency and reviewability of their decisions in these types of cases. Accordingly, at least in this limited scope, we will be forced to say farewell to paper.

An increase in the use of new trademarks by various businesses across the EU will definitely lead to developing the Sabel test further. The recognition of various non-verbal modes has brought a challenge to the verbal mode. In addressing such a challenge, it seems that the multimodal argumentation theory has a lot to offer. This will be more so if the EU at some point decides to take a broader perspective by also allowing taste, scent, or even texture marks.

References

Blair, Anthony. 2015. "Probative Norms for Multimodal Visual Arguments." *Argumentation*, 29 (2): 217–233.

Dutfield, Graham, Suthersanen, Uma. 2008. *Global Intellectual Property Law*. Cheltenham, UK, Northampton, MA, USA: Edward Elgar.

Eckstein, Justin. 2017. "Sound Arguments." *Argumentation and Advocacy*, 53 (1): 163–180.

Groarke, Leo. 2022. "Gilbert as Disrupter: Modes (of Many Sorts) in the Theory of Argument." *Informal Logic*, 42 (3): 507–520.

Kišiček, Gabrijela. 2018. "Can We Translate Sounds into Words? A Response to Leo Groarke's Auditory Arguments: The Logic of Sound Arguments." *Informal Logic*, 38 (3): 346–361.

Kjeldsen, Jens. 2015. "The Rhetoric of Thick Representation: How Pictures Render the Importance and Strength of an Argument Salient." *Argumentation*, 29: 197–215.

Kjeldsen, Jens. 2016. "Symbolic Condensation and Thick Representation in Visual and Multimodal Communication." *Argumentation and Advocacy*, 52 (4): 265–280.

Kress, Günther, van Leeuwen, Theo. 2006. *Reading Images: The Grammar of Visual Design*. London: Routledge.

Leborg, Christian. 2006. *Visual Grammar*. Princeton: Princeton Architectural Press.

Novak, Marko. 2020. "Multi-Modal Argumentation and Rhetoric in Judicial Proceedings." *Argumentation and Advocacy*, 56 (1): 41–60.

Tseronis, Assimakis. 2018. "Multimodal Argumentation: Beyond the Verbal/Visual Divide." *Semiotica*, 220: 41–67.

Tseronis, Assimakis, Forceville, Charles (Eds.). 2017. *Multimodal Argumentation and Rhetoric in Media Genres*. Amsterdam: John Benjamins Publishing Company.

Conclusion

Another Approach to the Rhetorical Tradition

Throughout history, theorists reflecting on law have navigated between rhetorical and dialectical approaches to legal argumentation to create their normative or descriptive models to explain what goes on when lawyers or judges justify their decisions. Even today, normativists in legal argumentation theory, who seek ideal solutions, would rather rely on a more dialectic understanding of law and legal practice, while legal realists in argumentation theory would stress that even dialectic argumentation is people's argumentation that is intended for an audience consisting of human beings, either as individuals or joined in social groups. Unlike the former, the latter would suggest that their rhetorical account of legal argumentation is closer to reality because a too ambitious dialectical project will never fulfill its ideal expectations. Thus, one may ask, what is the point of those very formal projects apart from their sheer utopia?

Many dialectical approaches to legal argumentation have indeed respectable goals and very interesting findings. In theory, they work perfectly. But their problem might be that their self-sufficiency is not in touch with social reality. Therefore, a legal argumentation theory that does not have, at least, a rhetorical part seems to be locked in a theoretical ivory tower, very much detached from everyday reality of legal practices. We need rhetoric to humanize (legal) argumentation – for better or worse. It seems that in North America, whose legal theory has to a greatest extent been influenced by legal realism, there is a better understanding for a rhetorical approach to legal argumentation than in Continental Europe, even though it was Belgium that produced one of the greatest (legal) rhetoricians of all times, namely, Perelman. Frankly, even today, there are some rhetorical islands on the Continent, like Trento and the Dutch isle, of strategic maneuvering as applied to law.

Multi-modal argumentation as used to explain legal argumentation seems to be a new chance to explain legal argumentation in a more rhetorical way. After Perelman, there has not been serious attempts in legal argumentation theory to embrace rhetoric in the law at a more comprehensive level. The already mentioned strategic maneuvering was only a rhetorical island in the midst of the dialectical sea in the pragma-dialectical theory of argumentation.

DOI: 10.4324/9781003433767-9

Its problem is that it sees (the goal of) rhetoric as (mere) effectiveness within the dialectical (goal of) reasonableness. But both rhetorical as well as dialectical argumentation – if we make this distinction – can, or not, be reasonable and effective.

Moreover, with the multi-modal approach to legal argumentation unlike the pragma-dialectical theory or argumentation (extended by strategic maneuvering), it seems to be the other way around: its necessary dialectical components (arguments as "products") are (to be) found within a much more complex rhetorical context of a human society, in which individuals argue against other individuals (as arguers) in front of another type of individuals or their groups (as audiences). Especially, in the context of law, the logical mode of argumentation is very important and indispensable for the rule of law to govern. But it is also important to know that it is not the only mode of argumentation to exist and that it is situated in a broader context of the totality of all the modes, which express the full dimension of a human personality and all its possibilities to argue.

A Closed Fist and an Open Hand

Going back to Zeno's metaphor of a closed fist being a description of the dialectical mode of argumentation and an open hand of the rhetorical mode, let us discuss first the need for dialectical argumentation. There are situations in legal cases that are clear, and we need to make decisions to resolve the dispute and then enforce it. In such a case, we need the certainty and authority of a closed fist. And we may remain certain about that for a very long time. However, we also have cases that are far from being clear but also need to be decided ("handed down") and enforced, even though there are several possible legal positions and decisions, but one of them needs to prevail because the case needs to be decided at some point. And that remains for some time even though we as society are, to some extent, uncertain about it. However, at another time or place, once prevailing legal position with respect to the decided issue might change subject to the changed context. After all, law and society are in no manner merely static. If unclear legal cases were decided by a closed fist, that would mean that we foreclose all potential changes from the position once made. An open hand that is perhaps expressed in concurring and dissenting opinions, and these are an especially valuable source to find the work of rhetorical means of persuasion, would mean an invitation to future individuals and groups to rethink the position taken in such a case.

Unlike majority decisions that are to close the fist at least to some extent, although sometimes they do not succeed in doing that firmly, separate opinions are meant to leave or make them open, for future deliberations. And there are many uncertainties that need to be addressed, both systemic and ideological, about which people argue before courts and which strive to make them certain to some extent and thereby resolve their disputes.

Finally, in anatomical textbooks, human hands are usually portrayed in a stretched and open manner. That seems to be their broadest context because, after all, are we able to deny that we do not spend more time daily with a stretched hand than a closed fist? Is that, therefore, its "normal" or even "natural" position? Hard to say. But, for sure, there are moments, and in the legal context very frequent ones, in which we need closed fists to ensure peace and justice.

Index

Note: Page numbers in **bold** indicate a table on the corresponding page.

Milton Keynes UK
Ingram Content Group UK Ltd.
UKHW051908230624
444477UK00005B/127

9 781032 557847